PENGUIN BOOKS

Colleges That Change Lives

LOREN POPE, a Washington newspaperman who led the fight for better schools in rural Loudoun County, Virginia, first began writing about education in a column for the *Gannett Newspapers* in 1952. His column led to his position as education editor of *The New York Times* during the height of the college-going chaos of the late '50s started by the GI bill. As an education journalist, and later as a top administrator of what is now Oakland University in Michigan, he became deeply concerned with the lack of information available to consumers on colleges. He believed that uninformed choices could account for heavy dropout, transfer, and failure rates. His interest was triggered by the poor advice he got for his own son from friends in the then Office of Education.

In 1965, he opened the College Placement Bureau in Washington to help families make informed, fruitful choices. Out of his reporting and research came a book, *The Right College: How to Get In, Stay In, Get Back In* (Macmillan, 1970), and several magazine articles, including the nationally syndicated "Twenty Myths That Can Jinx Your College Choice," first published in *The Washington Post Magazine. Reader's Digest* has sold a half-million reprints of its condensation, titled "Facts to Know in Picking a College."

These articles inspired his second book, *Looking Beyond the Ivy League: Finding the College That's Right for You*, which is now available from Penguin in a fully revised and updated edition.

Pope contributes to professional journals and speaks at meetings of the National Association of College Admissions Counselors. He has also appeared on radio and television.

He lives in Alexandria, Virginia.

Colleges That Change Lives

40 SCHOOLS YOU SHOULD KNOW ABOUT
EVEN IF YOU'RE NOT A STRAIGHT-A STUDENT

Loren Pope

Penguin Books

PENGUIN BOOKS

Published by the Penguin Group

Penguin Putnam Inc., 375 Hudson Street,
New York, New York 10014, U.S.A.
Penguin Books Ltd, 27 Wrights Lane,
London W8 5TZ, England
Penguin Books Australia Ltd, Ringwood,
Victoria, Australia
Penguin Books Canada Ltd, 10 Alcorn Avenue,
Toronto, Ontario, Canada M4V 3B2
Penguin Books (N.Z.) Ltd, 182–190 Wairau Road,
Auckland 10, New Zealand

Penguin Books Ltd, Registered Offices:
Harmondsworth, Middlesex, England

First published in the Penguin Books 1996
This revised edition published 2000

1 3 5 7 9 10 8 6 4 2

LIBRARY OF CONGRESS CATALOGING IN PUBLICATION DATA
Pope, Loren.
Colleges that change lives: 40 schools you should know about even if you're
not a straight-A student / Loren Pope.
p. cm.
Includes index.
ISBN 0 14 02.9616 6
1. Universities and colleges—United States—Directories.   2. School
environment—United States.   3. College choice—United States.   I. Title.
L901.P58   2000
378.73—dc21   00–027877

Printed in the United States of America
Set in Fairfield
Designed by Suvi Asch

To Viola, the copyreader and critic of my choice,
and Ann Garman Rittenberg, former client
(good small college, Eckerd),
who now has her own literary agency,
and who got me off dead center.

Acknowledgments

For such a book as this to be valid, the faculty members have to be, as an academic friend once observed they are, "stoop-shouldered with honesty." Professors, deans, and occasionally a president constituted a principal source of information at each of the colleges. I am indebted for their kindnesses and their readiness to discuss their colleges with candor. Their breadth of view was also crucial. Having been graduate assistants or faculty members at all the leading universities and many top colleges, they could make invaluable comparisons. At every one of these forty colleges they are daily demonstrating that teaching is an act of love.

I am equally indebted to the many students I talked with at each of these colleges, from freshmen to seniors, whose opinions were equally candid, and who often in their enthusiasm went beyond the faculty claims about nurturing or sense of belonging.

Able admissions staffs did much to make my visits more effective, provided accurate data, and often arranged special interviews or meetings at my request.

To Caroline White of Viking Penguin go my special thanks for her sharp eye and suggestions for making this a better book.

A good copyeditor is a humbling experience for a writer and Julia Lisella showed that "no pain, no gain" is still true.

Contents

SOUTH

MIDWEST

SOUTHWEST

NORTHWEST

Introduction

This country's educational system, the envy of the world, is responsible for its greatness, and for most of our history, just about anybody could go to just about any college if his father's check was good. Harvard did have an entrance exam for a while but brains weren't required; the "C" students like Franklin Roosevelt and Averell Harriman, the intelligentsia, and the ne'er-do-wells all went to college together. In high school there were no SATs and no Advanced Placement classes or tracking. In elementary school a bright student might skip a grade. What changed things was the college-going panic started by the GI bill after World War II.

The segregation of students by ability has been simply a commercial consequence of an exploding student population: too many are trying to get into a few well-known schools, and admissions people are lusting for valedictorians and National Merit Scholars. In the most sought-after colleges it has produced a barren arrogance in both faculty and students. As a young client told me, "It's hard to be humble at Amherst."

But for five decades what I call "no-name" colleges like those in this book have served a wide range of abilities yet produced higher proportions of scientists, scholars, and people who wind up in *Who's Who* than those who take only a fraction of the "A" students. That's a good story and significant to smart consumers concerned about their futures in a fast-changing world.

COLLEGES THAT CHANGE LIVES

A Lifetime Guarantee

This book is much more than a message of hope for the 97% who don't go to designer-label colleges or brand-name universities. It is a lifetime guarantee: Any one of the 40 colleges profiled here will do at least as much as, and usually far more than, an Ivy League school, an Ivy clone, or a major research university to give you a rich, full life, and to make you a winner.

They will do it for "A" students, "B" students, "C" students, students with learning disabilities or physical handicaps, and they will do it for dropouts, flunkouts, and those who lack confidence, so long as they have a desire to learn. They will raise trajectories, strengthen skills, double talents, develop value systems, and impart confidence because they do a much different and better job than the Ivies or the universities.

They do a better job because faculty and students work closely together, learning is collaborative rather than competitive, students are involved in their own education, there is much discussion of values, and there is a sense of family. Most of those things are of little concern to the schools the 97% don't go to. The 3% go to their name-brand colleges bright and full of self-assurance, get As and Bs, deserved or not, and come out pretty much unchanged and probably unfit for a new kind of competition.

I can give a surer guarantee even than Babe Ruth's when he pointed his bat at the grandstand where he subsequently hit a homer. In the case of these colleges the scores are already in. For the 70 years that records have been kept, many of these 40 that welcome "B" and "C" as well as "A" students have produced higher percentages of scientists and scholars than the prestige schools that take only a fraction of the "A" students who apply. Furthermore, many of them have matched most of the elite schools in the percentages of major achievers in *Who's Who*.

Talking to the students at these colleges shows why. The enthusiasm with which they describe what their experience is doing for them is often remarkable. One eager sophomore, with all the fervor he could summon, declared to me, "I come out of every class a better writer, a better thinker, and a better person!"

Talking with faculty members uncovers similar positive responses. Both men and women academics, Ivy Leaguers all the way, have often told me they wish they had gone to the colleges where they now teach. One who had just refused an offer from a major university said, "You couldn't blast me out of here!" In the university world, professors teaching at Harvard, Berkeley, and Texas, among others, have said their own undergraduate education at good small colleges was "unparalleled."

What is so important and so seldom recognized in the status-conscious higher education industry is that these schools have worked their magic on the "B" and "C" as well as on the "A" students. Indeed, the mix is an essential ingredient of the magic.

Also, SAT scores tend to be much, much less important at these schools. In fact, two deans at Clark, citing cases of students who were now doctors or university professors, said they preferred "the rough student with the mediocre SATs, the 500 verbal." And the dean at St. John's said, "All we want is people who read and who can do a little mathematics."

A Canadian once observed that the American practice of judging colleges by the academic records of the high school seniors they pick is like judging the quality of hospitals by the condition of the patients they admit. What happens during the stay is what counts.

The secret of these 40 colleges' magic is not in what they do, for they do many different things. It is in how they do it, and that is where they have so much in common. They attract strikingly different kinds of kids. They range from the two most intellectual colleges in the land—Reed and St. John's—to one where a professor said, "We take in kids who didn't do very well in high school and we turn out people who compete with the Ivies." In between these two are places for the venturesome and for those in need of nurture, including the naifs. Quite fittingly, curricular programs vary as dramatically, from the no-electives Great Books program of St. John's to the do-it-yourself challenges of Antioch, Hampshire, and Marlboro.

These schools share two essential elements: a familial sense of communal enterprise that gets students heavily involved in cooperative rather than competitive learning, and a faculty of scholars devoted to helping young people develop their powers, mentors who often become their valued friends.

When I asked students at these colleges my usual question, if they'd have dinner or spend a night at a faculty member's home on a visit five years hence, the usual response was, "I'd have trouble deciding which one."

These are the kinds of professors who make the difference because they put the focus on the student. In intelligence and qualifications, faculties are pretty much the same everywhere. But in the universities, professors are not usually part of a community or interested in their students' projects. Since Sputnik, research and publishing are where all the rewards are, and the top faculty at leading universities do little, if any, teaching, leaving that chore to graduate assistants and part-time faculty. In short, the university cheats the undergraduate. There is no other word for it. Education should include dialogue and involvement, not be just a monologue to the passive ears of note-takers busy because what they're hearing might be on the exam.

A young lawyer friend who quit Harvard in disgust after three years to transfer to Smith, a first-rate women's college, told me: "At Harvard I was being taught by students; six of them foreigners who could barely speak English. Everyone sitting around you in the dining hall was a class president or a star at something, so there was little chance to participate [if you weren't a star] and no sense of community, and no interaction with faculty. Faculty didn't have office hours. My roommate quit after one semester."

What high school seniors don't realize is that such experiences are typical at every large university, and even at small ones like Johns Hopkins, and if they go to one they'll get short-changed, often even if they're in an honors or some other program for a special group of students. (Undergraduate colleges that call themselves universities, such as Denison or Ohio Wesleyan, are exceptions, as is Clark, a research university that is one of this family.)

Even at the prestige colleges a student's encounters with faculty are likely to be, as a Carleton graduate spat out, "minimal!" This sentiment was also expressed by Wesleyan, Williams, and Oberlin students. The reason is similar; because the prestige schools put the greater emphasis on research and publishing, students come second.

The colleges discussed in this book develop people who can land on their feet—whether they are strong, intellectual students or those needing tender loving care—because they encourage a strong sense of community and interaction among students and between students and teachers. The greater such opportunities are in quantity and quality, the greater the effect. This is what a long-term study of 159 institutions, directed by Dr. Alexander Astin of the University of California at Los Angeles, showed. Dr. Astin has been the leader in investigating college outcomes for 40 years.

His results paralleled those reported by the late Dr. Ernest L. Boyer, head of the Carnegie Endowment for the Advancement of Teaching, in the book *College, the Undergraduate Experience in America*. Boyer's team surveyed 5,000 students in colleges and universities across the country. The accomplishments of these 40 colleges' graduates have for years offered textbook proof of these conclusions.

The nature of the course content or the kind of curricular program doesn't make much difference. The key is how it is delivered, and how the students work, collaboratively on class projects, rather than singly and competitively.

When students teach each other, a couple of good things happen. One is that they tend to go into greater depth because for part of the time each plays the role of tutor. The other is that knowing their work is going to be scrutinized by their peers keeps them on their toes.

The students wouldn't have it any other way. A sophomore girl told me, "I was about to flunk out because I thought I had to do it all by myself, that that was the only way to do it. Then I started working with others, and it's so much better, and so much more fun. It's wonderful!"

If faculty members are interested in their students' personal as well as academic endeavors—in other words if they become the students' friends—and work with students on research projects, things happen to young minds and spirits that don't happen at other places. In such a situation there is almost bound to be a strong sense of community, and that helps develop leadership, personality, and academic growth. The sense of community pervades the faculty as well. At several of these colleges I found professors exulting in the "warm collegiality" of the faculty, something they hadn't known in the universities where they got their doctorates or where they had previously taught. The implicit message to the students is effective: This is a cooperative, democratic enterprise.

Good things did not happen, both the Astin and the Boyer studies found, when students were commuters, when the size of the school was large, when teaching assistants taught, or when there was a lack of community. Dr. Boyer's team found these were the kinds of places where students were not happy or where they dropped out.

The effect of a mix of abilities hasn't been given the same official scrutiny, but faculty and students both testify that it makes for the best kind of learning atmosphere. A professor who'd gone to Carleton as an undergraduate said maybe 10% or 15% of his students could get in there and prosper, a middle group might get in but would have to work harder, while the bottom group could neither get in nor get through.

"That middle group," he said, "acts as the honest brokers in my classes. They ask the questions that the top group is ashamed to ask and that the bottom group doesn't think about."

Similarly, when I asked a girl who had transferred after three semesters at Wesleyan, where everyone is a top student, to Beloit, where there is a mix, if this was a valid assessment, she said, "Oh, yes! At Beloit everyone talks, nobody is afraid. At Wesleyan it was stifling; there was no discussion. I find I learn more at Beloit, even though it doesn't have the prestige." At Wesleyan "professors were distant, they'd only put a couple of negative comments on a paper and it was hard to get a conference with them. I liked the kids a lot but I thought they had tunnel vision, and there's more to life than that [study and grades]. At Beloit the professors are right there all the time; they can't do enough for you."

With this country fast becoming a cog in a global economy, a great virtue of these colleges is their array of foreign study programs, particularly at Kalamazoo, the pioneer in the field, where everyone spends two terms in study abroad.

Equally relevant is the emphasis on student research projects and the chance for students to work with professors on their research projects. Nearly a third of the papers faculty present at professional meetings are co-authored by students, as are about 5% of their books. When these students go on to graduate school they report they're ahead of the game; when they get jobs they demonstrate they're self-starters.

This is important because just about everyone now in college will in ten years or less be working at jobs that don't yet exist. In 1994 I was telling the director of institutional research at Franklin and Marshall that the Yale class of 1957 discovered at its 25th reunion that 75% of them were in jobs that hadn't existed when they were at Yale. His reply was better. "I've just been surveying our alumni who've been out ten years or more," he said, "and ninety percent of them are in jobs that didn't exist when they were at F&M."

While their price tags are higher than the public institutions, they are the investments that promise the long-term human and financial profit. Furthermore, they all are eager to help you pay the bill with all the financial aid for which you qualify on the standard forms. For good students they may give more, and you can dicker. (But don't think some outsider can find you a scholarship; that's a fraud.)

There could hardly be more persuasive testimony that college had better prepare people to be bold, imaginative, resourceful pioneers because the old establishment is crumbling and the old-boy network that helped staff it is becoming technologically unemployed. The colleges in this book develop the qualities needed to see opportunities in a changing world and to be smart and resourceful enough to act on them. They are the keys to the future for they create competence.

Required Reading

You're not as smart as you think you are if you believe:

1. Your college should be bigger than your high school (5,000 is the figure usually mentioned by girls, especially those from small private schools).
2. A name-brand college will give you a better education and assure your success.
3. A university will offer you more than a good small college.
4. You should go where your friends are going.
5. You don't need to examine yourself or the college.

Here briefly are some things you need to know about these myths that jinx thousands of college choices every year.

1. The best-size college:

Most good colleges are 1,000 to 2,000 for a reason; college is a time of internal exploration and the small familial community is more conducive to such an experience. What's important is not the number of people but the people themselves, the sense of community. The social life tends to be better at smaller colleges. Those are some of the reasons why I rarely recommend a college of 5,000 to a client. Good small colleges strive for all the variety they can get, while public institutions admit by formula. Most of their students are state residents less qualified than the out-of-staters and probably less sophisticated. The large private institutions tend to be compartmentalized by specialties. You get more effective diversity in a small college for the same reason it is easier to know everyone in a small community than in a great city. As a big-college freshman complained, "I miss the diversity we had in high school." She could have made her point by saying it's a lot better to have 600 available males than 3,000 unavailable ones.

2. Which type of school gives the best education and a jump start in life:

In nearly every chapter of this book, faculty members who have taught at Ivy schools say the work of their upperclass students is every bit as good as that of those in Ivy upper classes. The fact that many of these colleges consistently outperform the Ivy types in producing high achievers and contributors speaks for itself.

A visitor to one of these colleges will hear a lot about how much students feel changed by their experiences. They also talk about how envious their friends at big universities are of the attention they get and the opportunities they have. Typical of the comments I hear most often is this: "Just a year at Wooster has made a difference in my life, and I love my teachers. But my friends who go to Brown or Penn never talk about what their schools have done for them or about their teachers." If their schools are so great, why don't they? In nearly 30 years I have yet to have a client say that Amherst or Harvard or Michigan or Johns Hopkins has changed him or her.

In March 1994, *The New York Times* reported that a quarter of Harvard's class of 1958 had lost their jobs, were looking for work, or were on welfare, just when their careers should have been cresting. A headline said, "Many in the class of '58 thought their degrees ensured career success. They were wrong." The autobiographical sketches written for the 35th reunion "did not radiate with expressions of success and optimism," said author and Yale professor Erich Segal. "Quite the contrary, they seemed like a litany of loss and disillusion." The compiler of the sketches noted that "about 25 percent have tumbled out." Another class member, Senator John D. Rockefeller, pointed out, "The layoffs of managers and skilled technical people at IBM, or Xerox, or AT&T do not discriminate between graduates of Harvard and some lesser school. And when the layoffs come we are not prepared for non-success. We don't know how to deal with it."

In short, Harvard men failed because Harvard failed them. And Harvard was not alone. Alumni groups at other Ivy League schools, the story added, "are reporting that their members in growing numbers are suffering from the upheavals in corporate America. If there is a lesson in all this it is that a degree from a college like Harvard is no longer the lifetime guarantee of success in careers that it used to be."

Had these men gone to a different kind of college, *The Times* would have recorded a success story. They might still have been victims of the Big Bang of a new age, but their college experiences would have equipped them to land on their feet. As a recent graduate of such a college wrote me, "Antioch taught me to think. I learned how to learn. I developed a strong sense of confidence in myself. I know I could arrive anywhere in the world and not know the language, but I'd survive. In fact, I'd do more than survive; I'd immerse myself in the language and the culture and hopefully become a productive member of the community." Good as her word, she trained primary school teachers for the Peace Corps in Liberia until civil war there ended that. Then, after two months' immersion in the Sesotho language, she spent two years training teachers in a remote mountain village in Lesotho in West Africa. Now she's designing training programs for other volunteers at the Peace Corps's Washington, D.C. headquarters.

A graduate student on full fellowship, who is now listed

among the significant research scientists of all time, transferred from Harvard to Princeton because the only contacts he had with his adviser were Monday notes in the mailbox. Princeton profs were happy to one-up a rival.

A newly minted Ph.D. said she left Cornell after two years because "I could have gotten a degree without getting out of bed," except to take exams. For-hire note-takers could do the rest. And everybody gets As and Bs.

Two college presidents told me of their sons' "miserable" experiences at Yale. One son's adviser didn't even read his senior thesis. Several faculty members said their children had transferred to their colleges after disillusioning freshman years at prestige schools.

3. *The university as slack-filled merchandise:*

Many a former client has told me I was right, that the university cheats the undergraduate. It not only offers you less while claiming to do more, but also deprives you of your educational birthright. How? By not letting you get involved in your own education, by making you a passive ear in huge lecture classes, by consigning most of the teaching to graduate students, often foreigners who may barely speak English, and to other part-timers. You may never see a professor outside of class, you may never have a discussion in class, you may never even write a paper. That is not what education should be, nor is it preparation for a changing world. Furthermore, you may spend five years or more getting this hollow degree because you can't get into the classes you need to take in order to graduate.

The university's claim that it boasts great scholars is not just hogwash; it is false advertising. Most of them do little or no teaching, and when they do they are nothing more than performers behind a lectern in a big auditorium. Any great ideas they may have are already in the library. Involvement with good teachers is what helps young minds grow.

Outside of class, your chances of participating in some activity are slim to none unless you're one of the best. More likely you are sentenced to being a spectator. The salve has to be the Roman circus of the big football weekend.

4. Why you shouldn't be a teen-age sheep:

Going where your friends go is a common mistake across the country. This being afraid to leave one's friends is also one of the worst blunders of adolescence. Most of them you'll never see again, some you wouldn't buy a used car from. Forget them. A whole new set of friends is waiting, and as certain as the sun rises you will have a new set in less than three weeks. Guaranteed.

This herd mentality is one of the reasons why fewer than four in ten freshmen will be on the same campuses four years later, a figure that has been consistent for many years. But the consequences of following the crowd in deciding where to spend these four crucial years are much greater. They are blighted hopes, undeveloped abilities, and unrealized potential. Where a person goes literally can be more important than whether he goes. (He could educate himself in the library.)

5. Why you should examine both yourself and the merchandise:

Picking a college is a crucial decision because the experience profoundly affects the quality of one's future life. It can be the most exciting four years of your life. On the other hand you can plod through largely untouched and unaffected, or drop out or fail. Such unhappy results are common. Most teenagers give more thought to learning to drive or to water ski than to picking a college.

Confront yourself honestly. Why, really, are you going, for fun or for some other reason? What are your abilities and strengths, what are your weaknesses? What do you want out of life, or in life, something tangible or intangible? Are you supremely confident or hesitantly unsure of yourself? Do you want to give or to get? Are you a self-starter or in need of nurture and structure? Are you socially self-sufficient, marching to your own drummer, or do you need warm, familial support? Do you live in the fast track? And so on.

After you have questioned yourself you can effectively choose a college, but only after you have examined it, too. And the best way is to spend a working day and a night on the campus as part of the community. Be a consumer: Go to two or three classes, ask a couple dozen students and two or three faculty members the questions important to you. Spending a night in the dorm gives you time to think over what you've been told and to ask further questions.

Ask students what their chief gripes are, whether the experience has affected them and how, whether their teachers are also their valued friends, whether they are actively involved in their own education. Ask faculty members whether they think their students are there to learn or to get grades, and what they think of them. Go to the student union and question people on the newspaper or in student government. In short, don't go as a supplicant; be a hard-nosed, investigative reporter trying to find out if the school is good enough for you. If this one doesn't suit, don't worry; there are plenty more just as good or better that are eager to have you. Always remember that.

YOU'RE SMARTER THAN YOU THINK YOU ARE.

This whole book provides ample, comforting evidence that some colleges will indeed multiply your talents, raise your trajectories, impart confidence, make you a more effective, better person. They change the lives of "A" students, "B" students, "C" students, people with learning difficulties, late bloomers, the handicapped or disabled, or almost anyone with the desire to learn and to grow. In short, they make winners because they exert a special magic, intelligent caring, and tough love.

Long before Aesop wrote about the tortoise and the hare, an Old Testament writer observed, "Again I saw that under the sun the race is not to the swift . . . nor riches to the intelligent, but time and chance happen to them all." Not only are time and chance heavily weighted in favor of the tortoise, but the college experience that gets a youth involved and that works itself into his values dramatically increases the tortoise's power and speed.

If you read the chapter on St. Andrews you know they "take in kids who didn't do very well in high school and turn out people who compete with the Ivies." And the two deans at Clark made it crystal clear that they preferred "the rough student with the 500 verbal" who gets turned on by a professor, because he winds up being a doctor, a university professor, or something else he'd never in his wildest dreams imagined. At other colleges, faculty said their seniors' work was every bit as good as Ivy students'. So, a professor asked, "What does this say about our SAT system?" It says the SATs are a one-dimensional measure for a status industry but useless in judging human beings.

These points are typical of the evidence I have collected over the years of a truth long known: that there is no correlation between grades and achievement in life, except in mathematics, and mathematicians are born, they're not made. Indeed, the only long-term study of a very selective college's graduates—Haverford—showed that those at the top of their classes were the ones 20 years later who were most frustrated, who had the least satisfactory relationships with their wives and with their colleagues. (Haverford was all male during most of the study's 40-year span.)

Every year I have a few clients who have learning disabilities or physical handicaps, some severe, but all succeed. What they all have is that desire. My most recent example had a 450 verbal and terrible dyslexia. He graduated from college with a 3.5 in a tough engineering program and in 1994, when the firm was firing thousands, he was one of 200 graduates hired nationwide at a starting salary of $42,000.

Emerson wrote: " 'What will you have?' quoth God. 'Pay for it and take it.' " These are places eager and eminently able, if you are willing to pay for it with hard work, to empower you to take it.

The Learning Disabled of Today Will Be the Gifted of Tomorrow

Recently, a mother telephoned me with a request: "Please don't use the term 'learning disabled' to Ann when we come in for our interview."

Ann didn't even want to hear the word "disabled" mentioned. And she is not alone; some of my clients have even tried to deny that they learn any differently from anyone else. While no one really knows, the estimates are that 8 to 12 percent of the population has some kind of learning problem. But those percentages don't begin to reflect maternal anxiety.

Parents and students, relax!! This chapter can't cure adolescent indifference but it will prove the truth of its glad-tidings title. Not only can the high school student with a learning problem prosper in college, but by senior year he or she may be ahead of the problem-free peers. Furthermore, the skills of these people, who tend to be visual thinkers, will continue to grow in maturity and old age, and their productivity will increase, while the skills of logical thinkers will diminish.

Neurologists explain that dyslexia and other learning problems are simply biological differences in the way the two hemispheres of the brain are connected, or "wired." In general, the left thinks in words and numbers while the right thinks visually in pictures and in three-dimensional images.

In people with such problems, the connections between the

right and left hemispheres are different, and the different wiring, even as it creates difficulties with the spoken or written word, often produces a variety of creative abilities. Although the people with learning problems tend to mature more slowly, they go farther and reveal surprising strengths. They are the late bloomers, and contrary to what some parents think, late blooming is often a bonus. In nature, the most sophisticated kinds of life take the longest to mature. Thus the dyslexics often outdo the quick studies because they continue to grow and because they've had to overcome difficulties. So, away with the foolish shame!

Furthermore, the world increasingly puts a premium on the visual, spatial, conceptual, and creative abilities so characteristic of the dyslexics, the ADDs, and others now smugly and wrongly labeled "learning disabled." Today's verbal skills will take a backseat.

The era now coming to an end has been that of a literate society that communicates mainly by the printed and spoken word. Those skills have been the prized ones, and the ones on which the educational system has been centered. Even so, some of the greatest scientists, political leaders, generals, artists, writers, and poets from Leonardo da Vinci on have been people who had great trouble with words. They were, as such people often are, visual, conceptual and spatial thinkers.

Now, say some experts, the computer is changing everything. It has already replaced bank clerks. And with the advances in artificial intelligence, the computer will soon take over from the professionals in those areas where knowledge is routine, systematized, or conventional, for example, middle managers, attorneys, and scientists. The vast corporate downsizings of the early 1990s were a precursor of larger things to come.

But the computer's artificial intelligence hits a brick wall if the task requires imagination, creativity, intuition, the "lucky hunch," serendipity, seeing the possible connections, or taking the big leap. And this is where the dyslexics are outstanding.

We are entering a new era that has been called "the post–literate society," one in which the old adage, "one picture is worth a thousand words" will be an understatement. With the computer doing the routine and the formula work, the intelligence most in demand will be the one that can creatively and effectively find and make use of information, not the one with the greatest store of it. And that, incidentally, is where these catalytic colleges outdo the famous ones; students at two very different colleges in this book who'd been in off-campus programs with Ivy Leaguers told me the Ivies "might have had more information on a problem, but we could use it better."

Most of what I've said so far is the result of reading a terrific book by the dyslexic father of a dyslexic client, a former computer systems consultant, whose life is now devoted to research, writing, and lecturing on this cause, in which he is one of the world's leading experts. He is Thomas G. West and his scholarly, encyclopedic, and endlessly fascinating book is *In the Mind's Eye*, (Prometheus Books, 1997). This volume, which will answer just about every question you can think of on learning problems, is a great public service and one long overdue. Every family concerned about a learning problem—or even the usual problems of dealing with a teenage student—should have it in the house. To begin with, Chapters 2 and 3 will set minds at rest. And on page 172, he gives parents some good advice: relax, back off and wait a while; too much presure is counterproductive. Also, if I were dictator, every teacher everywhere would have to pass a test on it.

In his preface, Mr. West says this is a topic whose time has come: "As our technology, economy, and society are transformed at ever greater rates, while our institutions hold ever more tightly to outmoded ideas, perhaps it is time for some really fresh thinking . . . The old measurement scales do not quite fit, as many have long known, in spite of what they were told. And many have suffered for no good reason as a consequence." How true!

ADD, with its conflicting maze of traits, is a special problem to identify. Anxious parents, thinking a non-achieving teen-ager must have a learning problem, take him or her to a psychologist who may diagnose it as ADD, when all the teen is really suffering from is adolescence. It is often impossible to tell the difference!

To give some comfort to parents, Mr. West is at great pains to point out that the only pattern in learning problems, whatever names are given them, is that there is no pattern. The symptoms may overlap, get all mixed up, occur in crazy combinations, or defy diagnosis.

In the text of the book and in appendices, are lists of traits a person may have that are as long as your arm, but some of the more common ones—which are often contradictory and show up in many teens—include difficulty with handwriting; a general lack of organization; indifference to schedules; excessive daydreaming; difficulty with arithmetic (but not geometry, statistics, or higher mathematics); difficulty with speech (delayed speech development, hesitation, or occasionally, stuttering); ineptness or lack of tact socially, but in some cases showing exceptional powers of social perceptiveness. But parents should be of good cheer, says Mr. West, for many of them who've led fulfilling lives of outstanding achievements will recognize among these traits and in their children their own adolescent problems. And many of them will realize it has been a family pattern for generations.

To deal with students who have such a maze of traits, Mr. West observes that teachers have to use multisensory learning approaches. And that is exactly what tends to occur naturally in the colleges in this book. It occurs because learning is collaborative, and in small classes teachers tend to feel like surrogate parents in their concern for their students' welfare. A professor may give a student extra time on tests, let him tape a paper, and so on. The active ingredient is not a formal program; it is tender loving care, and it can work wonders.

However, a dyslexic student who has great trouble reading obviously would have trouble at St. John's where reading the

Great Books is central, or perhaps at Marlboro, where there is also a great deal of reading. A professor there said, "People may think that because this is such a friendly, informal, family-like place (just over 200 students) that it will be just right, but it's too intense." But that professor might be wrong. If a student with a reading problem really wants that experience badly enough, he or she should talk it over with a Marlboro admissions officer.

It is very important that anyone with a learning problem should make that known when applying to any college. Trying to hide it can only create problems. Call the admissions office and discuss the matter; ask what help the college offers and how students with learning problems fare at that school. Not only will they welcome your call, but you are likely to get some very reassuring information. I have been recommending clients with all kinds of learning problems to most of these colleges for well over thirty years, and they've all prospered because they've had one thing in common: desire to learn.

These colleges want to help you. Remember, as the president of Wabash emphasized to me, these colleges are inclusive, not exclusive; they want you. They also know that many of the world's geniuses come from this group: Winston Churchill, General George S. Patton, Jr., William Butler Yeats, Lewis Carroll, Thomas Edison, Albert Einstein, and Michael Faraday, not forgetting Leonardo da Vinci.

The morals (plural) of the story

The morals should be obvious. If you have a learning problem in today's literate society, you are likely to have the aptitude and talents needed to prosper in tomorrow's post–literate society. And that is the one in which you will make your own career, or more likely, two or three careers.

Also, you should take inspiration from the story of a client who as a high school senior told me, "When I was in the seventh grade I could read a whole page and not understand a word of it." To make a point he applied to sixteen colleges and was accepted by fourteen. He graduated in four years with a 2.5 average. And, he ran his own outside business all four years. All he had, but what he did have, was desire.

You, in the meantime, can do what others are doing; you can lick it, you can circumvent it, or you can compensate for it.

WHICH COLLEGE IS MOST CHALLENGING?
GUESS AGAIN

This question pops up all the time, usually from parents. "Challenging" really is a code word for "Which is the most selective, has the brightest students?"

Higher education being a status industry, the assumption is that selectivity equals rigor. Wrong, wrong, wrong. This is one of the worst myths jinxing college choices. Eighty years of official records testify that many colleges in this book dramatically outperform their very selective peers in producing the nation's scientists, scholars, and achievers. That's what this book is all about.

Neither of the two most intellectual colleges in the country—Reed and St. John's—is selective. But they are self-selective; few are willing to rise to their challenges.

Among the many life-changers in this book, Antioch, which has been selective only two or three years of its pioneering life, ranks number five among the 2,000 colleges and universities in Ph.D. production; Wooster number eleven; Earlham number thirteen; and Kalamazoo number fifteen.

Little Cornell College and mighty Ivy Cornell University provide a David-and-Goliath illustration. The university takes a few of its thousands of "A" applicants; the college accepts over 80% of all who apply. But a brand-new Ph.D. who left the University after two frustrating years, told me, "I was in classes of 2,000, sitting in the balcony; I could have gotten my degree without ever getting out of bed except to take an exam. I could have hired note-takers to do the rest." Also, she'd had only one conversation with a professor in two years.

At Cornell College, there is no such thing as a passive ear; every student is actively involved. Teachers and students work together in small classes, and mentoring is a vital part of their relationships. Students examine and discuss their values; there is much discourse and much writing. And the relationships continue outside of class.

A good college does indeed have to have some bright students. A mix of academic abilities is needed for good discussion; the middle group asks the questions the bright ones are afraid or ashamed to ask and the slower ones may not think of. However, the dean at intellectual St. John's said, "Some of the most useful questions are asked by the weaker students."

Unbelievable as it may seem today, no college was selective until the postwar college-going boom swamped the higher education establishment. That produced selectivity but did nothing about rigor; it only inflated status. Had selectivity affected rigor, a lot of these colleges' seniors wouldn't be making higher scores on such things as the Medical College Admissions Test than most of the Ivies, as they do.

Later, Sputnik turned the universities into money-grubbing research institutes and has left the chore of teaching to teaching assistants and part-timers, some of whom barely speak English. The scholars do little, if any, teaching. By January 2000, reported a U.S. Department of Education study, the fast-growing proportion of part-timers had reached 42.5%. If left unchecked, it said, this "threatens the university as a place of learning."

A mother told me she wanted her daughter to go to Stanford because, "That's where the high tech is." Her daughter, if she goes, is not likely to get anywhere near it until she becomes a graduate student. But in one of these colleges, she would be heavily involved in research as soon as she wanted.

Finally, in 35 years I've never had a client report that his very selective school had changed his or her life, or that they had to work especially hard. But I have had many testimonials that these colleges are Upward Bound experiences that have given those young people the confidence and power to do things they couldn't have imagined doing.

HOMESCHOOLERS ARE WELCOME HERE

Homeschooled students are a growing cohort that before long may outnumber those with learning problems. Their anxieties are different but every bit as great. Their questions are: How will the colleges view us? Are we at a disadvantage if we lack transcripts, laboratory sciences, languages?

The answer is, the colleges that change lives are eager to have homeschoolers apply. All these colleges will view them sympathetically and very carefully; in other words, as favorably as those with high school transcripts, and in some cases more favorably. Every applicant will be judged on his or her own merits, just like all the others.

Every admissions officer I talked to was enthusiastic about his or her experience with homeschoolers. More than one was predisposed in favor of them because they said these kids have had the initiative and the persistence to learn on their own, some for religious reasons, but more often because the local schools were bad.

However, homeschooled candidates do have to demonstrate three things: that they are socially ready for college life, that they have the motivation for college work, and the capability to handle the course load. Thus, they may be examined more closely than their peers with high school transcripts. The student's personal statement and essay are very important. These give the admissions people a glimpse of the individual that the objective data do not. Also, an interview is usually required, of parents as well as the student. Among other things, it can help tell whether this youth is socially ready for college. Also, if a parent has compiled a transcript, it can discover what his qualifications are.

Several admissions directors told me they've been impressed with the quality of their homeschool applicants. One said, "Ninety percent of the applicants we've had have been good. They tend to have high test scores and to be curious kids. In evaluating them we may rely much more on such standardized tests as the SAT IIs than we normally do." That's because the SAT IIs are explicitly tests of achievement rather than aptitude.

Another said, "They tend to be people with the initiative to be self-learners, and they work well in these colleges. We like to have a portfolio of their work if there is no transcript. We don't want the GED." Some admissions officers think the GED is not a very trustworthy measure for their purposes. Still another said, "I find they are strong readers with literate minds. The lack of laboratory science is no barrier if they have math and the science concepts." Most admissions officers, he added, would probably agree.

Colleges want all the documentation possible to support the application, such as academic work done outside the family, with appropriate evaluations, or courses at a community college.

Because values are central, as they should be, at these schools, there is much discussion of them. And if you are a homeschooler for religious reasons and have any concerns about a school's position or values, call the admissions office and discuss it with them to see if it is the right fit for you. They will be happy to oblige because they also want it to be a good fit.

Allegheny College
Meadville, Pennsylvania

A ttractive Allegheny, founded in 1815, is a shining example of what the exciting colleges in this book are doing to prepare their students for a new kind of world, things that make most of the prestige institutions look stodgy. It has a long and distinguished record of producing not only future scientists and scholars, but business leaders as well.

When I first visited Allegheny in 1994, it was all revved up with a great new curriculum featuring small freshman seminars, writing across the curriculum (even in math and science), independent study, and research, all designed to make its graduates even more effective in the next century.

Now it is enhancing the connections with the world of work with more emphasis on helping students make good decisions about their college and career opportunities. It is also requiring hands-on experiences such as internships or off-campus study. All residence halls are wired for Internet access, and information technology is being used in the classroom.

Allegheny is a spacious and handsome place. It has 36 buildings on 72 acres, an outdoor recreational complex of 182 acres, and a 283-acre nature preserve and environmental field station. It also has an observatory, a planetarium, art galleries, radio and TV stations, and a library of 539,000 volumes and 1,200 periodicals. It is located in Meadville, Pennsylvania, midway between Pittsburgh and Cleveland, close to six lakes and several state parks for boating, swimming, biking, and skiing.

Its new science building is worth a story in itself, and worth a detour for any science professor or budding scientist. Only Columbia University's graduate facility is better. Many colleges are proud of their new science facilities, but this one was faculty-designed—in collaboration with the architects, of course—and no expense was spared to provide the greatest possible protection from acid and other burns, with state-of-the-art hoods, shower heads right at hand, and eye-washer attachments at sinks and water faucets. Each lab contains glassed-in, soundproof, fireproof, odorproof rooms stocked with computers, desk space, and other needs so that a student can move right from his test tube or Bunsen burner to write up his experiment.

Another bright educational idea is the unique deployment of faculty offices to provide a new way of holding office hours and encouraging collaborative learning at the same time. Along a hall is a series of little bays forming reception areas, with semi-upholstered chairs and coffee tables holding a few magazines. Two faculty offices open off each bay; students can sit and read or discuss common problems while waiting for the prof.

As Dr. Ed Walsh, a chemistry professor who headed the faculty design team, said, "The idea is to say, 'come in,' not 'I'm busy.' We hold our office hours out there, often with two or three students with the same problem. Then they can discuss it and I'm not saying the same thing over and over again, and the teacher plays the role of moderator, letting the students discuss the problems by themselves, I can often sit there for 25 minutes and not say a word. This is team learning. So we call them collaborative areas because they're for collaborative learning."

Allegheny calls its new curriculum interactive because it involves tutorials and much independent study or research, perhaps with a faculty member. Even though there is a structured program of required courses, there nevertheless is a lot of freedom for those with special interests to design individual majors.

All this has required a lot of new faculty, and since many of them are in their late 20s or 30s, it is a group with a lot of zing and zest that has changed the whole complexion of the place.

Also, they work with a receptive group, students I found to be eager for a chance to tell others what the school had done for them, particularly some of the minority kids. As a group they are industrious and interested in the professions. Many are in their family's first generation to go to college, although this proportion has been shrinking. Nearly three-quarters receive financial aid, more than half come from out of state, 11% are minority or international, and nearly a fifth are following parents or relatives to Allegheny.

In shaping a new curriculum, Allegheny, like other forward-looking colleges, decided to put the emphasis on how to learn and the desire to learn, rather than on coverage of material. Former dean Jim Bulman, who went to Cornell and got his doctorate and taught at Yale, said a new program was needed for two reasons. One is that students come to college less well prepared than in the past. The other is that it was essential to prepare them for the new world, which everyone foresees except those families looking for colleges to prepare their children for the status quo.

Allegheny came up with solutions similar to those of other first-rate colleges. The seminar leader is the adviser for those 14 students for two years, nurturing a sense of belonging and close camaraderie. Everyone has to become informed in the sciences, the social sciences, and in the humanities, and everyone has to have a major and a minor, do a senior independent research project, and defend it in an open meeting.

What is new is a requirement that outsmarts those who always try to make a smorgasbord of the distribution requirements by taking the snap courses. Specific sets of three courses in each division ensure that a student comes out learned in that area of study.

The emphasis is on learning how to learn, on analytical thinking, and on the wholeness of knowledge, so there is a pervasive interdisciplinary thread. In a freshman seminar the discussion of a novel may be led by a physicist; a concentration in English will involve the study of artificial intelligence. There is also much emphasis on the moral life. Here is a place where values have long been out of the closet; students live by an honor code. And to develop analysis and good thinking, much writing is required all along, culminating in the senior project.

Results are already evident. The quality of writing is much better, the quality of senior theses is "dramatically" higher, and because they know from their freshman year that they will face this challenge, students have a stimulus to work harder and better. And some who have gotten out into the world have reported that the senior project, which made them tackle and analyze and synthesize and explain their idea, was the most valuable experience they had in college.

From the college's point of view, they've succeeded in preparing students for living and working in an economy and a world that values risk-taking, imagination, being able to see opportunities, and expressing oneself clearly.

About Allegheny's effect, its dean, Dr. Lloyd Michaels, makes a point that some anonymous Canadian has made in different words and that every catalytic college should be shouting from the rooftops:

"If the measure of a great college is the transformation that occurs between matriculation and graduation, rather than the academic accomplishments of entering students, then Allegheny ranks among the finest institutions of higher education."

Allegheny's new president, Richard Cook, formerly the provost at Kalamazoo, points out that Allegheny "has always had a daring spirit" as well as a commitment to the liberal arts ideal, so it's not surprising that it ranks among the top 4% in the production of business leaders. "In addition," he adds, "our alumni are disproportionately represented on volunteer boards, in service organizations, and in local and state government. Our educational philosophy is one of learning how to learn for a lifetime—an education for exploration and responsibility."

One mark of a good school is how much in accord are the stories of the faculty with those of the administration. Here they sing the same song. They say there is great interest in the art of teaching, that there are brown bag lunches on the subject, and week-long summer faculty workshops on teaching "beyond their disciplines." Every teacher is involved in working on curriculum matters and one important aspect is putting an emphasis on the moral (not religious) life because this is a place that believes it is central.

Most of them got their doctorates and earlier taught at Ivy League or Big Ten universities but agreed with an English professor who went to Cornell and then to Columbia when he said, "By and large, students get a better education here than at the larger school. There the graduate assistants (who do most of the teaching) are teachers in training, and you wouldn't want a doctor in training. In the big places the quality of teaching has little to do with getting tenure; here it's heavily weighted in favor of the quality of teaching."

Many talked of the close relationships with students. A chemistry professor called them "incredibly free-wheeling." Another added by way of contrast that at Yale, although he had an important responsibility—helping political science students with their schedules—no student ever came to see him.

A psychology professor summed it up with, "This is a very committed and dedicated faculty. We offer a lot of individual attention and students do a lot better than they ever thought they could. They get a larger share of doing their own education. The students are incredibly capable and talented but often not sophisticated intellectually, so they don't realize how capable they are, and when they get turned on they don't realize how far they've come."

The students' stories and attitudes certainly made honest people of all the administrators and faculty I had talked to. I was particularly struck by how many said they had learned how to think clearly and to write well. Several said that Allegheny's financial aid offers had made it possible for them to come to college and they thought the whole experience had enlightened and broadened them. They considered their teachers concerned and helpful friends. Some wanted to make a particular point of telling the world they didn't think they could get a better education anywhere else. A girl from India said she was trying to get her friends from India to come because this was "a wonderful place and it has done so much for me."

The fellow who made the deepest impression on me was an African-American who stayed behind when one group I'd been chatting with had to go to class. He very much wanted me to know that, "Allegheny made it possible for me to come to college, and it has made me a better student. In high school I had a 2.4 (low C+) average. Here I have a 3.0 (B), and I'm a junior."

Allegheny, as one administrator put it, is less "Eastern" than Ohio Wesleyan (which is west of it), less pretentious than Bucknell, which is east of it in the same state. "And," he added, "the comfort level is higher here. We bootstrap kids. This is a value-added school. Thirty-eight percent of our alumni contribute, and we only just started working on that."

I think he pretty much hit the nail on the head. Allegheny is a very comfortable school. Kids are comfortable with each other, there's no apparent sense of one-upmanship or competition. It is a thoroughly first-rate place and the only people not likely to find it comfortable might be those who have to drive in the fast lane. But Allegheny doesn't miss them.

Clark University
Worcester, Massachusetts

C lark offers something rare anywhere but unique in New England: a four-star academic experience at a major research university for a "B" student with SAT scores in the 500s, and the chance to do undergraduate research on big-league projects.

When Clark alumni wind up years later with Ph.D.s as tenured faculty members at top universities, that tends to prove the point. And that is not to say a "C" student with oomph couldn't do the same thing.

Such heady involvement in their own education is not limited to the science majors. Students in political science, sociology, and other disciplines have published papers as undergraduates or done such things as researching the problems of and drafting city housing policy for Worcester. And majors in philosophy and English, fields where publication is a different and tougher game, report that their profs work closely and individually with them.

Clark, the second oldest graduate institution in the country after Johns Hopkins, was founded in 1887 and opened its liberal arts college in 1902 with a commitment to combining research and undergraduate teaching, rather than polarizing the two as is done elsewhere.

Experience has given Clark faculty reason to be happy with and even to prefer the "500"/"B" students to the "700"/ "A"s. And Clark gets a lot of them; only a third of its freshman come from the top third of their high school classes.

Only 39% of its 2,900 students are from Massachusetts; 3.3% are African-American, 4% are Asian-American, and nearly 14% are foreign. By any definition—academic, economic, geographic, or ethnic—Clark gets a genuinely representative

American mix of kids. And it is doing very well by them, thank you.

Its location has its pluses and minuses. Worcester is only about 40 miles from Boston, every student's Mecca, but like Columbia and the University of Chicago, it's in a run-down part of the city. But that provides an opportunity for tutoring children who need it, teaching English as a second language, and for various helping internships.

Dean Sharon Krefetz, a political scientist, in the course of a long interview said, "We emphasize the autonomous citizen problem solver. We are concerned with social values. The citizen is a concern. If you want an educational place where students and staff are concerned with civic values, this is the place. We require a values perspective [one of the required courses]. Yes, Clark changes people. We make them more responsible and competent citizens."

Dr. Krefetz, who previously taught at Brandeis and Harvard, said the top students are the same at all three places but she preferred the "rough" ones. "A kid who's a wonderful writer had mediocre SATs. It shows there are a lot of opportunities here for kids from different paths. Our faculty is so dedicated they work with each student whether or not they have that spark. We look for students we can inspire and reach. We feel much more gratified when rough students blossom. This is a nurturing climate; three kids who were not impressive to begin with are now on the faculties at Harvard, Wisconsin, and Notre Dame."

Although Clark has traditionally been noted for its psychology and geography departments, the contributions of Robert Goddard, father of the space age, and other famed scientists, Dean Krefetz pointed out there are many other stars in its crown: "There are rare opportunities here for leadership and involvement in the community. Many different activities let each student find his or her niche. They foster leadership skills and a sense of responsibility, because we're not in an ivory tower but are dealing with real people with real problems.

Some students work as tutors to immigrants, teach English as a second language, or have internships in city government whose projects turn into actual city policy. For example, one girl researched and drafted city housing policy; another did a booklet on crime prevention that is distributed by the city. Such opportunities are greater than at a big university. Also, the city bureaucracy is not so big here as to defeat internships. And the city government leaps to our offers."

She has an abundance of achievements to talk about. The opportunities at Clark for future political scientists, urban planners, and sociologists are probably unmatched. For more than a decade the university has been building a partnership with its community. The University Park Partnership Program, that has revitalized its neighborhood. It has renovated nearly 200 homes, provided 175 units of affordable housing, started programs for children, a summer camp, a boys' club, and athletic facilities. It has created a rigorous secondary school for neighborhood children in which both students and faculty are involved. Clark students not only tutor neighborhood children, they babysit so the parents can attend school at night. The program has also built a $22 million K through 12 public school. And residents of the community can attend Clark tuition-free.

Clark also has two new interdisciplinary majors; one is Environmental Science and Policy, which combines environment, technology, and social science. The other is Communication and Culture, exploring how culture is both created and transmitted through communication.

Another program that Clark says is unique is the International Studies Stream in which students can meet the Liberal Studies requirements by taking internationally focused courses, becoming fluent in a foreign language, and studying abroad.

And if a student meets the academic standards, he can have a fifth year at Clark tuition-free and get a master's degree into the bargain.

As a good college should, Clark requires a shared intellectual experience and common intellectual achievements, not just any 32 courses, as Brown lets kids get away with. It is called The Program of Liberal Studies. Everyone must acquire skills in critical thinking and knowing that are essential for self-directed learning. Within a given framework a student can select an organized program of study that will give him a broad introduction to liberal learning and prepare him for lifelong learning. Major components are:

1. Critical thinking. Each student has to pass two courses: one in verbal expression, which may be offered in any one of many departments and which emphasizes the relationship between writing and critical thinking in that discipline, and the other, a formal analysis course that places special emphasis on logical and algebraic modes of thinking.

2. Perspectives courses. As perspective means seeing things in their true relation or relative importance, so these courses encourage breadth. They introduce students to the different ways in which various disciplines define thinking, learning, and knowing. This means everyone takes courses in other cultures, in art, history, language, scientific study, and last but not least, values.

These requirements apply whether one intends to major in physics or philosophy or anything in between. Furthermore, the faculty are fervent believers in these requirements; several volunteered comments on their importance. It was interesting to hear science profs boast about writing requirements. But that shouldn't be too surprising, because good writing is about 80% good thinking and good thinking is central to good science.

Anyone interested in becoming a geographer or cartographer—fields in which the demand in this uncertain world is both great and certain for the foreseeable future—would do well to go to Clark. Not only is its geography department justly famous, but 100 applicants apply each year for five places in its Ph.D. program, so those whose work is already known to the faculty will have a built-in edge for admission. All those accepted who don't have outside support receive remission of tuition and healthy stipends for which they work 17½ hours per week as teaching, research, or departmental assistants.

Clark is a major research university of small size, a place where a teenager can make things happen that he wants to happen, much as he can at a small liberal arts college. He will find a faculty concerned for his welfare, a faculty of the highest competence, and one that will set a high level of expectation, and care enough to see that he works to meet it.

Dean Alan Jones, professor of chemistry and noted research scientist, said Clark not only opens a door to the "B" student that is closed elsewhere in New England, but also that these kids who would be Ivy rejects get more out of college and contribute more: "The kids who get the most out of the college experience are the kids who are rougher. They meet a prof, get interested, blossom, set goals. They weren't number one in high school but they click in this environment. Consider the case of this student: He publishes three papers before he leaves Clark, goes to medical school. He had no idea of all this when he was sweeping floors in the school gym. Another, the son of high school teachers, was working with me in the lab and is now a prof at Stony Brook [State University of New York at Stony Brook].

"When Daddy is not a stockbroker they often don't know what the possibilities are or what they are to do. I'm more into working with kids who haven't had many opportunities—a dyslexic who came to Clark is now getting his Ph.D. in chemistry.

"The difference at Clark [from other liberal arts colleges] is the research atmosphere; we have big Federal grants that are competitive on the national scene, won in competition with MIT and Caltech [the top powers]. People with major research reputations are at Clark and they work with undergraduates.

"This is a very liberal place. We overcome parochialism, the views they're afraid of. They have to become more open; privileged kids have to deal with others who aren't; had they gone to an Ivy school they wouldn't have had to. We open kids' minds."

Dr. Robert Ross, a sociology prof, also believed the melting-pot diversity at Clark is good for the children of the affluent, but his rationale differed: "Kids are changing. In the middle class each year there's less of a burning thirst for knowledge. There's more a sense of entitlement, and college is more of a routine than rite of passage. They're more interested in accouterments than in the process. When I went to the University of Michigan coming to college was an adventure. Back then I could get them [the students] excited about learning. Now I have to work harder at reaching and activating than I did. These complacent, cosmopolitan children of affluent America may well benefit from going to college with kids for whom it is still an adventure."

Also, they—the complacent as well as the adventurous—do respond to the individual attention they get at Clark. One student's brother at Penn State, Dr. Ross said, "couldn't believe the attention he gets here." By any definition, he said, Clark gets a mix of students. On entrance tests they score below students at many other institutions, "but they finish above. And they're not more liberal when they graduate, but more reasoned."

He was also "very pleased" with the career achievements of his majors. They've become lawyers, foundation executives, environmental group executives, and social workers, among other things, and they've kept in touch with him.

Some took a more optimistic view of the students than the sociologist. One of them, Dr. Cynthia Enloe, head of the Government Department, credited students with doing much of the groundwork which led to creation of the Women's Studies Program.

In an interview for *The Clark Progressive*, she made another cogent point: Because Clark students don't feel they're the elite for having been accepted by an Ivy school, they understand the level of work they have to do to graduate. "They don't think they can sit back and slide through life."

She probably had in mind a stinging attack in *The Chronicle of Higher Education* by a Harvard English instructor—who surely has kissed his chances at tenure goodbye—on the debasing of grades there. The instructor quoted one professor as saying she could give one student "only a B+" because he hadn't turned in the one and only paper required for her course! In another story, a Harvard student tour guide was quoted as telling a prospective student, "You'll get all As and Bs."

"This place [Clark] is so alive," Dr. Enloe was quoted as saying, "I wouldn't leave it for anything."

Students who came from all points of the compass had favorable views of the school, if in varying degrees. A freshman girl from New Orleans found this New England community compatible and very diverse, as did one from St. Louis and another from Chicago. A couple of others thought there was so much diversity they didn't feel any great sense of community, while others disagreed.

A junior philosophy major planning to become a college professor was so enthusiastic about the help her teachers gave her with her papers that she insisted I go visit one of the teachers. I found him as interested in his young friends as she had claimed. He said that the kids at Clark were the equal of any others. An English professor who got his doctorate at Yale was as proud of his students' abilities and accomplishments as he was of the fact that "they call me Sarge"—in recognition, naturally, of his toughness in making them shape up their writing.

Several students said Clark had given them mind-opening experiences. A political science major said, "One thing I've learned is keeping an oen mind . . . critiquing and challenging myself . . . that's when you're really alive and really learning; and finally making sense of it all and being aware that a lot of different ideas I rejected when I came here can actually add to my radical ideals."

A prospective economics major said, "It's not so much the actual material you learn here but how you learn how to learn here, like teaching you different ways to think and to process information so whatever you go on to do later, you understand how to interpret it into your own world view."

These students also liked the fact that Dean Krefetz had just put in force a new, tougher, and more revealing rating-and-comment form for the students' evaluation of their teachers. Formerly, each department had designed its own form so it could play to its own strengths and blur any attempts at university-wide comparisons. Now all use the same form and everyone gets rated, from instructor to department head. But none of the faculty members I talked to were concerned enough about a new rating form to bring it up. The things they were eager to tell me reflected a liking for kids and a love of teaching. Furthermore, students sit in on faculty meetings; so it's something like a big family where things are laid out on the table.

Goucher College

Towson, Maryland

G oucher has several distinctions. It was long one of the best women's colleges. It is now one of the best-kept secrets among the top quality coed colleges, and it is one of the few first-rate undergraduate colleges in a major urban area—Baltimore.

Even though it lies close to the city's northern boundary, a visitor driving into the campus enters another world, a lovely, tree-lined spread of 287 acres. Not far beyond it is a Mecca for boaters and fishermen, Loch Haven Reservoir.

Another distinction is Goucher's dramatically successful pioneering in the career development field. Since 1920 it has had one of the best, most innovative, forward-looking, and effective career development offices in the nation, a result of its efforts to expand the job market for its women graduates. Since 1987, when it became coeducational, men also have been getting the benefit of all this expertise and wide-ranging networking that means prime job connections.

Goucher graduates' employment statistics are phenomenal. When the class of 1993 was surveyed in 1998, none of the 80% who responded was unemployed one year after graduation. Those who didn't have jobs were in graduate school or weren't in the job market. In the class of 1997, surveyed the same year, only 1% were unemployed and 72% of the class had responded. These are typical success stories. Any institution claiming a better record would be boasting. The moral is, if you're counting on your college experience to get you a job in a changing world, you'd be hard put to find a better bet than Goucher.

One reason is that Goucher had been very adroitly and effectively using internships long before most other schools caught on. It is one of the few colleges that require every student to have an off-campus experience, such as foreign study or internship, and at Goucher 80% choose internships. There are more than 200 of them and they cover just about every imaginable kind of job or enterprise in just about every part of the world. But that's not surprising when you consider Goucher adopted this program long ago as part of its strategy to open opportunities for women. Probably only Antioch, where every other term is an off-campus job and which started earlier, has done more in this area.

Supplementing this is a mentorship program that enables students to establish career contacts with Goucher graduates or with other friends of the college who are professionals in many fields. The mentors provide career advice and may open doors or offer jobs.

At the core of this success, naturally, is the product the Career Development Office has to offer. A Goucher graduate has had as good a liberal education as any institution in the nation can offer, and in the important ways, better than any prestige university. What are some of these ways? Richness of experience from being an active participant in independent study or student-faculty research projects, seminars, tutorials; from enjoying close relationships with scholar-teachers; and from being a contributing member of a community of learning, not just a passive ear earning course credits. All these things add up to the crucial 21st-century ability to go ahead on one's own. The Goucher graduate has met the highest standards, and has been the beneficiary of a superb faculty whose members love teaching and who take genuine interest in the individual student.

Goucher deserves, as do many other colleges in this book, much more attention from parents and their college-bound teenagers. For those who think they want to go to college in a city, Goucher is an ideal place. And until the college brings the percentage of men students from 31% closer to half, it will be a lot easier for men to get in than for women.

Twenty-seven percent of the admitted freshmen were in the top 10% of their high school classes, 24% in the second tenth, and 14% each in the third and fourth deciles. Four percent were in the bottom tenth, and for 37% there was no rank. The mean SAT total is about 1,180, which means as many below as above. What's more important than SAT scores is the interest in learning the applicant brings. Goucher no longer requires an interview. Instead it is one of the colleges that carefully reads all the material in your application. Except in unusual cases, the interview doesn't tell anything more than the written material, so do a careful job on it to tell your story accurately and fully. And if the admissions officer sees motivation and promise, he or she is going to say yes.

To attract top students, the college offers $8,500, $10,000, and full tuition merit awards and an array of others; indeed, 47% have merit grants ranging from $300 to full tuition. Slightly more than half get some need-based financial aid consisting of loans, grants, and campus jobs. It is often cheaper to go to Goucher than to some lower-cost public or private school.

About one-third of the college's 1,100 or so students come from Maryland, two-thirds from the mid-Atlantic region, 14% from the Midwest, 6% from other countries, and the rest from around the country. Fourteen percent are minority: black, Asian, Hispanic.

A dean called them "a very eclectic group; they are somewhat liberal; there are some risk-takers, since one reason for coming here is to be part of change, and this is more the case among men—it's more of an adventure for them." As is the case in several other colleges in this group, there is a strong commitment to volunteerism. For several years, students in the writing program, for example, have been working with underprivileged kids, many of whom have been helped from elementary right on through high school. There is also a partnership in science with an inner-city high school.

At Goucher everyone lives by the Honor Code. They also work hard, at least the students I talked to seemed to bear out the faculty descriptions of them as hardworking and interested in intellectual pursuits. The many merit awards are bringing in more and more serious students of high academic ability, which ensures a mix of abilities, something needed for good discussion classes.

Every freshman takes a seminar called Frontiers, an interdisciplinary exploration of a current topic, chosen by the instructor. Each class of a dozen or fewer is taught by professors from several disciplines, and the object is to integrate the various aspects of a liberal arts education.

At a lunch table, when a sociology major, a junior who had transferred in that year from a junior college and so hadn't had the freshman experience, complained the school wasn't challenging enough, one of his tablemates shot back that sociology was such a soft discipline that some schools had dropped it. A theater major thought there wasn't enough vocational emphasis. Another transfer said Rollins College in Florida was "frivolous" but Goucher was "fine." Everyone else I talked with during my visit, whether history, dance, theater, philosophy, teacher education majors, or athletes, said it was a choice they would repeat if they had it to do over again.

A few years ago, economics and related areas would have been the most popular majors. Now the humanities have taken over. More than one-third have gravitated to English, art, art history, communication, dance, dance therapy, languages, music, philosophy, and theater. Economics is now in the second tier, along with education, historic preservation, international relations, management, political science, and sociology. A quarter are in math and sciences, including computer science. And the math at Goucher, incidentally, is a hands-on affair focusing on real-world applications wherever possible and integrating it with computer science. Goucher was one of the first to introduce computer courses as well as to require computer literacy.

Beyond the freshmen seminars, students have to fill specific distribution requirements so that no one can leave Goucher as a specialized ignoramus. Goucher is also deeply concerned about preparing its graduates for the 21st century, and one of its efforts is a new major, the Cognitive Studies Program, which explores how people learn. In one of its courses, students are investigating with the aid of a mathematician, a computer scientist, a psychologist, and a philosopher, the possibilities of artificial intelligence.

Goucher has an array of support services that good students often find as useful as do those with problems or disabilities. One is a voluntary writing program to help students improve their skills to meet the writing proficiency requirement, or to do better in their other courses. More than one-third of the student body makes use of the Academic Center for Excellence (ACE); a lot of the bright students discover in college that they don't know how to study effectively. The ACE not only helps those with learning problems but also conducts sessions on test-taking techniques, test anxiety, and time management, and it is used by the "B" students as much as by anyone else.

Three years ago, the college had another bright idea, one that is reminiscent of the way Emory and Henry in Virginia helps those in dire straits. It spotted the toughest courses and assigned to them supplemental instructors who work with students in study groups. And it has been shown that students learn better and more effectively that way than by working on their own. It is another example of collaborative learning that helps make these colleges so effective.

As a result of this program, no student flunked chemistry the first semester of 1993, and poor grades in biology were reduced by two-thirds.

Freshmen get an introduction-to-college course, Transitions, that meets throughout first semester to enlighten them on things like time management, the college's expectations of them, rules, their own responsibilities, social problems, study abroad opportunities, career options, the Career Development Office, and graduation requirements. This has reduced bad grades by one-half.

These efforts not only improve the college's retention but also the student's own self-image and satisfaction. If a student doesn't realize his potential he will tend to externalize his frustrations and blame them on the institution. The imaginative approach that has long helped women realize their potential and has opened doors to them in a frosty world is now also getting the men up to speed.

A typical Goucher student, one professor said, is worldly and traveled, but as a high schooler was not committed or achieving enough for the Ivy schools. But they come here, he said, "and they get turned on." Another said his own son had been a "B" student in high school, came to Goucher, sampled a wide variety of courses, got excited about philosophy, and is now going to graduate school after getting top grades and scores in the 700s on the Graduate Record Exam (comparable to like scores on the SATs).

"This college," said a political science professor, "fits kids with basic skills. It is a nurturing environment. It is competitive but not a paper mill. They are transformed at the end of four years; the developmental curve is very high because the teachers here love their subject matter and what they are doing."

At Goucher, they said, students develop the capacity to read critically and to think critically, both crucial skills. They also said the level of expectation is high and that "the flow of good, noted speakers we have is important." One professor who had taught at Brown said there is no comparison between Goucher and Brown when it comes to close student-faculty relationships. "This," he added, "is everything I thought it was supposed to be."

Hampshire College
Amherst, Massachusetts

No college has ever been born of such distinguished parentage to such high expectation, so maligned in its adolescence, and matured to fulfill its promise so brilliantly as Hampshire. Dazzling might be a more accurate word. In only thirty years, two graduates have won MacArthur Foundation "genius awards," as has the college itself, one has had a Pulitzer prize, film industry alumni have had fifteen Academy Award nominations and three Oscars, as well as Emmy and Peabody awards; one in five has a terminal degree, several are publishing scholars. The famed Tuskegee Syphilis Study of

1997 was headed by an alumna M.D. And just in the last ten years, Hampshire seniors have won sixteen Fulbright Fellowships, three Truman Fellowships, two National Security Education Program grants, and nine other fellowships.

As Education Editor of *The New York Times* during the college-going panic of the late '50s, I did my part to extol the virtues and promise of the imaginative New College plan created by neighboring Amherst, Mount Holyoke, Smith, and the University of Massachusetts. At a time when getting into college, especially a good college, was the American family's high-voltage anxiety, this New College proposal was one that could live on tuition alone and thus could be replicated. It seemed a magic solution.

When it finally came into being as Hampshire College in 1970 in a former apple orchard on the southern edge of Amherst, it had what was hailed as a dream faculty, and its central idea was—and is—total immersion of the student in a broad liberal education that he himself would largely design.

With its four founding institutions it became part of a new Five College Consortium allowing students at one school to take classes at any of the other four. Some courses—dance, theater, Asian studies, astronomy—were cooperative ventures, and a bus system linked the campuses. But Hampshire would be unique: Grades were replaced by written faculty evaluations; there were no academic departments, no freshmen, sophomores, juniors, or seniors, no fraternities or sororities, and no intercollegiate athletics (although the school now has intercollegiate soccer and basketball).

Within a framework intended to prevent his coming out a narrow dilettante—as one can at Amherst, Brown, and others—every student, with faculty advice, was his own intellectual architect and builder. He had to provide the ideas.

Hampshire suddenly was one of the most sought-after schools in the country and it attracted throngs of independent, energetic, and imaginative people. It also lured youths who chose not to notice the responsibilities required by this intoxicating freedom. Most teenagers have a planning span of eight to ten hours and to them it looked like the primrose path or the yellow brick road.

When the dilettantes found it took more work, structure, and planning than they had bargained for, dropout rates and parental disaffection grew. Also, the academic freedom was often seen as frivolity, especially when a news story in 1984 described an upper level thesis titled, "A Career in the Field of Flying Disc Entertainment and Education" (frisbees). What wasn't publicized a few years later was that the thesis author had become a product-development and marketing consultant for two firms. Hampshire was getting a bad rap, and it lasted for several years.

Happily, those days are long past. Hampshire's 1,200 students—from nearly every state and a dozen foreign countries—are there because a very able admissions staff does its best to make sure Hampshire is the right place for them. It takes about 60% of its applicants, which means that whether the student and college are right for each other is more important than the grade point average or test scores. More than once admissions director Audrey Smith has said no to someone with As and taken another with Bs and Cs.

Today no college has students whose intellectual thyroids are more active or whose minds are more passionately engaged. A few equal it, but most don't come close, including Hampshire's neighbors. Students are not only happy, they feel free to declare that their peers in the other colleges are missing something important.

The effect persists. Although it's only been awarding diplomas for 25 years and its oldest alumnus was 47 in 1999, more than half the graduates have advanced degrees. Remarkably, Hampshire ranks 16th among all the institutions in the country in the percentage of future psychology Ph.D.s.

Its record in the film industry is simply astounding. In two decades it has outperformed even the major schools, such as UCLA and NYU, in turning out writing, producing, and directing stars. Best known is Ken Burns, creator of *The Civil War* and *Baseball* documentaries. Others include Paul Margolis, who wrote the TV series *MacGyver* and is now executive story editor for the TV series *Sirens*; John Falsey, whose *St. Elsewhere, Northern Exposure,* and *I'll Fly Away* have set new standards in network TV programming; and Jeff Maguire, whose screenplay *In the Line of Fire* was nominated for an Academy Award. These alums also are opening doors to Hampshire students with all kinds of internship opportunities.

The *Alumni News* reports such a variety of jobs and achievements around the world that it actually makes fascinating reading. A dozen graduates reported books published, one reviewed on the front page of *The New York Times Book Review*; a few were short story writers; one was a producer for Czech TV; a dozen others had professorships at places like Tufts, Columbia, University of California, and Ohio State; some were just getting doctorates; there were newspaper and TV correspondents in Alaska, Tokyo, Moscow, and in several U.S. cities. There were psychiatrists, owners of business firms, actresses, a magazine editor, a man working for the Israeli Forest Services as a result of his Division III thesis, and a tattoo artist working on his master's thesis in film at UCLA.

Many ended their squibs urging other alumni to call or visit them, including this one from Moscow: "There are four Hamp alums here. Call or let us know if you're going to be in the area."

There are two reasons why Hampshire graduates achieve so much. One is the kind of person the college attracts. The other is what the college does for them by equipping them to become their own wide-ranging explorers and connection-seers. As one Hampshire student said of a Five College seminar on another campus, "Some of the others had more information on a topic, but I can take information and turn it around, use it better."

In another 15 years, Hampshire alumni will probably be leading the pack as cutting-edge innovators in many fields and in developing new technologies with potential business applications in the new world of global entrepreneurship. The man who has more patents than any living American, Jerome Lemuelson, has given the college $3.2 million to develop courses and programs designed to stimulate innovation and entrepreneurship.

Some now under way—in artificial intelligence, digital imaging in film, river ecology, animal behavior, innovation in farming, and aquaculture—are already affecting the learning process. A physics professor involved in the farm course said, "The Lemuelson Program has broken down the walls between a liberal arts education and the search for solutions to real world problems, so that what we're doing is no longer just a theoretical exercise."

Several student inventions have come out of the Lemuelson program, and at this writing, two students are awaiting a patent for an accessible snowboard for people with physical disabilities.

In his first two years a student takes work in four of the college's five interdisciplinary schools that replace traditional departments. They are: Humanities and Cultural Studies, Social Science, Natural Science, Cognitive Science, and Interdisciplinary Arts. He can take two courses in each school or do an independent research project in each.

Taking the courses could be the easier way; the project is no mere term paper. A topic such as Historical Forces and the Erosion of American Soil means learning something about geology, geography, weather, agriculture, economics, and history, among other things. The student quickly discovers the ankle bone connection to the leg bone is only the beginning. In fact, he may have started on an inquiry that will engage him for four years and take him into areas he had no original intention of exploring. This is Division I.

For Division II, which he starts thinking about in his second year, he selects two professors to serve on his concentration committee and discusses with them how he might best address his interests and goals. He drafts a concentration statement describing his learning plans for the next two or three semesters. It must meet the professors' concern for intellectual rigor and breadth.

And by its nature it is a broad gauge. Such topics as Education and Social Mobility, or The Influence of Schooling on Moral Development, like the erosion topic, become wide ranges of inquiry and are far more flexible and demanding than the confines of a simple history, sociology, or geology major.

This richness is largely responsible for the intellectual excitement. Everyone is embarked on a learning adventure that may take them to places they never dreamed of. It's not surprising that a prime conversational topic is "What are you doing?", or that the Hampshire students tell a visitor that on the Five College buses they are the only ones talking about their work.

As a student works his way along his Division II project, the teachers provide criticism, advice, and evaluation. The examination is no written test. It is a serious and lengthy evaluation of a portfolio of papers he has produced in his course work or for his research project, or an evaluation of an internship or some artistic products. An additional component has been added to the Division II requirements; namely, some exposure to and understanding of issues involving Third World and minority cultures.

There is nary a grade on his Hampshire transcript because a student learns much more from thoughtful written critiques of his work, of his strengths, and in suggestions for improvement than from an A, a B, or a C. This system has proved a boon in the real world. Such detailed pictures of the students give them a distinct advantage when they apply for jobs or for admission to graduate school. However, they do get grades for courses taken at one of the four other schools in the Five College Consortium, and these will appear on their transcripts.

Values are important at Hampshire. The experience is intended to foster a concern for others as well as to develop individual talents, so before moving on to Division III, a student must perform some service to the college or to the community. It may be anything from participating in the college governance to working with disabled citizens.

The final year, Division III, is largely spent on a major independent study project under the guidance of two Hampshire faculty members and a professor from a neighboring college or a professional working in that field. Usually, the project explores in depth a specific aspect of the Division II project.

Two other advanced activities are required. At least one must be an advanced-level course or a teaching activity, such as helping a faculty member with an introductory course, or serving as a second reader on a Division I exam committee.

As at many other colleges, there is a January term which allows for any one of a multitude of adventures, from foreign study to trying an otherwise unavailable course at another college.

A computer science professor who went to Oberlin as an undergraduate summed it up this way: "This is the only place for those who can see an educational opportunity and pursue it. I have two second-year student co-authors doing research on a graduate level, and another doing publishable research. Some are even working on artificial intelligence (a graduate level area). Hampshire is the only place where this could happen. Hampshire is a unique opportunity for people with drive. Encouragement does it; it helps pull him up to the level where he can do it. Somewhere else he'd be spinning his wheels."

A theater professor added that she has students directing plays after the first semester, they are so eager to get busy and reinvent the wheel, another way of saying they're caught up in the enterprise.

Others said anyone who comes to Hampshire "has to care about the world of ideas because here they have to be engaged.

And they are passionately engaged. They work on weekends; when they get going on a project, their stopping point is when the job is done."

They also offered these opinions about their students:

- They are concerned with ethics, actively involved in social service, and tolerant.
- Hampshire students have built-in crap detectors, much initiative and flexibility, they invent new careers, and the graduate schools want more of them.

These professors had all gone to traditional, prestige colleges but all thought that Hampshire prepared young people better. Its students develop good study habits and good instincts for what's important. They know how to write a good job report, and they have developed a broad view. They've also been forced to think. Some courses, for example, require students to write one-page summaries of what they've done and how they arrived at a problem's solution.

Another teacher attested to the computer science professor's claim that encouragement was the secret. She said, "There's something that happens and you see it happen before your eyes. Kids get transformed. I'm supervising a Division III project of a student who's always tried very hard and always before this when she'd bring in her papers I'd say 'you're not analytical enough' and her eyes would almost fill with tears and she'd say, 'but I tried so hard.' And we'd explain, and finally, this year, she got it and she's going to do a great job, and she said to me, 'I love it so much I can't bear to graduate now that I've discovered what it's about.' And that's really a pretty exciting thing.

"What do you need to do to get it? It's tolerance for uncertainty; everything isn't cut and dried."

Students I spoke with had two recurring themes. One was the kind of person who should come to Hampshire. He should be interested, motivated, and feel strongly about doing independent work, and "be a little bit of a self-starter—you'll learn how to be a self-starter." He also has to have a reason for coming; he may not know what it is, but it isn't just going to college. He should be able to tolerate uncertainty and know the value of it, and be able to imagine.

The other theme was even more frequently expressed, and that was how much diversity there is. A New York City boy from a high school class of 850 that embraced 75 to 80 ethnic groups said he found much more diversity at Hampshire. "They were all middle class. Here there are all sorts of people; for example, I met my first gay [person] here. But the real reason is that here you get identified by the work you do; the question is; 'What are you doing?' "

In addition, they had a lot to say about being deeply interested in their work, and being convinced of the superior quality of the classes at Hampshire. One girl added, "I took a class at Amherst and thought it was terrible."

The sense of community also came through strongly and consistently. "Here," as one said, "everybody's together. You know all the profs. It's small and intimate and everybody's so friendly."

As at so many of the other schools in this book, Hampshire students said their experience deeply affected their values. One girl expressed a common feeling when she said, "Moral judgments are definitely affected. People are so much more moral and non-judgmental here. You learn how to listen."

Hampshire is in a class by itself for those who have the drive to profit from it.

Juniata College

Huntingdon, Pennsylvania

F or as long as I've been interested in colleges, Juniata in rural middle Pennsylvania has shown up in the top ranks of the National Resources Council's surveys of which colleges produce the nation's scholars and scientists. A recent visit showed why. This school is not on every suburban high school senior's lips and is not very selective, but it deserves to be. It has a powerful sense of mission. It has a powerhouse faculty trained at the top universities. And it has eager young customers who become high achievers. Testimony to Juniata's excellence is the fact that one of its alumni, Dr. William Phillips, was co-recipient of the Nobel Prize for Physics in 1997.

That combination produces dramatic results, especially in science, Juniata's strong suit. Ninety percent of its applicants to medical, dental, veterinary, and optometry schools are accepted. For medical school alone it it is a grand slam, 100%. Furthermore, science professors emphasized, unlike many schools, they don't weed out anybody, even someone with a combined SAT score of 900 who requires nurturing. More than half the science students get involved in undergraduate research; some years all do.

In the last few years Juniata has received grants of $1.7 million from the National Science Foundation to further strengthen their science programs and to work with high schools. The college also got a Merck innovation award. A chemistry prof pointed out, "We have outstanding lab equipment. We throw away equipment other colleges would be glad to have."

With a $900,000 Howard Hughes Foundation grant, Juniata is doing something unique. It has a combined chemistry and biology lab which integrates the study of both disciplines, teaching students cutting-edge research techniques in molecular biology. The college is also building a new center for science in which about ten percent of the space will be devoted to student-led research. Though many of the faculty have research grants, the school's attitudes is that scholarship is not something apart from teaching but a way of modeling.

In the crowded school teaching market, 90% of Juniata's graduates get secure jobs immediately after graduation. Of its 1997 class responding to surveys, 98% were employed, in graduate school, or in other planned post-graduate activities within six months of getting their diplomas.

Worth special note are two facts: One is that Juniata has an outstanding record of inspiring women to become scientists and doctors—60% of the freshman chemistry class usually are women. Another is that nearly half (47%) of their enthusiastic alumni contribute financially. Few colleges can make such a claim.

A dean said, "This is a value-added place. We serve students from rural communities. We provide upward mobility. There is a heavy emphasis on faculty-student contact. There is a strong sense of community, with no fraternities or sororities. The sense of community is enhanced by Mountain Day, when the school closes down on some unannounced day and everyone goes to a nearby state park and plays for a day. And at Christmas, Madrigal Dinner, faculty and administrators wait on the students."

Juniata is a place where women not only get as much attention in the classroom as men, but is also a place where they have many role models among the faculty. Indeed, there could hardly be a better place for women to develop. There are four women professors in biology, chemistry, and mathematics, as well as women on the Allied Health Committee, which makes graduate and medical school recommendations. Biologist Debra Kirchhof-Glazier, who heads the committee, said, "Our classes are female friendly. Women tend to respond to relationships, so I know every name in my classes, and all the students know each other, even in big classes. We put name tags in a basket and mix them up. Each student picks one, then locates that person and becomes acquainted. In our classes the women are definitely vocal, and I pick on women to be sure they speak up. We had one shy woman run a large class on eating disorders, and another on how to study."

A remarkable 80% of the student body participate in intra-murals and their intercollegiate teams are all bona fide students. The men's volleyball team in 1994 was the Division III champion, and the women's team has been in the playoffs the last 19 years.

Over 80% of the students receive financial aid that averages more than $4,000 a year. Juniata's 1,700 students aren't all from rural areas; three-quarters of them are from Pennsylvania, and the rest come from 29 states and ten foreign countries. About 78% of the applicants are accepted. The middle 50% of acceptees have total SAT scores in the 1050–1250 range, and most were in the top half of their high school classes, but many of those were rural schools.

Whatever their backgrounds when they come, students soon acquire worldly perspectives. There are always some foreign faculty members and exchange students on campus. Everyone is encouraged to study abroad for at least one semester in their major area during junior year. They can choose from an array of 21 programs, which include direct exchanges of both students and faculty with universities in France, Germany, Japan, and Mexico.

Whether direct exchange or not, every foreign term involves total immersion. The Juniata student becomes a member of the host university's student body and community. A junior may go as a business major but he or she comes back knowing some of the host country's culture. In contrast to most other univer-sities' foreign study programs, which provide separate enclaves for the U.S. students apart from the host country's, Juniata's foreign programs are much more international. Thus the experience is more intense and the feedback and the rewards are greater.

Students are free to design their own majors with the advice of two faculty members, but their study must include the core curriculum providing the framework of a liberal education. It has cross-cultural requirements. One, for example, is called Heart of India, team-taught by an Indian professor and a student with the help of Juniata profs of chemistry, geology, religion, and history, all of whom have been to India. Another, less elaborate, is The Greek Mind.

As at many other good colleges, seniors must prepare a research project over two semesters, develop it, and present it in a colloquium of students and faculty. They also must take a course called Values Study, which is just what the name says, and which is team-taught by faculty members from several different disciplines.

On just about every campus I visited, faculty members were happy with and proud of their students. Here I got the feeling that by the time they were seniors Juniata students must be ten feet tall. The words most used to describe them were "honest," "highly motivated," "hard working," "professionally or vocationally oriented," and "having a strong desire to serve." Many of them when they arrive are unsophisticated but bright and eager. Their good qualities are what sell most faculty on coming to Juniata.

Other faculty went further. One who had taught at those places said the kids at the top were just as bright as those at Middlebury or Haverford. Another, a science prof, said, "Our kids are performing at a higher level in grad and medical schools than they did in college. They often find they've done some of the work here. We take the average kid and open doors for him."

To underscore her points she told these two stories:

"One of our seniors who was rejected by the medical schools he applied to in 1986 went to grad school at the University of California at Davis and has been hired by Harvard as associate professor in charge of the cardiology lab at Brigham and Women's Hospital.

"Last year at Harvard medical school, a Yale graduate asked two of ours where they'd gone to college. When they told him, he said, 'Juniata, where's that?' But on the first exam, both our graduates got As and the Yale man got a C. Showing him their papers they said, 'This is where.'" A chemistry professor could hardly wait to add that in 1993 the world-famous Mayo Clinic in Rochester, Minnesota, accepted six applicants nationwide for its grad school clinic and two of them were from Juniata.

All these things don't happen just because teachers are interested in the students and the students' work. As at other colleges in this book, Juniata's faculty is committed to improving its teaching methods. They confer with each other, comparing notes on what works; they have a team of faculty that will consult with any teacher who wishes help, and they sit in on each other's classes. They call "fantastic" both the interest in teaching that has been aroused and the fact that many profs have revised their teaching methods to make them more effective.

As one might expect, the students would write enthusiastic letters of recommendation for their profs anytime. The volleyball players were naturally proud of their success but wouldn't want to be anyplace else anyway. Science students were even prouder than the athletes, sure they could lick twice their weight in Ivy Leaguers, an attitude that was pervasive in the science buildings. It was not just the students who were infected; one secretary told me: "We're good!"

The English, business, and other majors sang the same song. One called the learning environment "fantastic" and the faculty challenging and full of parental concern for their progress. It was clear the teachers were friends and mentors as well. And to a favorite question about being able to have dinner or spend a night at a faculty member's home five years from now, several said the problem would be in deciding which one to choose. A couple of housewives taking courses part-time were as enthusiastic as the kids.

One little group of upperclass students felt so strongly about the quality of their experiences that they asked me, "What's the difference between this school and Amherst?"

My answer was that Amherst has more very bright, more sophisticated, and more well-to-do freshmen than Juniata, but by the time they're seniors the situation has been reversed. The Juniata seniors' talents have been doubled and sharpened, and they have been better equipped to cope, to adapt, and to take risks—things they will have to do in this new world. And women could not have more encouragement or better role models than at Juniata. Amherst, on the other hand, has turned out pretty much the same kind of person it took in; there, getting in was the great achievement of life: Juniata students seemed to like my answer.

What kind of person would be happy at Juniata? Most teenagers would unless they need the big city, want to be in the fast lane, or aren't interested in learning. If they want to be able to feel that they belong and that people are eager to help them, they will be happy here. Twenty years ago most of the students were first-generation college and from mid-Pennsylvania. That is no longer true and there is more diversity—a quarter of the freshmen are from out of state—and there's a good contingent of international students. Also, the college's heavy emphasis on foreign study as well as foreign student and faculty exchanges has helped changed things.

And anyone interested in the health professions could hardly find a surer entrée into a graduate program or medical or veterinary school. Not only is Juniata's record phenomenal, but it has been achieved with students who did not come to college with impressive test scores. The person with that 900 SAT score will be turned on, and if medical school turns out not to be the realistic choice, another way will be found into a health profession.

A teenage girl, especially one who may lack confidence, should know that no place will make a greater effort to see that she feels at least as important as any male, and that she flowers.

Things like these are some of the reasons Juniata's alumni are so eager to help and to contribute financially. "Alumni fly in from Oregon to do volunteer jobs," said a professor. "It's absolutely fantastic!" Satisfied customers are the proof of the pudding; there should be more places like this and more people should know about them.

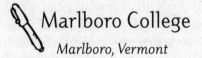

Marlboro College
Marlboro, Vermont

Marlboro College, nestled in one of Vermont's scenic hills near Brattleboro, has fewer than 300 students. They design their own programs—a poor idea for most collegians—but if I had $100 million I'd give a third of it to endow this school. There is no other college experience like it. The rest would go to Antioch and Hampshire, where students also design their own programs. Reed and St. John's—where they don't—would be included if they were as needy.

Each of these schools has an ethos that demands commitment and performance and turns out democracy's essential leaven: bold, clear thinkers, people of vision and character.

One of the fruits of the GI Bill, Marlboro was founded by returning veterans in 1946. Walter Hendricks, who had been teaching GIs in France, gave his old hill farm to realize his vision of a college where education would take place "mind to mind." He had the help of Robert Frost, Dorothy Canfield Fisher, Ambassador Ellsworth Bunker, and the famed scientist, educator, and regent of the Smithsonian Institution, Dr. Caryl P. Haskins.

What tiny Marlboro has given to society in its short life is simply astounding for a college so little known and so little sought after. It shows what kind of young people it draws and what it does for them.

In just five decades Marlboro has produced an impressive array of alumni that includes editors at *The New York Times* and *The Wall Street Journal,* a newspaper publisher, college and university professors, bankers, CEOs in business, doctors, lawyers, research scientists, artists, and poets. An amazing 60% go on to graduate or professional schools, and to the top ones.

Even more dramatic are the figures on Marlboro's exalted rank in the production of future scientists and scholars. Only three schools—California Institute of Technology, University of Chicago, and Reed—turn out higher percentages of future Ph.D.s in the life sciences. Only ten do better in theology and religious studies. Just 17 top it in math and computer sciences.

And as it should be, it's a good mind in a sound body. Its cross-country ski teams were second in NCAA Division II in New England in 1985 and third in 1986, pretty good for a student body a fraction the size of its competitors. It also has teams in volleyball, tennis, basketball, ultimate frisbee, and touch football.

The founders provided for a self-governing community modeled on the New England town meeting, with everyone on a first-name basis and, as at St. John's, with no faculty ranks. The basic tenet is that academic learning is inseparable from the community in which it occurs. Students, faculty, staff, and administration all are equal voting members. The town meeting can even vote down faculty decisions on academic policy, but the faculty can override by a two-thirds majority.

At first glance, Marlboro looks like a homey, old-shoe, nurturing place in the country for someone who needs help, the plain white frame buildings are so informal and the people so friendly. Indeed, in their first life, some of the buildings were barns and a farmhouse. But that impression is deceiving. Marlboro's academic program is rigorous, and someone who is dysfunctional is likely to be hurt. Nor would physically disabled people find the slopes easy to negotiate. This is a place for self-reliant persons who are interested in ideas and the life of the mind. Students here tend to be a year or so older than other college students, and that makes a significant difference in the level of maturity.

As for admission requirements, if you really want to go to Marlboro and can show the admissions committee in an interview that you belong there, you're in. You will be asked if you really understand the writing requirement and the Plan of Concentration, and you'll be told that the demands are tough.

Two-thirds of the applicants are accepted, about one-third are in the top third of their high school classes, and their SAT scores average around 1,100.

For graduation there are only two requirements beyond the usual one of earning 120 credits with Cs or better, plus a sort of family obligation to the place. The first is that every freshman has to pass muster with a 20-page work of clear writing by the end of the year. Because good writing is mainly good thinking, this is quite demanding. Otherwise, he can have the comparative luxury of taking a variety of liberal arts courses for the first two years. These provide for breadth and for introductory courses to one's areas of interest.

The second requirement is a Plan of Concentration designed by the student and one or two faculty advisers that fully occupies the junior and senior years and involves putting together a whole thesis. It is a focused course of study, but the range and the variety have no limits. Marlboro may have only 42 faculty members and its physical plant may lack the expensive new science buildings that many other colleges have, but that faculty and the outside resources available can satisfy any intellectual bent. The fact that 60% go to graduate and professional schools in a multitude of different fields says so.

A Plan may be cross-disciplinary and it often changes, deepens, and broadens as the learning progresses, raising new questions and the need to explore new areas. A concentration in World Studies, for example, requires two terms in two different cultures.

As for the common obligation, one day a semester, everybody pitches in to work on some of the things that need fixing or cleaning up. Indeed, some of the buildings were built by students, staff, and faculty.

Instead of going to a class three hours a week, a junior or senior will meet one hour a week with one of his or her tutors, to report on what has been done, to plan, or to discuss. For example, someone doing a project on environmental science and environmental policy and ecology may be having tutorials with a biology, a political science, an economics, and perhaps a sociology professor. Otherwise the student is very much left to his own devices and self-discipline.

As one girl said, "there is no place to hide." Everything is riding on what she is doing on her own—and on her own initiative. It is a far heavier responsibility and a good deal more work than the conventional way. It takes someone able to go ahead on her own to handle this kind of freedom. It is the reliance on student initiative that separates Marlboro education from one-on-one elsewhere.

The Plan is a heady adventure, one that attracts transfer students to Marlboro, and it is what alumni talk about as their most exciting and stimulating experience. Juniors and seniors were telling me the same kinds of things Reed students did about how rewarding it was to work on their projects or foreign experiences on their World Studies internships.

Whatever his or her particular Plan, all Marlboro graduates have proved to themselves that they can define a problem, set clear limits on an area of inquiry, analyze that object of study, evaluate the result, and report thoughtfully on the outcome of a worthy project.

One of the great things about the Plan is that it puts teachers and students on the same side of the fence. The final evaluation of every student's Plan—which includes a three-hour oral exam—is conducted by an outside examiner, an expert in the particular field who may be from Amherst, Columbia, Harvard, Williams or elsewhere, along with Marlboro faculty members. So the student's teachers are being evaluated too.

The outside examiners often give better grades than do the Marlboro faculty. A Cornell professor said the one he examined compared very favorably to Cornell's top honors students in English. An MIT professor went further. He said a senior physics major's knowledge of relativity was "greater than that of all but the rarest MIT graduate." Marlboro's physics lab may not be as showy as some at other schools, but in the summer of this student's junior year it got her an internship at the Argonne National Laboratory working on the Hera Electron–Proton Particle Accelerator. A Yale divinity school evaluator called another student's work "quite extraordinary."

The attitudes of students here echoed those at a few other places in this book. I have talked to no group of young people more thoroughly sold on what they are doing. Marlboro is a do-it-yourself kind of place, said one, "and if you want something to happen, you've got to make it happen yourself." That's a virtue, he added, because the world is full of people waiting for someone to tell them what to do. Another felt that Marlboro's little democracy gave her a sense of personal power and independence, and "I'm no longer satisfied to leave decisions that affect me up to someone else."

Nor is there anywhere else a more palpable sense of trust and of being engaged in a common enterprise, if one of infinite variety, than at Marlboro. The library is open 24 hours a day and operates on the honor system; nobody is monitoring the borrowed books. The student leaves a dated, signed card in a checkout box by the door. The computer center is also open around the clock.

Not once during my visit did anyone make that frequent small-college gripe that everyone knows your business. That certainly is the case, but here it tends to make people think of the consequences of any action or churlish attitude that is going to be known to the whole community.

The loyalty to the college seemed incredible, and I was told that was true even of those who'd left without graduating. Everyone I talked to spoke with evident interest in their projects and their plans for now and for after graduation.

They also seemed more mature than most, which is not surprising because the average age here is a little higher than at most other colleges. These are people interested in ideas, so while they may come expecting to study religion or theater or whatever, they may wind up going to graduate school in philosophy or Russian studies, or even graduate schools of business. The experience has helped them find themselves.

Students also become self-sufficient socially. Marlboro is not even a hamlet. What after the Revolutionary War was a town of 3,000 now has a very good inn, a post office, and about 30 houses scattered about; Brattleboro is ten miles away. So a Saturday evening's entertainment may evolve from someone's bringing music to the student center to an impromptu party with dancing. The college also has a full schedule of imported concerts and lectures by noted people. In the summer it is the scene of the Marlboro Music Festival.

It is not just a conceit that causes Marlboro to use many pages in its catalog to describe individual faculty members as people with many interests in addition to their scholarly ones. One, for example, went to Cornell, got doctorates in divinity and in literature, started Outward Bound programs at Skidmore College and at the State University of New York at Potsdam, had his own wilderness programs, was also a university professor in New Zealand, and is at Marlboro because he loves the outdoors and the kind of place Marlboro is. He is, in short, one lively person, and typical in his enthusiasms and his love of what the college is doing.

Marlboro is an egalitarian place where respect is shown. There is more intimacy in the best sense and more interaction than at other colleges, thanks especially to the two years of one-on-one tutorials. Students are heavily involved in their own education, which is a collaborative effort of student and mentor, with the mentor risking some judgment too. For all the demands, it is a place of relaxed camaraderie. During a mid-afternoon visit, I watched the president and a faculty member in a pickup basketball game with students, and the whole place made me think of an extended family hanging out in shirt-sleeves.

Who should come here? First off, one has to be self-sufficient socially because this campus is at the end of the road. It is rural, pastoral, and hilly. Next, one must like people and be prepared to be a working part of a small self-governing community.

But above all, a Marlboro student should be a person who isn't going to be scared off by what one professor said: "The more you demand the more you're going to draw. We expect a lot of our seniors. People who come here should be interested in ideas, the life of the mind. That's central here. And they must be self-reliant."

That number, like the number attracted to Reed or Antioch, or St. John's or Hampshire, is small, but they constitute a Gideon's army. Gideon, in one of Israel's crises, culled an army of a few hundred from a host of thousands and defeated the Mideanite oppressors. The analogy is apt.

Ursinus College
Collegeville, Pennsylvania

About 30 miles northwest of Philadelphia is a new star of the first magnitude in the small galaxy of colleges that change lives. It is 130-year-old Ursinus, named for a sixteenth-century German scholar. It is a friendly and un-pretentious place of just the right size—1,200 students—on a scenic campus of 160 acres.

Until a decade ago, reflecting the German religious roots of the area, Ursinus had kept its light under a bushel; recruiting, for example, was a no-no. Now it is casting its net more widely and has students from twenty-six states and twenty foreign countries. The minority population is 10 percent and growing. They have their own activity house, which they named Unity, where they put on programs both for the whole school and for the townspeople. Here, everyone belongs.

Ursinus's academic emphasis also changed in the last decade, from a career-oriented to a pure liberal arts school as the result of the synergy of a faculty and a new president both making commitments to the liberal arts ideal. The president, John Strassburger, a former Knox dean, and the faculty set out to make Ursinus a life-changing community of learning. And they have succeeded.

It is one of the 8% of colleges good enough to have a chapter of Phi Beta Kappa, the scholastic honor society. But it is the only college I know of whose athletic director is a former academic dean. Furthermore, faculty members of both sexes are honorary "coaches of the week," who give home game pep talks and may even design a play which the coach will use sometime during the game.

The athletic director, Dr. William E. Akin, became a historian but was born a sports fan. He once even gave a course in sports history. When a new prexy brought his own new dean, he chose to be athletic director. "When I took this job," he said, "I asked, 'What can we do to make a better connection between the athletic and the academic sides?' I wanted to show that athletics are not separate, but part of what we're trying to do as a community of learning."

His brainchild has been a success, both on and off the field. The first year, 1997, Ursinus won every home football game as well as its first conference championship ever. Two years later, the faculty has a winning record, as you will see later on.

The college accepts slightly more than three quarters of its applicants, whose median SAT scores are in the 1,100–1,300 range, and nearly half of whom were in the top tenth of their high school classes. Ninety-two percent of its 116 faculty members have Ph.D.s or terminal degrees. The faculty-student ratio is 12–1, often a bragging statistic elsewhere but an understatement here. It fails to reflect how much the teachers are involved in their students' lives.

This is a place where professors talk proudly about how dramatically their students grow in skills and in self-confidence in four years, how their aspirations rise, and their perspectives broaden. The startling fact that three-fourths of Ursinus's seniors will be in graduate or professional schools within five years is ample proof. The students for their part see themselves in such a different and brighter light than when they arrived on campus that everyone I asked the question of said they would want their children to come here to have the same kind of experience.

Its center line is a core curriculum, which means everyone has a shared liberal arts foundation, one in which there is much discussion of values. Just as important, every student is actively involved in his or her own education. He or she has to have a capstone experience, such as a senior thesis, and also works on some other independent project.

Almost everyone goes beyond the requirements and does some independent research as well. Many of them present their papers at professional meetings or collaborate with faculty members and become co-authors as undergraduates. In 1998, 153 students presented papers in 13 disciplines at conferences, and that was no spike in the pattern. The college provides access to a wealth of internships. At least 25% study abroad, and the percentage is growing.

Writing across the curriculum, even in biology and mathematics, is one of the hallmarks of good colleges. Ursinus, however, carries it to a higher level. Every senior has to pass a course in which he writes as a professional in his field would write. "This," said a biology prof, "is the transformation from an amateur to a professional."

The professors are mentors rather than lecturers. Dr. Victor Tortorelli, a Pied Piper who is also chairman of the chemistry department, takes great pride in the fact that the newly remodeled science building, with its state-of-the-art designs pioneered by Allegheny and Kalamazoo, promotes collaborative learning. Here, professors and students do their research not in separate labs and offices, but side by side. They are fellow workers. Such closeness may boost a student's confidence that he too can do what his teacher is doing, and that's what often happens.

As another professor said, "Students come to us as passive recipients and leave as active learners. We transform them!" One of the newer faculty members added, "I've been here four years, so I've seen my first class through, and the change in them is striking." "How do we transform them?" asked economics professor and faculty coach Dr. Heather O'Neil. "We have high expectations. As seniors they do as good work as Ivy students."

The students agree. Nearly everyone I talked to said his or her life had been changed, whether by seeing new worlds opened, by having their horizons broadened, or by becoming more tolerant. But more especially, nearly everyone spoke of having a solid new confidence in their ability to do things they never before would have thought possible, or even thought of. And it seemed clear that these were not the kind of teenagers who had come to college full of self-assurance.

When I read to a group of junior and senior girls the testimony of a Hiram junior that "many catalytical things have happened to me. These are incredible people, they love to teach; they are always making cross connections from one area or discipline to another, always pushing me to do better . . .", they said that was just what was happening to them. Because the school had opened new worlds to them, everyone in the group was working on a different major than the one she had planned to pursue as a freshman. Many had had no idea when they arrived that they'd be so heavily engaged in their own educations or that they'd have to work so hard. Nor did they have any idea they'd find the work so satisfying or feel so good about themselves.

One of the facts of life that even some of the campus leaders had learned the hard way was that getting involved was the key to the happy experience. Time after time, both black and white students would say something like, "I wasn't happy at first, but then I got involved." The involvement can be almost any kind of activity: an internship, a foreign study term, working on a project with a professor, starting a new club or team. Whatever it is, students say their instructors are always supportive. And such support often continues for years after graduation.

The interest and pride faculty members take in their students just spills out. A conversation with a group of them turns into a bragging session with a group of proud parents, they are so eager to tell what their young charges are doing. Here are a few of the things they wanted the world to know:

- "Almost everybody does independent research. In psychology it's 100%."
- "We send students to professional conferences to show their work and they come back with ribbons."
- "It's a rare biology major who graduates without doing independent research, although we don't require it."
- "Our literary magazine illustrates one of our differences. At one college in our conference their glossy job is put out by professionals and carries stuff few students read. Ours is written and produced by students, and students read it." Reading something a fellow student has written is more likely to stimulate an uncertain teenager to think, "I can do as well as that," than is the polished work of a professional.

> ■ "The students are putting on a show of their art
> work in the Berman Museum this afternoon. You
> should go see it; it's a good show and it's all theirs."

This kind of atmosphere changes the lives of professors as well as those of students. They get a new value system seeing their young friends doing the sophisticated kind of work they couldn't have done last year or even last semester. It becomes their achievement as well, so they keep pushing, suggesting. It is axiomatic that in a caring community, where standards and expectations are high, students will rise to meet them. That is one of the things that makes a distinctive college, where the result is greater than the sum of the parts.

While some new Ph.D.s know that teaching is their real love, it is common at colleges such as Ursinus to hear professors say they'd arrived intending to go on to research universities but then something happened. They find they're in the kind of academic world they didn't know existed, a warm and supportive community they'd not known as university graduate students and teaching assistants. They also discover that seeing their students blossom under their care changes their outlook, and their values.

Some see the light for other reasons. One of these was a classics professor who credited the school's increasing diversity for his epiphany. "Here's how it has transformed me: For the first time ever, in my 101 Western Civ class, I have about an even number of black students and white students, and for me that's kind of scary; it makes me aware of my need to teach them the failings of the Western intellectual tradition, how colonialism and oppression can be presented or explained by the Western way of thought. And the other night I went to the Martin Luther King vigil at Unity House. I went there mainly because I was hoping some of my students would be there. I wanted them to know that I was trying to reach out. I never would have done that a few years ago when we had only a very few minority students."

The attitude of the minority students is reciprocal, so much so in fact that it can make things difficult for an activist. The co-founder of the black awareness organization which operates Unity House is an emphatic young lady, a sophomore planning to become a doctor. She thinks her African-American sisters and brothers are "apathetic." She said, "They don't feel like there's a problem. I do." Asked if it wasn't true that everybody got along very well at Ursinus, her activist frustration showed: "That's the point. People are not uncomfortable, but there's a line."

But then she herself started talking much like the others: "The school does listen to students," and in fact its "very personal" atmosphere influenced her decision to come here. She likes it better now that she is involved. Then she went on to concede that she'd pick Ursinus if she had to do it all over again, and that she would "definitely" recommend it to her children.

This girl had come from a small, predominantly black high school. However, the multicultural advisor explained, that was not a big factor in her attitude. She said that coming to a predominantly white college is a culture shock for African-American students, whether they'd gone to white or black high schools. For the first time, she said, they found themselves living with white students around the clock, rather than dealing with them only five or six hours a day at a commuter high school.

An African-American chemistry major, who'd gone to a predominantly white Philadelphia high school and who had already been accepted in a Ph.D. program at Purdue, said, "Ursinus opened my mind." Otherwise, she meant, she wouldn't be going to graduate school, in chemistry or anything else.

Others that I spoke with said Ursinus had made them look at themselves, had opened new areas of interest that had caused them to change majors. Every one said he or she would send their kids to Ursinus. They said such things as: "Faculty relations are excellent!" "Most definitely changed me!" "Definitely want my kids to come here!" "Exposed me to how others think, broadened my horizons, made me see all the options out there." "Ursinus is different and better."

In short, they were saying the same things that students all over the campus were saying. Typical was that of a senior girl who was headed for a Ph.D. program in art history. She said, "I wasn't happy at first, but I realized I had to get involved. I had been concentrating on my studies. I became a house coordinator, I interned in the multicultural house, and I went to Spain as a junior. That term changed my view of myself and it changed my major from international relations to art history. At a big school, I wouldn't have gotten the attention that changed me. All my teachers have been very supportive. I now have the confidence to say I'm qualified to be the leader or to get the internship, or to present myself well."

At Ursinus, every prospect pleases the student who wants to do something to improve himself or herself. Summer research programs are plentiful and grants are there for the taking with a good proposal. Internships abound, and a student interested in his subject may work with a professor on a project and wind up seeing his name on a paper or book as co-author while he or she is still an undergraduate.

A couple of students also had urged me to see the student art show, so I went. The exhibits filled most of the gallery's first floor, one very large and three smaller exhibit rooms. While quite a few of the works were very good, what was impressive was their great number. There simply couldn't be enough art majors in a school of 1,200 to produce that many exhibits. A lot of non-art majors were being exposed to art courses and showing their work. The place was full of interested teachers as well as students, seeing what others had done, enjoying the refreshments, and balloting for the best in the various categories.

In the faculty coach-of-the-week plan a professor can hang out with the football team, go to team meetings, design a play, join players for the Saturday pregame breakfast, give a pep talk, and then stand on the sideline looking official. And sometime during the game, the coach will use the professor's play. In the championship year, two of the honorary coaches were women, an art historian and an economist.

Ursinus's league includes Dickinson, Franklin and Marshall, Gettysburg, Haverford, Johns Hopkins, Muhlenberg, Swarthmore, Washington, and Western Maryland. Before the Muhlenberg game, the political science professor giving the pep talk wore a tie with the opponent's colors, and at the climactic moment of his talk cut it off, shouting, "We cannot settle for a tie!" For the final home game against powerhouse Dickinson, English professor Dr. Jon Volkmer's pep talk paraphrased Shakespeare. He used what he calls "the greatest pregame pep talk in history," the St. Crispin Day speech of Henry V before the battle of Agincourt. For the team, it was the same kind of epic event. Here's his version:

> *This day will be called Ursinus Day.*
> *Every year on this day you will strip off*
> *your shirt and show your scars, and say,*
> *"These wounds I got on Ursinus Day."*
> *You will grow old and forgetful, but*
> *even when your hair is all gray*
> *You will not forget the names of this day:*
> *Gilbers the coach, Rhodenbaugh, Barrera,*
> *Orlando, Oliver, Faso and Floyd,*
> *Hagenberg, Parks, and all the rest—*
> *You will teach your sons these names*
> *And every day on Ursinus Day*
> *You will raise a toast and say,*
> *"We few, we happy few, we band of brothers."*
> *And whoever hears you will be jealous*
> *And hold their own lives a little cheaper*
> *Because they were not here today*
> *They were not here on Ursinus Day.*

Ursinus won, 14–0.

Professional football teams may sometimes look to prayer to

win games, but Ursinus, as befits a serious liberal arts college, is finding its more intellectual, albeit more secular, approach very effective, thank you. For two full seasons, the home game win-loss record is 10–5, while the away game record is 5–9.

To say that teaching is an act of love doesn't tell the whole story. Ursinus is the kind of challenging, encouraging place that develops confident thinkers and doers who will cope well in a new world.

Western Maryland College

Westminster, Maryland

Western Maryland was created in 1867 as a "creative and innovative liberal arts college." For those days, the word "radical" would have been more accurate—it was the first coeducational college south of the Mason–Dixon Line, and one of the few anywhere in the nation open to all, regardless of sex, color, race, religion, or ethnic origin.

In the thirties it displayed creativity and innovation sufficient to beat Boston College, the University of Maryland, and other big boys in football, with teams coached by a botany professor, Dick Harlow. As a scientist he was also distinguished enough to be hired later by Harvard as zoology museum curator—and as football coach. (The college competes in the NCAAA Division III Centennial Conference, often called "The Ivy League of small colleges.")

More important, in recent decades the college has been one of the top 50 producers of future Ph.D.s in the sciences, as well as in its seniors' scores on the Medical College Aptitude Test. In fact, Western Maryland has produced better test credentials for medical school than four of the Ivy universities.

And among other things, it numbers 154 college and university faculty members among its alumni.

The attractive 160-acre campus, 31 miles from Baltimore and 56 from Washington, sits atop a prominence overlooking the little town of Westminster, and from the rear lounge area of its stunning new library is one of the loveliest views on any campus, across a central Maryland farm and woodland vista to the Catoctin Mountains, site of the Presidential retreat of Camp David. In half an hour, students can be in that area for hiking, picnicking, swimming, or canoeing. The reason the college's name doesn't fit the region is because one of the founders owned the Western Maryland Railroad, one of whose ancient cabooses stands waiting on a bit of siding inside the football stadium.

Of the campus's 40 buildings that give it a familiar, good college look, the new library is the crown jewel, with its stunning architecture and the tranquil charm of its interior spaces. Homey little wedge-shaped enclaves of stacks and reading nooks done in polished dark wood and soft pastel carpeting fan out from an atriumlike staircase. It would be hard to find a more satisfying spot to spend an afternoon or evening. The library's 200,000 volumes are on-line, which also means the resources of other university and college libraries are available to students and faculty. A major project of restoration and remodeling of six classroom buildings was completed in 1999 with the opening of the new Science Center, the better to continue to develop the college's future scientists whose scores on the Medical College Admission Test put most of the famous schools to shame.

Ninety percent of the faculty of 90 hold the most advanced degrees in their fields; the student-faculty ratio is 14:1 and there are no teaching assistants, but statistics don't reveal either the quality of the teaching or the sense of family enterprise they bring the development of their young friends.

From 1993 to 1999, the college grew from 1,200 to 1,500 students, who come from twenty-three states and a dozen foreign countries. About 60% are from Maryland, a percentage that has been steadily dropping as the able Dean of Admissions Martha O'Connell spreads the word farther afield. Eighty percent of the students get some form of financial aid, scholarships, grants, loans, or work-study jobs on campus. About 60% get need-based awards ranging from $200 to full tuition.

One of the recent attractions has been a branch campus in Budapest, Hungary, which President Robert Chambers established in 1995. Students from that part of the world do their first two years there and then transfer to the main campus to complete their degree work. Naturally, this program offers students on the Westminster campus an easy opportunity for study abroad, since they can use part of their financial aid awards to cover the cost.

An average of 1,500 part-time graduate students take courses on or off campus in any one semester, most of them in the college's internationally recognized program for training teachers for the deaf. These courses are also open to undergraduates.

This is another college that can boast of taking "B" and "C" students and making them success stories. The median SAT scores for freshmen are about 561 verbal and 560 math, which means there are as many scores below those figures as above. And 80% of all who apply are accepted.

President Chambers observed, "They may come here provincial but they leave sophisticated. They are homebodies, but the January term for study abroad is the plus." This is an observation made at many other good colleges, that students come back "changed" as a result of their foreign study exposures. And all students must have this experience.

Here students are involved in the governance of the college as well as in their own education. They hold full voting memberships on most policy-making committees, right along with the professors and administrators. There are also three student visitors to the Board of Trustees, and two student representatives on most Trustee committees.

As at many other schools, there is a mix of rural, small town, urban, and cosmopolitan backgrounds, and a student can find his or her own group or a cross section of people to talk to. Fewer than 20% of the students belong to fraternities or sororities, which they may join in their sophomore year. Although members have the option of living together in a section of a residence hall designated by the college, the Greek system isn't divisive nor does it dominate the social scene.

Mainly, this is a community of nice, earnest, unassuming, quietly self-assured teenagers who realize they are getting a first-rate education and who regard their teachers as their friends and mentors. As one senior testified, "I took the Graduate Record Exam [chemistry] in December and I knew every question; that's how well prepared I was."

President Chambers naturally had some other points to make. A daughter at the University of Pennsylvania and a son at the University of Colorado were both disappointed by their choices. The son had transferred from Western Maryland to Colorado in search of what he thought would be the benefits of size and it turned out to be a mirage.

"I have been at Yale, Bucknell, Brown, and Duke," President Chambers said, "and this place works best as a community. It is a kind of home to faculty, students, and staff. At Bucknell the size, 3,200, was enough to give a sense of bigness. If I were going to college now I'd choose a small college. If they have one thing it's a sense of community; faculty members watch football practice; the kids are in their classes."

Deans, faculty members, and students agreed with him on the feeling of family, but they all emphasized that it was a family in which expectations were high and the standards firm. For example, Dean Leroy Panek said Western Maryland is the toughest grader—gives more Ds and Fs—than any of the other 14 Maryland and Pennsylvania colleges in its group, most of them better known and much more selective. Perhaps one reason for its gold standard in grading is the way the requirement for competence in that crucial area—writing—is enforced. The instructor doesn't do his own grading. Everyone has to pass a composition course by writing an essay on a topic chosen by the instructor, but the essay is then graded by two other professors, allowing for no favoritism.

This kind of atmosphere may be one of the reasons faculty members in political science, economics, chemistry, and English all boasted that their kids get into the best graduate and professional schools because they're "so outstanding." A Stanford professor asked the English prof to send him more graduate students, a political science prof who had taught at Georgetown thinks her students at Western Maryland are just as able, and an economics professor said that at Harvard Business School two of his students got higher grades than some Ivy classmates.

Technology has ended lecture and note-taking, at least in biology classes. Professor Esther Iglich said she wanted a class of participants in discussion, not a bunch of stenographers. So she puts her lecture notes on the Web in advance, so students can go over them beforehand. Then they can ask questions and have discussions in class.

The teachers' pride in their students is reciprocated. A senior history major, who had been accepted by Penn State, paid her deposit, and been assigned a dorm room, decided to make a second visit to Western Maryland. A full day there made her realize she'd be in much smaller classes and that she'd be able to talk to her professors and not be just a number.

Four years later, she feels she has several advantages in the competition to get into one of the best Ph.D. programs: her profs know her well and as a result will be able to give persuasive recommendations, and she feels better prepared than if she'd gone to Penn State. "We write a lot and we do oral presentations [not possible with large classes]. Do I know how to solve a problem? Oh yes! The profs try to show that a problem can be solved in more than one way, and that you may not have the whole truth, or that other views may be true. We learned to collaborate. I wouldn't change and my friends wouldn't either." She will tout Western Maryland to her own children.

Others echoed what she had to say about learning how to solve problems and added that the four years there had affected their values and had made them more open and aware.

One senior said, "Some of my classes have been so small that the prof said we could take the final exam any day of the week that suited us. There's a lot of trust here."

Another added, "It's very homey here. There's a lot of interplay among freshmen and upperclassmen and it's very valuable. It has helped me grow."

Three chemistry majors all said they had their names on research papers; a sophomore already had her name on three. As one of them said, "There is more opportunity here; we can do research." To have been co-authors of published papers while undergraduates will not only help them get into the best doctoral programs, but will be stars in their crowns later on when they start job hunting.

A communications-writing major who had been sold on the college because "everyone was so nice" has had three internships—at a radio station, a TV station, and writing a funding proposal for a low-cost housing project—all of which will stand her in good stead when she applies to graduate school.

A senior from Sri Lanka who also came to Western Maryland because everyone was so friendly, although he'd also been accepted by Southern Methodist and Babson, said, "It's incredible; I expected to be treated differently but I wasn't. Teachers would give me a full hour after class to be sure I understood everything. Now I'm going to get a Master of Business Administration degree and my brother is coming here."

What they and others were saying was clear: Faculty members were eager to help students to go as much in depth or as far as they wanted; they set no limits. Several students made a particular point of saying that the readiness of faculty members to take time out to talk to them or show them around when they had visited was what really won them over.

As those students have testified, Western Maryland is a friendly, democratic place where there truly is a sense of family and of caring. It is not for the person who has to live in the fast lane; he or she wouldn't like it and wouldn't add anything. But for anyone who's interested in learning, gaining self-confidence, and developing his or her abilities and powers, this is a place that will do that job, and do it with TLC to spare.

Agnes Scott College
Decatur, Georgia

If high school girls knew what life is really like in exciting places like Agnes Scott in Atlanta, women's colleges would regain their attraction.

A day's visit to this warm and happy producer of outstanding women with its lovely campus would make them ask why anyone needed a coed college. Here women know and are quick to say they have the best of both worlds. They say: We are in full control of our social lives, just as we are queen bees in the classroom; the coeds are the deprived ones. Besides, they add, we graduate with a confidence and power to manage our own lives that few colleges bestow. The proof is that hardly more than a baker's dozen of the nation's colleges and universities produce such a high percentage of future doctorates, and other kinds of achievers, as Agnes Scott. In 1999, this century-old college reached its goal of 1,000 students a year ahead of schedule. President Helen Bullock said, "We have great depth of resources and faculty. One hundred percent have terminal degrees. The student-faculty ratio is 9 to 1. We are adding twelve new positions and five are being replaced." Three-fourths of the applicants are accepted. A little over half are from the top tenth of their high school classes, 60% had SAT verbal scores over 600 (Recentered), and 40% had math scores over 600 (Recentered).

The student body is diverse, with 18% being African-American, (22% in the 1999 freshman class). But it is one community, and the students really mix. Furthermore, students told me, it is one family. The black students put on a Christmas production that includes white students. There is no need, one girl said, to go to predominantly black Spelman College: "I know who I am here." Students come from 36 states, half of them from Georgia, and 4 percent from eight foreign countries. Five percent are Asians, and 3 percent Hispanic. While most of the students come from the South or Southwest, a visitor wouldn't think of this as a Southern school. Instead, the words most likely to spring to mind would be warm, diverse and cosmopolitan.

Financial aid is another area where Agnes Scott shines. Nearly two-thirds of the students get need-based aid, and Agnes Scott is one of the few that meets 100% of every applicant's need. Furthermore, the average aid package for 1999 is worth $16,300. In addition there are nearly 40 merit scholarships that average $8,800.

Downtown Atlanta is just a handy subway ride away, and it is a major metropolitan center with rich cultural, financial, and scientific resources. They include the famous art museum designed by the English architect, John Portman. Almost all major corporations have Atlanta offices. The Atlanta Federal Reserve Bank offers both wonderful internships and future job opportunities.

Biology students are especially lucky, since the nation's Center for Disease Control offers unmatched opportunities for internships with scientists working on the nation's major health problems. The biology faculty takes full advantage of this opportunity; two of the students I talked to were having such experiences. But that was just a sample. A biology professor said, "Over half of the biology students are doing research, and the Center for Disease Control is our Federal Reserve."

The first knot of students I encountered on campus set the tone for my visit. They were half a dozen African-American women chatting outside a building between classes. And even though it was just before finals their mood was relaxed and happy. Two seniors all set for graduate school had special reason to be, but the sophomores and juniors who were still far from jobs or graduate school were just as confident.

"The personal relationships here are so great," said one, and later in the day a professor would echo: "We are ambitious for our students. We take a lot of risks for them." That was typical. Students and teachers were both expressing respect and support for each other.

The incentive for a shy or uncertain girl to be herself and to do things starts in the classroom. The classes are very small—seminar size—and usually discussion-oriented and she can lead the discussion.

When males are wanted, there are plenty of attentive ones calling: from Emory, from Georgia Tech, from Georgia State, and half a dozen other schools in the city. To a vigorous nodding of heads and assenting words, a junior said: "Put this in your book: Agnes Scott is a great choice for a woman who wants to have a social life because it is in Atlanta, and there are so many boys. There's a balance between academic and social life. Any girl who complains she's not having a good social life is not making it happen, because she can totally take that in her own hands."

With equal force she continued, "It's so wonderful, going to class and not worrying about what you're saying or what you're wearing. In a coed school I've never heard a girl leading a discussion, never!" She also had visited all the selective New England women's colleges before choosing Agnes Scott.

Her enthusiasms reflected a pride that reminded me of the way the men at Wabash, the nonpareil men's college in Indiana, talk about their school. Furthermore, it was often the chance, unplanned visit that had altered their views of what they wanted in a college and sold them on Agnes Scott. Five of the girls I talked to had come to Atlanta intending to apply to Emory but fell in love with this campus where, unlike Emory, everyone was warm and friendly and the sense of community was palpable.

Several girls were eager to testify that it was 'neither Southern nor typically women's. The first, from Jacksonville, Florida, who had applied to fifteen schools, including Emory, said, "At the other schools I found the girls flaky and aloof. Not so here. This is a totally different set of girls. You have real conversations, and people are a lot more open-minded here. There are more diverse backgrounds here. I applied to Ivy schools but I thought the opportunities were better here. You get more help here. There are excellent internships and foreign study programs. It is more participatory here."

A friend added: "Tell girls that here girls are not like my image of a girl's school. I became more open. It's not stuffy here, as it is at Emory."

Others were eager to testify, including one who declared, "Agnes Scott definitely affects values. After I came here I was appalled and wondered how I ever could have been so closed-minded. How could I live 18 years and not see other points of view? Here you have to argue the other side; you have to be open and evaluate the other side so you can argue persuasively. You find there's no black and white—the whole world's gray."

Most eloquent was that emphatic junior, a hard-sell advocate for women's colleges: "It's so intellectually alive here! It's not like high school where we were fighting over boys. We have Atlanta with all its attractions and Emory and Georgia Tech. It's a great choice for girls who want a social life! Women's colleges have so much to offer it's not even funny. I think women can get a better education there. Coed colleges can't educate women in the environment they need the way women's colleges can. They can thrive better in a women's college environment." Like some of the others who had shopped the women's colleges, she didn't find any like Agnes Scott. "At Smith the professors were trying to draw out these women and none of them would talk, and I know these women were intelligent. Then I came to Agnes Scott and everyone was talking. I even came to a biology class and everyone was talking. The women at Agnes Scott seemed so much more intellectually alive than the women at Smith. I was just so amazed by that. Also, everybody smiled at me and smiled at each other and they smiled at my parents and I was so embarrassed to have my parents along. So I found that this intellectual community was also very friendly. I'm totally for women's colleges and I'm going to force my daughters to go to women's colleges!"

After saying, "I don't want to follow that act," a girl from Virginia for whom Agnes Scott had not been her first choice, said she was happy she'd landed there because, "it is not stuffy but happy, and there's no reason why you shouldn't do your best; the professors want to help you." Another noted that even though it's next to a big city there is such a sense of community that "I have professors call if I miss a class. They will not let you fail here!"

Another who'd been a shopper said she'd found no other school as alive or the students as involved. She agreed that on no other campus were the kids so warm or open, but also said Agnes Scott had special advantages. The Honor System was very important to her, and besides, "What more can you ask than Atlanta, or the Kaufman program for Women Entrepreneurs?"

A girl who had been nodding at all this wanted to be sure I appreciated the Agnes Scott differences: "My boyfriend is at Harvard and he was telling me how happy he was that he had even had a chance to talk to one of his profs." She was in a different world, one where professors share students' hopes and inspire new ones. They also start them on the way to realizing them. For example:

- The economics department tells freshmen that the field needs women and is rich with promise. So, a professor said, "We have nine majors in graduate school from a college of 800 [in 1998]. Why so many? Because we're able to talk to them early. We have five interns in the Federal Reserve Bank in Atlanta, and a music major is one of them. Here women become leaders."

▪ An Atlanta Semester program, the only one of its kind according to its director, is designed to start women on the way to leadership roles in business and in society. It combines internships in city betterment activities with academic work.

The dean of students, summed it all up this way: "Women here have the feeling they have the power to choose the option they want for their lives. They are told, 'You are the author of that story.' And they are achievers. We talk about values a lot; we come out of a faith tradition. We try to get students to think beyond themselves, to be of service to the community. And finally, the Honor System is the cornerstone of life at Agnes Scott."

The Honor System is run by students, exams are not proctored, and it just goes without saying that each student will live up to the compact with her conscience that she put her name to as a freshman. The document for each current class is framed and hangs on a broad stair landing, a public statement reflecting the high expectations of each member of this family.

Collaborative learning is encouraged with "talking study halls," two centers equipped with tables and comfortable chairs where students can work together on projects or do routine assignments. The curriculum has requirements that ensure exposure to the elements of a liberal education, but there is much flexibility. Everyone must take freshman composition, and be exposed to the sciences, humanities, social sciences, and a foreign language. A year-long "Global experience" in the sophomore year expands horizons and enforces at least a rudimentary working knowledge of the language of the country they'll be studying and visiting that year.

When they come back, there are internships and research opportunities to fit every interest, as well as independent study projects that are expected in most departments. After hours they can use the school's state-of-the-art physical activities building or try out for one of the five intercollegiate teams: basketball, cross country, soccer, tennis, and volleyball.

The college has something more important than a formal program for those with learning disabilities. The faculty provides a full measure of tender loving care, and anyone with a learning problem can take risks and get full support. Students with learning problems are welcomed, and they prosper. Agnes Scott is a hospitable place for them. For those with physical disabilities, the college has gone to great lengths to make its facilities accessible and to make life there pleasant and convenient.

For many years, decades in fact, I had known from all the published indicators of quality that Agnes Scott had few peers in developing women who helped make this a better society, but only seeing this community in action can impart the full force of its happy élan and its sense of mission.

Birmingham–Southern College

Birmingham, Alabama

Birmingham–Southern, like Hendrix, Millsaps, Rhodes, and Eckerd, belies the popular notion of Deep South schools as sleepy havens, just as the city it inhabits belies its reputation as the Pittsburgh of the South. Like Pittsburgh, Birmingham has had a renaissance; both are now cities of professionals, white collar businesses, and attractive downtown parks. In spirit Birmingham's renaissance has gone beyond Pittsburgh's and is exemplified by its outstanding new museum, the Civil Rights Institute, whose no-holds-barred exhibits chronicle the history of the civil rights struggle.

The college is a warm, friendly, and increasingly diverse place with nearly 10% African-Americans, 3% Asians, and nearly 2% international students. Able, imaginative administrators and an enthusiastic, high-quality faculty are making good things happen. The social concerns Birmingham–Southern displays put to shame many colleges I've visited north of the Mason–Dixon line. What's more, it is institutionalizing them. In its infancy and still under development is a required core course intended to produce citizens capable of and willing to take leadership roles in dealing with community and national problems.

An African-American freshman who said her mother had made her attend this college of 1,800 mostly middle-class, middle-of-the-road and motivated white teenagers said she'd been converted by the way both students and faculty reached out to make her feel she belonged. Now, she said, "I really like it." No longer did she want to hide safely away in the huge University of Alabama.

Her affection for her school was echoed by students from Croatia, Korea, China, and many towns big and small in this country. And the college's high retention figures are eloquent confirmation: 92% of the freshmen return for the sophomore year, and three-quarters of an entering class graduates in four years, percentages that put it in the top 10% of private colleges and far above any public institutions except the University of Virginia and Berkeley.

Most of the students come from the South, 70% from Alabama, but the admissions staff is now actively recruiting in other parts of the country, particularly in the Midwest and Southwest.

Birmingham–Southern accepts nearly three-fourths of its applicants, and for nearly half of them the school is their first choice, which tends to mean that morale is high; students don't feel they're rejects or that theirs is a fallback choice.

The mean SAT scores are in the low 500s verbal for both men and women and in the middle 500s for math for men. Twenty-three percent score over 600 on the verbal and 34% over 600 on the math. Nearly 40% were in the top tenth of their high school classes.

What all this means—and people take colleges' SAT averages and class ranks far too seriously—is that anyone with a "B" record in a solid program, and a lot of those with lesser records, will be welcome, but they had better be serious about planning to work, and have some evidence to back it up. As the director of financial aid said, "We're looking for potential for success, and we want to make it possible to come here."

DeeDee Bruns, Dean of Admissions and Financial Aid, describes Birmingham–Southern's students as "motivated, focused, [with] a healthy balance of interests, upper middle class, middle-of-the-road conservative, much less of the 'me' and more of the 'we,' less consumerism, and much more community service activity. Indeed, a remarkable 70% of the students are involved at some time during the year in Southern Volunteer Services." It is a multifaceted affair; students may help in projects as diverse as landscaping, repairing homes, helping in homeless shelters, tutoring, or working in Calcutta, India, alongside Mother Teresa's volunteers.

The college's most exciting project—which was the idea of President Neal R. Berte—is the developing leadership program, for which the Luce Foundation has provided $175,000. It seeks to produce people who can and will take leading roles as citizens. Unlike other leadership programs, it has nothing whatever to do with getting ahead in one's job; its goal is to realize John Donne's devotion "No man is an island . . ." The centerpiece is an interdisciplinary core course the English Department is developing on leadership activities. It ties into classroom discussions the issues being argued nationwide. A political science prof discusses elite behavior; a mathematician discusses decision-making; a classicist provides the literary text or background; and a black judge has a team-teaching role in classes on leadership in civil rights. In addition, every student has a term of hands-on experience with service in some local organization.

When the program is under full steam, not only will the entire college community be involved, the word will also be spread. In the summer of 1995 it sponsored the first annual week-long civil rights seminar for high school students with civil rights leaders as speakers. In the future the program aims to attract students from all parts of the country.

Offering students such a broad and comprehensive concept with the whole faculty contributing to it would be impossible at a university, where every professor's survival depends on his standing in his own specialty and to hell with students if they get in the way.

The faculty, many of whom have taught at major universities, say that relations with students are close, that they get a lot of pleasure "when you see a kid from a small town in Alabama open up." They also say that students are willing to share their personal problems with their teachers. All this helps explain why they say Birmingham–Southern has an impact on its students. A lot of faculty members believe it enough to send their own children here.

A history professor said so many alumni are eager to find spots for interns, to help in the job hunt for graduates, or to otherwise help their alma mater that "we can't find work for all of them." A sociologist who had taught at the University of Georgia said, "Alumni treasure their experience here, and for the right reasons—not football weekends—but for academic as well as personal growth. That certainly was not the case at Georgia."

A political science prof who had taught at the University of Florida put his finger on a central difference between the good college and the university when he said, "There is a great difference in teaching at public and private schools. There you identify with school as football and partying; academics are secondary. Students go to class almost as observers. You can do that in a class of 200; you can't here." His burgeoning Latin-American Studies program sends 100 students to Latin-

American countries every year; it sponsored a faculty colloquium on the North American Free Trade Agreement, and it
awards travel grants to the best proposals for foreign study
projects.

A music professor said, "Most of the professors from other
schools I know are jealous of our students; they win most of
the scholarships in competitions." He then produced a list of
nearly 50 who had major scholarships or fellowships in this
country and abroad, who held important jobs, had roles on
Broadway, or were members of major opera companies.

Nearly every conversation I had with a student elicited some
comment about what a close-knit community it was. A sophomore girl struck a common chord when she said, "When I
visited here I was really impressed. The students here are
really accepting. They tell you the same things the admissions
people do."

A couple of fellows on athletic scholarships were as emphatic as a religion and philosophy major had been that this
college had made them question and think through their attitudes and values. As one of them said, "I think this school
builds character. Students live by the honor code. We are challenged to think so that we don't just accept."

Some who had been accepted at Vanderbilt, Duke, Rice,
Emory, and elsewhere, and the Croatian girl who had considered a score of other schools, all said the high standards, the
sense of family, and the close relationships of students and
teachers had won them over.

What all of this says is that Birmingham–Southern is a
high-quality, caring place where a person from any part of the
country would not only be comfortable but would grow intellectually, morally, and personally. That is not to say that the activist who marches to his own drummer at a place like Antioch
should come here expecting to turn it upside down. Nor will
the big-football-weekend addict be fulfilled. But the community here will accept and tolerate both. And if they stay long
enough it will do them a lot of good.

Centre College
Danville, Kentucky

If one were to put activist Antioch at one end of the spectrum of high-quality colleges, and life-of-the-mind St. John's with its Great Books and no-electives curriculum at the other, Centre would probably find its name appropriate to its position.

Centre students are bright, wholesome, polite, friendly and personable, eager to do well, and serious about what life holds for them. Intellectually curious, they take many courses outside of their majors, but they are neither future philosophers or college professors nor Antiochian risk-takers or revolutionaries. For the most part, they might be called the intelligent, responsible (and very engaging) center.

Why should they be revolutionaries? It would be hard to incite rebellion in such a familial community. They never had it so good. A caring faculty does so much hand-holding students feel (as they do at Antioch) that they own the place. Class sizes average a clubby and conversational 16; each faculty member teaches seven courses and has a heavy responsibility for his advisees as well.

If a student misses two classes in a row the instructor will call to see if anything's wrong and alert his adviser. Dean Milton Reigelman said, "We're so small, a problem can't fall between the chairs." (After much faculty agonizing the college recently decided to increase enrollment from its traditional 900 to 1,000.)

Walking around its beautiful campus, whose majestic trees look like they have been there since the college was founded in 1819, one would imagine a community twice that size. At one end of its architectural spectrum are historic landmark gems from the 1800s. At the other, modern end is a lovely structure that Centre claims is the finest arts center in the nation for a college its size; indeed, a university would be proud to have it. It was designed by The Taliesin Associated Architects, the firm of Frank Lloyd Wright's students.

This impressive art center gives the historic and charming town of Danville cultural bragging rights. It has brought such performers and shows as Rudolf Nureyev, Mikhail Baryshnikov, Twyla Tharp, Bolshoi Ballet, Alvin Ailey American Dance Theater, National Dance Company of Senegal, Dave Brubeck, Ella Fitzgerald, Ray Charles, Leontyne Price, Joan Sutherland, Philadelphia Orchestra, Le Orchestre de Paris, Czech Philharmonic, Itzhak Perlman, *42nd Street, Cats, Amadeus*, and the New York City National Opera Company. In one two-week period The Empire Brass, *Meet Me in St. Louis,* Menaheim Pressler, and Vinson Cole all performed here. The center also regularly presents major exhibitions of great art.

All this plus an impressive new Integrative Studies curriculum coupled with a foreign study program give Centre students a sure confidence as well as intellectual sophistication and a sound value system. It's not surprising that as adults they demonstrate a more impressive allegiance to their alma mater than do the alumni of any other college or university. Centre ranks number one in the percentage of alumni who make financial contributions to it.

Another bit of testimony to its quality is the high number of children of faculty and administrators who choose Centre in spite of the liability of having a parent around, or who come back—often against parental wishes—after having tried a different, distant, or more famous place.

Centre's seniors, if they have good records, can be sure of getting into the best graduate or professional schools. That also goes for getting jobs. Very few colleges or universities can boast that during the recession of 1992, 96% of its graduates were either in graduate or professional school or had jobs within six months of graduation.

Centre's enviable retention record also testifies to its quality and character. Even though, unlike the Ivies, hordes of high school seniors aren't pushing and shoving to get in, 90% of its freshmen return for the sophomore year, and, more than three out of every four graduate in four years. And Centre accepts 85% of its applicants.

Two-thirds of the acceptees were in the top 20% of their high school classes, and that figure includes all kinds and sizes of high schools. The middle 50% of the class has SAT scores ranging from 480 to 600 verbal and 530 to 650 math, and ACT scores ranging from 25 to 29. All of this means another half had scores above or below those ranges.

Financially, the school is a bargain, costing several thousand dollars less than quality colleges in the North. Sixty percent of the students receive financial aid, and the average aid package is about $10,000. If the scholarships awarded on merit are added, the percentage receiving aid rises to 82.

Its faculty—as can be said of the other colleges in this book—is earnestly committed to and excels at the art of teaching. It is obvious that they like the kids they're teaching and enjoy working with them. Moreover, not only is there an unusual sense of community and mutual regard among the faculty, but between the faculty and administration as well, which is a rarity. Profs who've been at the most famous universities said they've never experienced the kind of collegiality they enjoy at Centre.

No university faculty compares with Centre's in the impact it has on the growth of young minds and personalities. Ninety percent of Centre's teachers hold Ph.D.s or terminal degrees earned at the best institutions, and they are active scholars. They not only publish, they draw students into their research as co-authors and often take them to professional meetings.

One of the indicators of the leverage a college exerts is the percentage going on to further education, and not only is Centre's 49% impressive, but those with the good records can get in anywhere, and do. Thanks to a new state-of-the-art science facility, a gift of the Olin Foundation, the percentage of fresh-men (including increasingly more women) planning to major in one of the sciences has climbed to 50%. That bespeaks a cli-mate that draws women into careers where they've often been shunned or afraid to enter.

Centre holds another mark of distinction as the place that runs the Governor's Scholars Program. This is a state-financed program in which gifted Kentucky high school students are brought to the campus for special summer courses.

The faculty, in its diversity of origin, is more representative of the United States than is the student body of 1,000, which is two-thirds Kentuckians, although 40 states and territories are represented. The college is now embarked on a recruiting campaign to increase the percentage of students from other parts of the country, as well as that of minority students.

The faculty, one professor said, is also more liberal than the students, whom a sociology prof described as "the corporate class of Kentucky." He called the college "the ruling-class col-lege of Kentucky. We have no competition [from state col-leges]. For a Kentucky teenager the choice is a prestige college or Centre. And if they pick a prestige college they often come back here after a year or two.

"The dominant culture" at Centre, he said, "is working to-gether to do what is expected. It is not an intellectual student body. We in sociology draw our majors from the oddballs; the students are 60% Greek [fraternity and sorority members]." He was one of those who was struck by the faculty attitudes: "The faculty politics here are the best I know of, [in terms of] the collegiality," and he'd been at Swarthmore and at Yale.

Like others, he remarked that change is in the air, and is changing the students. Besides increasing the size of the stu-dent body and seeking greater diversity, the Integrative Pro-gram improves on the traditional core curriculum idea of a shared intellectual experience. It is designed to develop in stu-dents the ability to imagine and create, to think and reason analytically, to solve problems, to integrate and synthesize complex information, to use language clearly and persuasively, and to make responsible choices. To achieve these goals, students are exposed to three aesthetics courses; three scientific and technological and perhaps one in math; three in social sciences, one cross-cultural, two in fundamental questions; and one in Integrative Studies. There are also foreign language and English composition competency requirements, and there is much emphasis on writing throughout the four years.

The Integrative Studies and the Fundamental Questions courses are interdisciplinary and are team-taught. One course, for example, Civil Rights in America, involves political science, history, economics, and theology, and might be taught by profs from two or even three of those disciplines. A course titled Business, Society, and Ethics uses case studies to examine the scores of values and competing concerns, in addition to profits, in the modern corporation, such as environmental issues, employee rights, employer responsibilities, consumer protection, working conditions, and so on.

Another force for change is a foreign studies requirement involving a study term either in Strasbourg or in London. Several professors said this was making a great contribution and that students returned with a broader vision in addition to a new sophistication.

A breezy, live-wire economics professor, an Oklahoman and a Harvard Ph.D., who previously taught at Harvard and at Middlebury, had, as might be expected, a much different slant than the sociologist. He preferred the Centre students to those he'd had elsewhere. And he thought change had already taken place in student attitudes and outlooks. He said, "I'm an entrepreneur and the kids from this background are winners; they're gonna hustle more than the Ivies. I'd bet on one of these before I'd bet on one of the Ivies. The profs here are more liberal than they, and the Integrative Studies Program has had an effect on them. I know personally I've had an impact."

A recent faculty addition, an economist who had taught at Duke, considered its and Centre's students "comparable, very similar in quality, and very motivated to learn; [with] a zest for knowledge." He was impressed that a large number want to go on to graduate school, and he thought Centre had a real impact on its students, especially in learning how to learn.

A classics prof who had taught at the universities of North Carolina, Florida, and Texas, agreed but said Centre's students don't represent the extremes at the big institutions. "These are really outstanding students; they are outgoing, polite, and not very adventurous. The school has an impact; particularly now that we have a foreign program, the kids come back wonderfully changed. Also, the undergraduate research in which students co-author papers and get to go to professional meetings is a wonderful thing."

A philosophy prof, a former Jesuit priest who had taught at Notre Dame as well as at Texas, drew a double parallel: Centre's and Notre Dame's students are not only similar in ability but in sophistication; neither group is urban or streetwise. He also noted a major change in the student body; students are less interested in fraternities and sororities, and the tempo of scholarly activity has greatly increased.

"The faculty is much more representative of the United States than it was, and the level of decency and collegiality is extraordinary, not only among the faculty, but between the faculty and the administration as well," he declared. "Our students are wholesome and intelligent; what we are pushing for now is diversity. This is a wonderfully nurturing place with a lot of writing."

The students reciprocate. Every one I talked to would make the same choice over again, even a senior history major from Richmond, Virginia, headed for graduate school, who said at first he wasn't "gung-ho" about it because Danville didn't offer such metropolitan divertissements as opera or ballet. He had tried Washington and Lee University, "despised it," then East Tennessee State, same verdict. He came to Centre "by accident" and stayed. Centre, he said, "is vastly superior to W&L educationally; it reinforces your values and helps you think things through and arrive at good and valid conclusions." Another said, "It has opened my eyes and is changing my way of thinking and is teaching me to trust my own judgment."

A senior from New Orleans added that the atmosphere was warm and friendly, but that the social scene was changing because of "administrative interference" in students' social events.

Every student I talked to said that while the majority were in fraternities or sororities, that wasn't essential to a good social life or to being a big woman or man on campus. There was total agreement also that anyone who came back to visit after five years would have dinner or spend the night at any one of several faculty member's homes. In my random sampling not one said he or she would make another choice or fail to tout Centre to their own kids.

A young woman disputed faculty descriptions of Centre students as not being venturesome. She pointed out that in off-campus programs in which she'd been involved with students from prestigious institutions, she had always been impressed by Centre students' comparative intellectual curiosity and venturesomeness because they took so many courses outside of their majors. In fact she considered Centre unique for this reason, and she wondered if the Ivy type students weren't scaredy-cats protecting their grade point averages because their eyes were on law, medicine, or business school.

The level of satisfaction is high at Centre, among the students, the faculty, and the administrators. They like their lovely surroundings, their teachers, their colleagues, and the civility of their community. And as this young woman implied, they are happy that the new Centre is helping them become something better and beyond "the corporate class of Kentucky" to pioneers in a new world.

As at most colleges, almost everyone can find his own niche. But the person who needs the dominantly intellectual discourse of a St. John's or a Reed, or an intense scientific seminary like Caltech or Harvey Mudd, or the independent-as-a-hog-on-ice feeling of Antioch probably won't feel fulfilled here. Centre is, in short, a happy, high-class bargain for the "A" students who aren't at either extreme, as well as for their "B" and "C" siblings.

Eckerd College
St. Petersburg, Florida

Eckerd, one of the country's most attractive academic bargains, is a hot growth stock; in a few years it may not take the "B" student it accepts today. It's likely to sail out of sight for a book like this by becoming as selective as an Ivy school; when that happens, the "B" student will need some substantial accomplishment other than grades to get in.

Eckerd admitted its first freshman in 1960. By 1985, it had joined the ranks of the elite—the top 50 in the production of graduates who go on to get doctorates in the sciences and in the humanities. Today, Dr. Richard Hallin, the admissions director, won't look at the "C+" clients he would have taken a few years back; they must have solid "B" or "B+" records in very solid programs.

Any college that rates in the top 50 is Dean's List material; a young, unselective one with such status is dramatic testimony to its community of learning. Eckerd exerts a leverage on the youths whose development is its reason for being. And that sets it apart from all but a very few colleges (many of which are in this book).

In the field of marine science, Eckerd is in a class by itself by virtue of its magnificent, and unique, new state-of-the-art marine laboratory. No Ivy or any other school has anything to match it. The structure is set back from the water to preserve the shore line, but a dock with a large underwater tube reaches out into the Gulf of Mexico and sea water circulates through every room, where sea animals are in their native habitats so students can observe and work with them as they live. As a faculty member said, "It is a unique way to teach our courses."

Eckerd is too young to show a record of alumni achievement such as percentages in *Who's Who,* Pulitzer Prize winners, corporate executives, creators of new enterprises, or major benefactors, but the effects of a good college experience aren't limited to a single area; they show up across the board. And they will.

My client sample naturally is limited, but in over 30 years in which two or three or more clients a year have gone there, none has ever expressed any dissatisfaction. The college's own survey of graduates over a 15-year span offers a more definitive and glowing response. One alumna, now a very successful literary agent, wrote to me 15 years after graduation: "Going to Eckerd was a delightful experience, one, needless to say, I will never forget, and I feel confident that my education was as good as can be found anywhere in this country . . . (And I shouldn't put it in the past tense. Eckerd taught me, among other things, that education never stops)." She is married to a Princeton alumnus.

Eckerd's president, Peter Armacost, and the academic dean, Lloyd Chapin, go her one better; they say Eckerd's students get a better education than at the Ivies. Why? First, Dr. Armacost: "Because students here are involved in their own education; because faculty members work at improving their teaching; they are actively engaged in comparing techniques.

"Our Academy of Senior Professionals program in which distinguished retirees provide a different point of view in the freshman Western Heritage or in the senior Judeo-Christian Perspectives classes are unique in the way they work. The retirees live on campus and act occasionally as counselors or career advisers or on personal problems.

"The faculty here are as good as at the Ivies. They not only publish but their principal interest is teaching.

"Here there is a sense of community."

Dean Lloyd Chapin makes the often unappreciated point that the faculty at any good college is every bit as well qualified as any Ivy staff; after all, they all got their doctorates at the same elite graduate schools.

"The Eckerd faculty publishes." He pointed to a five-foot-long row of recent books. "They haven't published as much as the Ivy faculties but they are working on the cutting edges. They are as good as faculty members anywhere, and I staked my own kid's welfare on the belief they are. My daughter had a better experience here than my older children did at Colgate or Emory. Furthermore, the Eckerd faculty does more for its students than do the Ivies' faculties. There is a great deal of involvement; we have faculty retreats on taking each student seriously, and as an individual.

"Elsewhere, faculty members tend to regard their classrooms as their castles, but here we have teachers' forums in which groups of 20 will share teaching techniques and discuss things that will or that won't work. Over half the faculty is involved in these forums. There's a lot going on in this area.

"Our faculty members' tenure depends on teaching. They can't get tenure unless they're good teachers. That's why our students do course evaluations every year. And the stiff graders don't suffer. Students regard the profs who set very high standards and grade hard as 'compassionate hardasses.'

"Also, mentoring [personal and academic advising] is taken seriously here. We try to evaluate it; the students fill out questionnaires at the end of each term evaluating both teachers and mentors. The results tend to be bipolar; both the brickbats and the bouquets are very positive."

Eckerd's freshmen and faculty get a head start on getting acquainted with a multipurpose month-long autumn term before school starts. Freshmen can study any one of a dozen or more topics: The Behavioral Bases of Stress, Coastal Oceanography, American Politics, Religion and Public Policy, or The Sociology of Sex Roles. The teacher for each group of 20 becomes the academic and personal mentor for each of them for the year, and each group stays together as a Western Heritage class. Autumn term is thus an orientation with no upperclass students around and promotes bonding among the freshmen and with their mentors. They also get a course credit, and placement testing is done.

At the end of the year, each freshman chooses a second mentor in his intended major or field of concentration and both stay with him from then on. He thus has a second opinion for general help and for making his big decisions, such as if he wants to design his own major.

Eckerd is on a 4-1-4 schedule [January term in the middle of the year], so everyone uses the winter term for a change of pace: a term at another college, international study tours, a project on campus, or something very different, like studying poverty in Appalachia, pottery in New England, or languages in upstate New York.

The Academy of Senior Professionals—300 of them—gives Eckerd freshman and senior classes a unique zip. It is a group of people, some retired, who've had distinguished careers in a broad range of fields and who act as sort of adjunct faculty. They may act as resource persons in the classroom, counsel students on academic or career matters, or give talks or conduct colloquia. Some live in college housing on campus and some nearby. The program is run by a retired college president who decides whether an interested applicant is likely to pass muster in this new kind of role.

The Western Heritage and Judeo-Christian Perspectives classes they help teach are both value-oriented, and the mature viewpoints of retired corporate executives, generals, professors, writers, and others bring a different and usually nonacademic viewpoint to class discussions, besides offering a counterpoint to the authority of the professor. For example, a sociology prof who is a pacifist has as his Professional a retired major general. There is a mutual respect but the class is a lively one.

In a writing class, the late Pulitzer Prize–winning author

James Michener critiqued students' efforts and had a reputation of always finding something good to say about every paper, no matter how bad. Michener also gave the college $1 million.

Dean Chapin says, "I like these students best, compared to Emory and Colgate. In basic intellectual quality they're as good, and they're more enthusiastic and less cynical. Emory is cold and competitive, with much social ambition and grade grubbing. Here there's a sense of community and a lot of student involvement."

Prof. John Reynolds, chairman of Marine Sciences, raves:

"The students here are superb. Eckerd attracts kids who want to give something back to the community. They are superb human beings who will also contribute.

"What we accomplish: We give them the tools. We are blessed with capable, fine teachers who confront values and make linkages across seemingly unrelated disciplines. Our research crosses boundaries, our environmental program is interdisciplinary. We are concerned with ethics and issues; I have to think about how I feel about mammals and articulate that. The autumn term class involves not only learning about mammals but also such questions as, do we manage or mismanage them? What are our values in this matter and how do we face them?"

Eckerd has an honors program providing two years of independent study and research for students of outstanding ability; and for those who might someday be college faculty members a two-year Apprentice Scholar Program, financed by the Ford Foundation, develops the skills and habits of professional scholars.

In this, my second visit to Eckerd, all the students I questioned expressed some form of satisfaction with what the community was doing for them. I was also impressed, as I had been on a previous visit, that the minority students seemed particularly integrated into the mix. A dark-skinned senior from Curaçao said he felt such a warm sense of family he didn't particularly want to go home, and that the school had broadened his horizons and taught him time management.

More than one student felt that the absence of fraternities and sororities contributed to the sense of community. A literature and religion major, also a senior, said that if it had not been for the mentor program and a caring faculty when he got into drugs and alcohol his freshman year, "I wouldn't be here." But now he thinks he'll go to a seminary, work in the Peace Corps, or do some kind of ministry.

They, like others, said Eckerd had challenged their points of view and their value systems and had affected the development of the latter. Two pre-med seniors said the Western Heritage class had had an impact "from day one." One of them added, "Eckerd taught me how to balance my life; I find I can do so much."

These comments are in line with what seniors have been saying for many years in the school's own survey of graduates. More than 90% have said their values have been affected, as have their abilities to think critically, to work independently, and to define and solve problems, their enjoyment of learning, their understanding of self, satisfaction with life, competence as a person, ability to get along with others, and openness to new ideas. Few thought it had affected their religious beliefs, although 70% said it had influenced their understanding of the Judeo-Christian tradition.

Ninety-six percent said Eckerd was a good choice and nearly two-thirds even approved of the food, a standard complaint on many campuses.

But more immediate is the recent comparative testimony of a former client who came to me after a year at the University of Pittsburgh, who then chose Bryn Mawr over Eckerd, and after a semester there is now at Eckerd. She has this to say about Bryn Mawr, which is as Ivy as a women's college can get:

"I think Bryn Mawr is an excellent school, and it is unique . . . one fits in very well, or one does not fit in at all. One of the things I could not get used to was the aloofness with which most of the students treated each other. I thought that at a women's college everyone would feel more comfortable and open with each other because we were 'all girls,' but I found just the opposite to be true. It seemed there was a lot of competition and a lot of stress. I also couldn't get used to all the political correctness that was going on.

"My problems with finding out about my French requirement in the beginning of the semester made me feel like I was back in a big university, caught up in red tape . . . I was also surprised at how little contact the students had with the professors outside of class, and how formal the relationships between the students and the professors were."

After she'd been at Eckerd a while she wrote me:

"I love Eckerd. I love my classes, I love the weather, and I've met three girls in my dorm who are the first good friends I've made since high school. I play soccer every Friday, I have a blues show every week on the Eckerd radio station. I'm auditing an extra literature class, and I've signed up to be on the staff of Eckerd's literary magazine. I also took beginning sailing lessons, and I can sign out for a two-person sailboat at any time on the waterfront. The warm, sunny weather down here is wonderful, and all the people are very friendly. I started feeling comfortable here right away . . . and the school is big enough so that new people don't stick out."

Emory and Henry College
Emory, Virginia

Little Emory and Henry is a case study in the parable of the talents. It does more for its human material—and thus comparatively for society—than do the three most selective institutions in the same state of Virginia. The very selective trio take in four- and five-talent freshmen and turn out four- and five-talent seniors, sometimes less. Emory and Henry doubles the talents of most of the kids it gets, and contributes to their moral development as well. It is a caring, nurturing college and it may be unique in the way it works with parents to spot and help kids in need of help.

All this happens on a charming campus of lovely buildings and great trees in colorful, hilly southwest Virginia. Set in a village near the small town of Abingdon, which is famous as the home of the Barter Theater, Emory and Henry's hilly countryside is lovely but rural, appealing more to the outdoor and the environmental than to the worldly city types.

Nearly half the students come from a radius of 100 miles and some are the first generation to go to college. Seventy percent are from Virginia, with a sizable chunk from Richmond. Recently, the college has been working to increase its out-of-state percentage.

It is a place where everyone smiles and speaks to you, a warm and friendly small "d" democracy with a strong sense of family.

The personable Dr. Thomas R. Morris, a widely quoted expert on the Constitution and on Virginia politics who left the chairmanship of the University of Richmond's political science department to come to Emory and Henry, is the rare college president with a sense of mission.

He is rare in another way that reflects the kind of person he is; he is deeply concerned for the well-being of his community. He lived the first full week of his presidency—bag and baggage—in a freshman dorm because he'd heard there'd been a lot of complaints about a lack of hot water and nobody had paid any attention to them. Now there's plenty of hot water, and he became an instant hero. Of course, as a survivor of Virginia Military Institute's notoriously rough first—Rat—year, he was tough enough to stand a freshman dorm for a week.

Some members of the Board of Trustees worried that because he has written several books and is frequently interviewed by television and newspaper reporters he might not be sufficiently interested in the school's athletic program; and students worried they might be getting a stuffy pedant. But about five feet of one wall of his office is alive with a blood-red-and-white portrayal of the Washington Redskin's football great, that 180-pound David, Larry Brown, slashing his way through the Goliaths of the New York Giants' defensive line. And at lunch half a dozen students chorused of their new president, "He hasn't missed a game!"

The beauty of the campus undoubtedly played a part in the original decisions, but kids are here because they want to be here, they love it, they take a warm pride in it, and their regular-guy president, and they want to learn. I didn't meet anyone who wished he'd gotten into some other school, which is unusual, because at nearly every college, except maybe Harvard, there is a sullen cohort of rejected suitors of another institution.

It is also a rare educational bargain, boasting not only a talented as well as caring faculty, but a solid core curriculum—the sine qua non of a shared intellectual experience—that provides a liberal education on which students can build in graduate school and in later life. Everyone takes a Western Traditions sequence, a Great Books course, a religion course, one Value Inquiry, and a Global Study sequence. And everyone is also required to develop his or her writing skills.

The college offers need-based financial aid, and many more than half the students receive aid. It also has a new Bonner Scholarship program in which 26 freshmen each year get grants of $3,700 a year for such community service projects as teaching or working with the disabled while going to college.

Few colleges work so closely with parents to help their students prosper. Dean Rick Pfau said, "We ask all parents to send us letters telling us what they think the needs of their son or daughter are for prospering here."

One mother wrote that she wanted her son to wear a coat and tie. That request somehow fell between the chairs. "But often," he said, "the letters alert us to needs we might otherwise be unaware of, such as learning disabilities, personality matters, and so on. They help us serve the students more effectively."

There have been some dramatic cases of growth as a result. Dr. Ron Diss who runs the Learning Resources Center says, "all the learning disabled students succeed when they want to." When challenged he re-emphasized the word "all."

My own experiences support his claim. In more than a 30-year span every single client I've had who worked to overcome his or her disability succeeded in college, some with Dean's List records; and some went on to professional or graduate school.

When a parent's letter says a student has or may have an attention-span deficit, some form of dyslexia, or some other problem, the Center alerts the faculty adviser. It then follows up weekly with faculty members.

The Center gets grade reports of every student and calls in for conferences those who get a D or an F. The Center also gives tests where necessary or provides study skill sessions, remedial work, or tutoring.

"Everything is cross-referenced," said Dr. Diss. "We know who the at-risk students are, and they get the help they need when it is needed." As a result, the percentage of Ds and Fs, and hence dropouts or flunkouts, is now very low.

The college emphasizes discussion classes and writing for two reasons: One is to involve students in their own education, the other is that much more teacher preparation is involved in a discussion than a lecture class because the instructor must have a question to cover every point he wants to make. At the same time, more is demanded of the student; he not only has to have read the material to be discussed, but he must have thought about it because he must be able to talk about it in an insightful way.

The dean sits in on classes because he is looking for empathy with students and for good teaching. Tenure depends on both; being an active researcher isn't enough to keep a faculty job here.

Several faculty members testified that what the college is doing to develop abilities and talents in students produces results. One of them, a teacher with empathy enough to win teaching awards, professor of history John Roper, said E&H students, even those who come less well prepared than others, do well in graduate school. "The kids here are better than they think they are. They are eager, they are genuine. They never worry about asking the naive question. The white students are not as racist as kids elsewhere. Many of these kids live in the same houses their grandfathers did. They have a country shrewdness; if the train's leaving, they've got to catch it. They're not as well prepared as some, but that troubles me little. We're an add-on school.

"I've enjoyed teaching these kids more than any others I've ever taught [at U. of South Carolina and U. of North Carolina]."

Not only do they do well in graduate school, he added, but the General George Marshall Library in Lexington will take any E&H student as an intern because the scholarly work of their predecessors has been so good.

Dr. George Treadwell, sciences chairman, agreed that many of them aren't well prepared when they come, but that when they're seniors they go on to the better graduate and medical schools, "and they write well."

He added that the college has a definite influence on the youths' development, not only because of the value-oriented courses they must take but also because there's "a great deal of personal contact with faculty members. In fact, fairly often faculty members will come here for less money simply because of the E&H philosophy."

Dr. Ed. Damer, author of a best-selling philosophy textbook, *Attacking Faculty Reasoning,* said, "This is a challenging place; it excites me, and I've been teaching here for 25 years. These students are here because they want to be here, because they're interested in learning."

In conversations with a couple dozen different students, not one said he or she would go someplace else if he or she had to do it all over again. All of them spoke warmly of their relationships with their teachers and with their fellow students. And the answers to one of my standard questions—"If you came back here five years after graduation would you have good enough friends on the faculty that you'd have dinner or spend the night at a faculty member's home?"—the answers were either "yes," "certainly," or "you bet."

Surprisingly, no one had a gripe about a prof who was a clunk. More than one spoke with pride about their undefeated football team in which the star halfback could practice only three days a week because of labs, and the best lineman's class schedule was so full he could practice only one day. The students' pride in the team's achievement and in the rightly ordered priorities of players, coach, and college was at least equalled by Dr. Morris's when he proudly described the players' commitments and their accomplishments.

Anybody's reaction to those students would be, "What a nice, genuine, open bunch of kids; honest, unassuming, warm, and emanating a quiet self-confidence."

What former students think of their alma mater is one of the true tests: How do its graduates believe 15, 20, and 30 years later that this experience has affected the quality of their lives?

If the theory is true that a person puts his money where his mouth is, few colleges or universities, Ivy or otherwise, could match the esteem in which Emory and Henry is held by its graduates. In the 1990–91 academic year, more than 51% of its alumni contributed. That ranks it number 21 in the percentage of alumni giving, among the nation's more than 2,000 four-year colleges and universities.

E&H is a friendly, homey kind of place that is likely to give you strengths you didn't know you had if you've felt put off by the competition for grades in high school. If you're interested in learning, don't worry about your SAT scores; E&H acceptees show a wide range of them.

And if you think you might need help—and more people do

than admit it—this is a place where caring people will help you over the hump.

Finally, the fact that faculty members say the students are here to learn says something very important about the nature of a place, and it's not too often I get that kind of response.

Guilford College
Greensboro, North Carolina

O ne would never guess that the country's hottest producer of oil geologists is a Quaker college of 1,400 students founded in 1837 in Greensboro, North Carolina, that accepts 75% of its applicants. It is.

Six of its geology majors have key positions in the four major oil companies. Three Guilford graduates—two of them women—head the oil explorations in Southeast Asia for Amoco, Chevron, and Texaco. The one at Chevron, the youngest ever to hold such a job, hit on her first two drillings. Another woman heads Amoco's explorations research. A male alum is an advanced exploration geologist for Texaco, and the sixth graduate is exploration geologist for Exxon in Calgary, Canada. In addition, Texaco chose two Guilford graduates for their Frontier Division, which makes global decisions for the company. Several other Guilford alumni are in staff positions with major or independent oil companies, or are doing consulting.

Guilford has several other claims to fame; it has led all institutions in the state in winning prestigious Danforth Fellowships. And it produces such achievers from a stock of teenagers with SAT verbal scores in the 500 range and high school records that put just a little more than a third of them in the top decile of their classes.

Guilford has a major observatory on top of the Frank Family Science Center and is one of 16 colleges and universities picked by the National Aeronautics and Space Administration to participate in a joint venture of special programs at flight and space centers and research laboratories to prepare NASA leaders of the future.

For the South it is a liberal institution. Being Quaker, it truly is a friendly place. The individual, values, and social concerns are the important things. There is an honor code, but an atmosphere of trust has been created that makes it unnecessary in the view of a math professor whose family has gone to Guilford for five generations. "In 20 years," he said, "we've had six cheating cases. The atmosphere is noncompetitive; it's 'I'm competing against myself.' We encourage collaborative work, but of course each student draws his own conclusions and makes his own arguments."

In the intense competition for African-American students, Guilford has done well; 7% of the student body are African-Americans, and they graduate at the same rate as whites, more than 70%. Significant is the way my question was answered: "While I haven't bothered to look, blacks do as well as whites and graduate at the same rate." Even when I first visited more than 15 years ago Guilford stood out as one integrated community, in dramatic contrast with many other places. On a more recent visit, when I was hearing from a black secretary only good things about Guilford students, I asked her if she'd send her own child here. She said, "My daughter's a sophomore here."

President Donald W. McNemar, who taught international relations at Dartmouth and came to Guilford after serving as headmaster of Phillips Academy in Andover, Massachusetts, said, "We combine the liberal arts and preparation for a career on a value-based education. These unique programs prepare students to be leaders in a rapidly changing world. Guilford graduates leave with values, skills, and commitments which enable them to make a difference."

Guilford's wooded 340-acre campus in a northwestern suburb is a lovely place in which to have the experience the school offers. Many campuses are attractive, but this one has a special charm, and Quakers, like New Englanders, keep everything picked up, painted up, and fixed up. No visitor has ever said a Guilford building—or even a dorm—looked anything but fresh as a daisy.

Especially charming is Guilford's Carnegie library, which houses 250,000 volumes, and fiber optic linkages to other libraries make it the equal of that in a major university. The original 1908 building has been renovated and greatly enlarged with a two-story, atriumlike addition that provides 400 inviting places to study, and a seven-room art gallery. It has both cozy carrels and a light and airy openness that is both alluring and good for grade-point averages. Among its special and endowed collections is a comprehensive Friends Historical Collection of rare books and periodicals and 600 volumes of Carolina Quaker records dating from 1680.

It is one of the few colleges in the South that has intercollegiate teams in lacrosse as well as in the more usual ones of baseball, basketball, football, golf, and tennis, in which it is formidable.

Although Guilford's fame in geology is a great coup, and there is much student research here, chemistry professor Dr. David MacInnes and his students are also doing leading-edge research in metal-free batteries (important to pacemakers and to all kinds of portable gadgets). One professor did a major piece of the research that made a plastic battery possible. Math and physics students publish in undergraduate journals.

Involvement is required in other fields as well. Everyone goes through a core curriculum planned to ensure a liberal education. Most classes involve discussion and have 18 or fewer students, which means there's no place to hide. Majors in sociology, government, and religious studies must do internships. Government students may spend a term working in Congress with a North Carolina representative. Sports medicine majors must get experience in two jobs.

About a third of the students take a foreign study program in China, Mexico, Central America, Italy, Ghana, England, France, Germany, or Japan. They go with a professor in groups of 20 to 25.

There is a special sense of family here as palpable as at Earlham, the Quaker college in Indiana. As is Quaker custom, students and teachers are on a first-name basis. Dr. Elwood Parker, the mathematician of long family ties, said, "As a fundraiser, the first question I invariably get from an alumnus is about some faculty member, how he is, that reflects a kind of relationship that is more powerful here than at any other place. We're all in this together. There is a lot of team teaching."

Dr. Parker taught one such class without a textbook, which was a challenge to his philosopher teammate. In departmental meetings, faculty members not only discuss how they're teaching and trade tips, but also ask about how particular students are doing.

In an introductory geology class I visited, a dozen students working in teams of two or three were poring over great sheets of a gigantic three-dimensional jigsaw puzzle simulating a section of the earth 26 miles by 16 miles and 5 miles deep called the Quaker Quadrangle, its geology invented 25 years ago by Dr. Cyril Harvey. He, incidentally, had been a whiz kid who went to the University of Chicago after the tenth grade. He came to Guilford 30 years ago after ten years with Chevron. Dissatisfied with existing manuals, he decided to write his own lab program. His idea was to design a tool he could use not only to simulate geology, but also to give the experience of scientific research and discovery with three-dimensional thinking. The students were arguing points about its history or whether it was a logical place to expect to find oil. Such facts as rock configurations and drilling costs at a given spot were all stored in the computer, and as students checked things out they were solving their problems by using the information in the textbook. "As they solve," Dr. Harvey explained, "they make their own discoveries, the principles in the book become real and it's a personal experience, an emotional kick—in fact it's almost magical the way they're thinking for themselves."

It must be; one of the Texaco exploration directors hadn't intended to be a geology major until he got hooked on the Quaker Quad. It may also be one reason why the first three holes ever proposed by Guilford graduates were discoveries. One of those who hit said this was the most important course she ever took, even counting graduate school, that prepared her for her job.

Two other anecdotes are apropos. A senior geology and English major told me she'd been a "C+" student in high school but that now Dr. Harvey was recommending her for graduate school. "You realize your potential here," she said. "Ninety-eight percent of the profs are caring. I think we're spoiled." She was trying to get her sister, who was not having a good experience at Brown, to transfer.

Amoco's exploration head, as a brand-new Ph.D. from the University of North Carolina, failed at first to get the job after an interview. She went back to Guilford, not to UNC, to get advice, because "You told me I was good." Dr. Harvey told her Amoco had made a mistake and to go back. She bought another airplane ticket, told the bosses they'd made a mistake and they hired her.

The rest of Guilford's faculty also think their students are good. They think they benefit from comparisons with those at some of the other places where they've taught, including Emory, Vanderbilt, Clemson, Colorado College, and Carleton. They described Guilford students as much more serious than those at Colorado College; they are not grade-grubbers and they don't cheat, as students at Emory did; they don't mind working at something they're interested in even if it means a low grade; they will try things; they're outspoken and thoughtful; they feel they have authority, and they challenge; they want to go to graduate school but it's not a track as it is at Carleton. And there's simply no comparison with the Clemson football factory, where instructors were under pressure to favor athletes.

A math professor added: "We care. If we have a genius we know what to do with him or her, where to send him; we're going to do what will contribute to the person's best development; we won't try to keep him because he's a good student. The Quaker ethos of peace and collegiality is strong. Race issues are discussed here, unlike some places where one faculty member won't speak to another holding different views."

The student view is much the same. They said that most work hard—though there's always a bottom group making minimal effort. Like the geology/English major, they were practically rhapsodic about how good the teaching was. "It's a great environment in which to learn," said a sophomore from a magnet school in New Orleans. A senior girl thought Guilford had changed her life. Two different students took a special pride in the fact that faculty members who had inventions or other outside achievements didn't brag about them.

Although the sample I took was small, I was mightily impressed that every black student I talked to was at least as enthusiastic about the school, if not more so, than the white ones. This attitude conveyed not just a strong sense of community but also a feeling of ownership.

There is no Guilford type, students agreed. Not only do two-thirds of them come from out of state, but they represent a diversity of backgrounds, geographical areas, and 30 foreign countries. The secretary whose daughter is a student said, "There are some Ivy types, and some obviously not, that you would see in a shopping mall downtown, so it would be difficult to pick out a Guilford student as you would spot a Bennett College girl."

Many kinds of students would be happy at Guilford. The admissions director had as good as answer as anyone. When asked at a college fair what kind of shoe Guilford would be, he said it would be a sandal, because it is so open and comfortable. There certainly is a broad range of types, but basically it is a place where people trust and like each other.

It is also a stimulating place where the teachers care, where they expect a lot, and where they provide the encouragement as well as the challenge to get young people to do things they had no idea they could do. Guilford is a fine example of a college family that is doubling talents.

Hendrix College
Conway, Arkansas

On a balmy April day, as one enters the 50-acre enclave of masses of red and white azaleas, dogwoods, giant willow oaks, and manicured lawns that set off Hendrix's attractive buildings, the overwhelming impression is that this Shangri-La in Conway, Arkansas, 30 miles north of Little Rock, must be the most beautiful campus of them all. And inside this lovely setting is a warm community that offers an educational experience to match, one without peer.

No city street intrudes; the outside world is walled off by the trees and shrubbery. Even the parking is way out of sight. A walkway high over the street takes visitors to a 120-acre parklike expanse of recreation and sports facilities. There are tennis courts, intercollegiate playing fields, including one for rugby, and a fitness trail in the woods. A giant indoor activities center has more tennis as well as basketball courts, and its Nautilus fitness area might dwarf even those of some professional teams. Students said it is more used by the girls than by the boys.

Close by are the streams, lakes, forests, and hills of that outdoorsman's paradise, the Ozark Mountains, offering canoeing, whitewater rafting, spelunking, rock-climbing, horseback riding, hot-air ballooning, hiking, and camping, not to mention some beautiful country. The college takes full advantage of this bounty with a comprehensive outdoors program for every interest and every range of skill.

These attractions are bonuses offered by one of the country's academic gems. It truly is a too-secret treasure that is both a financial bargain, with 93% of students receiving financial aid, and a great opportunity for a better educational experience than you'd find in most name-brand places. It really is a shame that this century-old college of 1,100 students isn't more widely known. Partly because it's in Arkansas and partly because of modesty stemming from its church origins (Methodist), Hendrix has blushed unseen rather than trumpeted its virtues. Only recently has it begun recruiting students from outside its region.

Hendrix accepts almost 90% of its applicants, two-thirds of whom are from Arkansas. However, since the college started casting its net farther and wider, the out-of-state percentage is growing. The middle 50% have SAT totals in the 1,250 range, which means a lot of scores are below as well as above. Half of those accepted were in the top half of their high school class, but that includes many small rural ones, so it is a good bet for "B" students with good programs from larger and more competitive high schools. And that also goes for "C" students who mean business.

There are no fraternities or sororities. As a student from Alaska said, "You make friends with people from different departments, different parts of the country, different cultures. Your 'group' becomes the whole campus."

Nearly 90% of the faculty hold doctoral degrees from the great American and European universities. All the rest have terminal degrees in their fields. In the last decade, the faculty has grown from sixty to eighty although enrollment is only up by 10 percent. New majors have been added in international relations, anthropology, and computer science, while more strength and diversity have been added to existing fields. The student-faculty ratio has been lowered to 12-1, and the average class size to 15.

To accommodate all this growth, the college has added new centers for the physical and life sciences as well as two new dormitories and six small residences housing 16 to 18 students each to provide opportunities for residential programs. It has installed a new pipe organ in a renovated chapel and has added intramural and regulation soccer fields to its already well-equipped recreation area.

Sixty percent of the graduates go on to graduate or professional school. And they are welcomed. They score in the 98th and 99th percentiles in the graduate tests because they've already been doing what graduate students do; research. Each year students accompany faculty members to professional meetings to present the results of collaborative student-faculty research. The chances of a student getting this kind of experience at a great university are close to none.

It is not surprising that Hendrix has had ten Fulbright Scholars and ten Watson Scholars in the last ten years, as well as eight Goldwater scholars in the last seven years. Nor is it surprising that one in eight of the state's doctors went to Hendrix, or that another alumnus, Dr. Harry Meyer, was one of the team that found a vaccine for dreaded German measles.

Indeed, Hendrix, despite its size, ranks 12th among all the four-year institutions in the country in the proportion of chemistry majors, 13th in physics, and 23rd in biology.

Hendrix offers so much partly because it is such a warm community of learning, one in which the minority students are an active and integral part, and in which campus employees not only call students and teachers by their first names but also put on the Christmas banquet because they said they could do it better than the caterers who had been hired by the president, Dr. Ann Die, just so that all of the college's employees could be guests at the banquet. That is the way she thinks. Part of the college's drive and sparkle emanate from this practicing psychologist of wide and lively interests. Of the college's mission she says:

"Hendrix is a classic institution that has never deviated from its commitment to the liberal arts foundations. We do not offer a 'drive-through' education where students come to pick up grades and go home. We are involved in every aspect of our students' lives—we foster their intellectual, social, moral, physical, and spiritual development."

And Hendrix is deeply concerned with moral (not religious) development. As its very able academic vice president, John Churchill, a Rhodes Scholar, Yale Ph.D., and former head of the national Rhodes Scholar office, said, "It is places like this that incubate the continuity of democratic values." He himself came to Hendrix from the Rhodes office out of a sense of mission to the South. He would improve any school.

Dr. Churchill's sense of mission is shared by his colleagues, from President Die on through the faculty. "Why are we doing good work?" he asked, "We've had the advantage from the start of having strong people, with a sense of mission; we've never gone off course or astray. We have tremendous human resource strength, people committed to education. A big part of the key to a successful, fulfilling career here is liking students.

"It's very hard here to avoid getting into courses or conversations about big issues, such as duties of government, nature of citizenship, definition of culture, because this institution will not let you specialize in a very narrow field. The objective of students at good small colleges is not vocational but educational.

"Values? No question the experience at Hendrix affects values. Obviously, we have no agenda of values; that would be antithetical to developing the values that really belong to people. I have far less confidence in teaching for developing a person of good moral character than I have in the intense discussion of important exemplary cases—Aeschylus, Homer, Freud, St. Augustine. These are the grist of the mill that develop some acuity in ethical thinking. Students are engaged in a common dialogue."

A music professor said, "I came out of an undergraduate education (University of Texas) not much different than when I went in, except that I had a lot more knowledge. What's amazing to me is that the kids who come in here are unrecognizable when they leave. They learn to cope with challenges and to understand other ways and points of view, partly because of the foreign programs." To which another professor added, "I told a kid just today, 'You couldn't possibly have done something this sophisticated six months ago.' "

Collaborative learning is emphasized. Built with this idea in mind, the new library has small study rooms where little groups can work together. There is no cutthroat competitiveness.

As at other colleges in this book, the faculty's enthusiasm for their students is one of the two main reasons they have stayed at Hendrix instead of moving on to a university. The other is the faculty belief in a shared enterprise and the strong sense of fellowship. A history professor recalled, "I was only going to stay three or four years, and mine is the standard story, and it's the students, it's not the Arkansas climate. One of my students is a combined physics and history major, another designed his own interdisciplinary major. They're interested in many things, not just pre-professional or vocational."

A music professor said he came 14 years ago not intending to stay long, "but now you couldn't blast me out of here. The commitment of the students was a new world for me. Students are interested in music who aren't music majors. Both students and faculty are interested in worlds other than their own. The collegiality here was unbelievable, no factions at all, no infighting. This is a more appropriate kind of education; you get opened up earlier and specialize later."

A biologist who had come to Hendrix as a temporary stop on his way to being a researcher summed it up with, "I was blown away by the collegiality, a feeling that there was something special happening, that everybody was in this together, that they really were changing students' lives, and that that was something important, the most important thing you could do with your life. I've now been here 22 years. We don't have disciplinary problems, whether they attend class. We've got good people, good counseling, and a positive atmosphere, and this is critical to a student looking for a place. We have very high standards and I think that is why our students are so successful in graduate and professional schools—that and collaborative learning and critical learning."

The process of bonding starts for freshmen before the fall term, with a three-day orientation camp-out with faculty members. The school year comprises three terms and in each term students concentrate their energies on only three courses. For two of the first year's terms freshmen are divided into seminar groups to study Western intellectual traditions, a program that is designed to make them think rather than acquire information, and that demands much writing.

Later, students must take courses in the humanities, natural sciences, and social sciences, as well as complete a major. With faculty guidance, the major may take any one of countless forms. There are honors courses, much independent study, and ample opportunities to do research projects, alone or working with a teacher.

Off-campus study opportunities are many. There's a Washington Semester Program, a Hendrix-in-Oxford Program in England, and many others around the world. Students interested in marine biology can take courses in the Gulf Coast Research Laboratory in Ocean Springs, Mississippi. Often these are heady experiences the student couldn't have imagined having when he was a freshman. For instance, the high point of one political science major's college career was a summer internship in the White House where, among other things, his duties included the exciting work of drafting political speeches.

Hendrix is an easygoing, unpretentious, democratic place. A senior from Missouri headed for medical school said she had been "charmed by the people and by the community atmosphere," to which a freshman added, "this is a really unique community. You can relate to your profs; they are your friends and they are involved in the volunteer programs." (Long before she's a senior I'm sure she won't try to modify 'unique.') A senior from Texas called it the most welcoming and friendly place he had visited, noting that after he got here he found the work "challenging."

It was a student who proudly told me about the annual Christmas party. President Die had ordered the first one catered so the kitchen staff could attend. But afterward they said they could do it better, so they do. "At Hendrix," she said, "a real emphasis is put on every person. We know the names of people on the ground crew, the janitor knows me and calls me by my first name." She and a couple of others said they go back to their high schools to spread the word about Hendrix.

They all talked about how important their out-of-class experiences had been to them. Some mentioned activities and some the excitement and broadening experiences of the foreign study programs, but the common thread was that getting involved was essential to getting what you should out of the experience. "This is no place where you can fall through the cracks," one student said.

The kind of person who should come here, they said, should be willing to be involved in the life of the community, be "open-minded, accepting, and willing to grow, because this is a most diverse place." He especially should want to take an active part in his own education. This was not the place, they felt, for anyone who wouldn't be happy in a completely unpretentious place. It's not for the fast-track person.

Little Rock is only 30 miles away but students and faculty alike felt the richness of the campus cultural programs, the variety of activities, and the limitless outdoors attractions were more than enough compensation for not being next door to a major metropolis. There is a good cultural life on campus. The generosity of a foundation has enabled the college to put on some first-rate festivals. In 1994, for example, it was the exploration of many worlds—scientific, social, political, and artistic—that opened up in the Victorian era. There were lectures, demonstrations, musical and theatrical events, and exhibits in which faculty and guest performers both took part.

This is an ideal place for African-American students. They are very active. They have a pep music group that plays at games, and a choir. As one said, "I know that I can do what I want at this school." A black sophomore said she came here because "I was ready to take on a challenge, academically and socially, a positive challenge." And she's glad she did.

At first I was a little puzzled that none of the black students had mentioned Hendrix' charismatic black English professor, Dr. Alice Hines, the kind of teacher there should be more of. I concluded they didn't feel a need to mention race any more than she had in lovingly relating the successes of some of her late-blooming students. She didn't mention color until I asked whether the black students felt they were part of the community. "Absolutely!" she said, "Black students are very active at Hendrix and are part of the community. When they come here they know where they're going; it's not a new culture, and they're self-starters."

Like some of the faculty members, I was unexpectedly blown away by Hendrix. It is an exemplary college and teenagers of a wide range of abilities and interests would find this a very happy fit socially. It is a far nicer and more sophisticated place, besides being infinitely more exciting academically, than the retreaded teachers colleges that are now universities in most states, or the state universities. There should be at least one college as good as Hendrix in every state.

Lynchburg College
Lynchburg, Virginia

Lynchburg College is a 214-acre spread of exceptional beauty, complete with a lake and a view of Virginia's Blue Ridge Mountains, that is no longer a traditional little Southern college. In its rebirth it is making productive citizens by taking average students and developing in them powers they didn't know they had, with a special emphasis on minority students.

Seventy percent of the 1,850 full-time students are from New England, Middle Atlantic, or Midwestern states, and there's a large contingent from the Atlanta area. Their SAT totals are in the 900 to 1,000 range, half of them are in the upper half of their high school classes, and about 85% of the applicants are accepted. Students dress neatly; there's no green hair, no far-out look, or grungy type here. They are more conventional and conservative, nice-looking teenagers happy to be on this nice campus. And at Lynchburg they're in a community that operates on a student-run honor code.

For 20 freshmen who had high grades and SAT scores, Advanced Placement courses, and extracurricular activities, there is an honors program that provides special courses, lectures and trips, independent study in the senior year, and their own dorm.

Lynchburg is something of a financial bargain; Virginia provides $1,500 tuition grants [the 1993 figure] to state residents, aid is given to those in need, and $5,000 scholarships are awarded to high school seniors chosen for the new Involving Leadership Program. The college also offers a variety of other scholarships out of its own funds, as well as all of the federal grant and loan funds.

Twenty years ago the faculty saw that the job the college was doing had to change if it was going to prepare people to live productive lives in a new kind of world. Lynchburg brought back Great Books courses to encourage students to think about life's and society's problems; it required writing and speaking across the curriculum to equip students to communicate their ideas clearly; it created an Involving Leaders Program to help students develop the confidence to be contributors at school and in life. And it committed itself to an institution-wide change to attract minority students and to help them succeed.

What might seem a nonacademic wrinkle was also introduced. It is an Outward Bound–type Adventure Program with

a challenging rope-climbing course the freshmen have to negotiate. The college calls this "another form of education," because as in Outward Bound, surmounting obstacles raises one's
self-image and builds self-esteem.

These things are the work of a faculty with vision and of the
late Dr. George Rainsford, who was president for ten years
starting in 1983. When I visited him, he talked about what he
thought a college must do today. Its job is changing, he said, for
two reasons. First, in the next decade or so, one of three people
in this country won't be white. This means not just providing
more opportunities for minorities, but making them equally
prosperous parts of the family. Second, he said, to be able to
compete in a more sophisticated, global economy, every college
student will need more sophisticated preparation. Instead of
being a store of soon-to-be-obsolete information, students need
to be able to think, to see connections, to organize information,
and to write and speak clearly.

The faculty, having decided to require writing across the
curriculum, realized there had to be something meaty to think
and write about, so they introduced Great Books courses, now
called the Lynchburg College Symposium Readings (LCSR),
to be taken all four years, by everybody, whether business, music, physics, English, or philosophy majors. And they're not just
lectures to passive listeners. At least 20% of each course must
consist of writing. A program evaluator from Harvard reported
that he was amazed to see "a literate, scholarly paper using a
classical source emerge from a course on a subject like accounting."

The Communications Department argued that speaking was
as important as writing, so many classes became oral presentations by students instead of lectures by a professor.

Every student has to take six courses that deal with some of
mankind's major concerns. It starts in the freshman year, so
that the student gets to know John Locke, for example, all the
way along. And the senior year LCSR course is a capstone to
pull together the 32 courses he takes in his college career.

A college faculty often will accept change only grudgingly, but most of Lynchburg's is enthusiastic about theirs. They sit in on each other's classes—something that's a no-no at most institutions. They have discussions on what's working and what isn't. Some of them are elated about what it has done for their teaching as well as for their students.

A history prof said, "LCSR has shown me that lectures are not the most efficient way of teaching. Most of my classes now are conducted by questions; I only lecture when I'm introducing new material. The result is that I never know where the class is going. Furthermore, it has taken me from being isolated in my own discipline to seeing how it fits into the whole picture.

"In a model U.N. class where oral presentations are required, a very shy student had to talk, and it worked an incredible change in her. Group oral presentations I videotape so they can see themselves later, how effectively they talked, and it's amazing how it builds confidence."

With obvious pride in what the new program was achieving, one prof said, "A few years ago a boy who wasn't ready to work flunked out, realized after a term what he was missing, came back, graduated with honors and won a major award as a senior. We're producing productive citizens!"

The faculty does business research and provides lectures for the business community. They also give people older than 25 a chance to complete or augment their education in a part-time program called ACCESS, which is open to anyone and which has more than 700 participants.

Value development is a principal object of the Involving Leadership Program. And it's been having an effect. Among other things, the hours of community service put in by the students have grown enormously.

High school seniors who win the leadership awards take a weeklong summer workshop before entering college. During freshman year they have weekly meetings on such topics as motivation. They advise the college on ways to get more students involved in activities and have a leadership internship in the junior or senior year.

Upperclass students gave the leadership program uniformly good notices. Even if they had not been among the scholarship winners when they came, they believed it had helped them overcome inferiority complexes by making them active participants who had to deal with people, thus developing their self-confidence. Several said they felt the leadership experiences would help them present themselves more effectively in job interviews.

If the effect on one of my clients is any indication, just the recognition of getting one of these $5,000 awards has a dramatic effect. Ever since this personable young woman, an average student, got one because of work with her church youth group for Head Start, and for operating a summer day-care camp at her home, she has radiated a new and happy air of self-assurance.

The program for minority students may well become a model. It began with efforts to encourage campus recognition of minority cultures, and to hire minority staff and faculty where possible. In the first private college–public school partnership in Virginia, the college and the two elementary schools with the largest minority populations started working together. Education students do their practice teaching there; college faculty offer the schools' teachers professional courses and other aid.

This partnership offers the earliest opportunity to raise youngsters' aspirations and get them thinking about college and the future. Summer programs help them along, and "there is a lot of outreach" to keep in touch with the young people. Each fall, minority high school seniors chosen by their guidance counselors spend three days on campus getting a full taste of college life. There's a similar program in the spring for juniors.

The result is that Lynchburg's enrollment is now 13.5% minority, a remarkable feat given the cutthroat competition for minority—especially African-American—students. In 1986,

Lynchburg had five black applicants; in 2000 it had 212, and managed to get 28 of them. That was eloquent testimony to the effectiveness of its efforts, because the bidding for minority students is so intense that they not only get much greater aid packages than white ones, but get them when the family is affluent and has no need; some such have been my clients.

Those who decide on Lynchburg find a staff of minority professionals ready to counsel, to answer questions, to help, or just to give an encouraging pat on the back. Their welcoming demeanor, their obvious competence, and interest in their visitors would make anyone feel better. The director, an alumna, said, "I'm giving something back."

Special events throughout the year highlight black culture. National speakers are brought in for black history programs that involve both the campus and the community, and the college bookstore is well-stocked with multicultural merchandise.

The college's efforts are paying off; minority graduation rates are double the national norm. Every minority student I talked to was happy he or she had come to Lynchburg. A black alumna who had quit another, good job to work in the development office because she believes in the school, said, "It has the potential to make a lot of leaders, black and white." Another said, "It wipes out stereotypes." Every one of them said they would want their children to come here.

Lynchburg's students are heavily pre-professional; 30% are business majors and 42% go into business or graduate schools of business. A total of 20% go to graduate or professional schools and about 10% go into education, mainly elementary and secondary school teaching.

All of the students I talked to said Lynchburg was a place where you felt you should be involved and that if you weren't you were a bit of a deviate or a shirker. "This is not a wallflower school," as one put it, "it definitely encourages involvement." More than one of them said the whole attitude of the place had fostered independence and built their self-confidence. A couple of seniors said that as freshmen they'd been shy and afraid to speak out, but Lynchburg had helped them learn to assert themselves. "It helps in becoming your own person," added a senior girl.

Whether it's part of a nationwide phenomenon or a consequence of the new Lynchburg, the dean of students thinks the students here are less materialistic and more service-oriented than a decade or so ago, and in addition that they have a more practical, hands-on attitude.

Every student answered my stock question about whether they'd have good enough friends on the faculty to have dinner or spend night at their homes five years from now with emphatic responses like, "Sure, with lots of them," or, "We have dinner at their homes now."

Of Lynchburg's new vision, President Rainsford told me, "We do a superb job. What we do is take the average kid and prepare him to compete with the best. Our approach is the opposite of most." Lynchburg is blessed to have a successor in Dr. Charles O. Warren, a research scientist with a sense of mission, who is making the college a model for others to follow.

So far the Lynchburg approach has the full endorsement of its customers. They agree with the college's claim that it is empowering them; they feel good about themselves and grateful for a confidence they didn't come to college with. The successes of the minority programs help make a happy campus and set an example for other colleges.

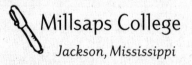

Millsaps College

Jackson, Mississippi

After that searing sixties movie about Mississippi rednecks, *Easy Rider,* fed the latent prejudices of Easterners, clients often told me they didn't want to consider a college in the South, except maybe in Florida. (They already had qualms about the quality of life in that rustic expanse between the Alleghenies and the Colorado ski slopes.) They didn't know that both the quality of education and the quality of life at a college like Millsaps in Jackson, Mississippi, were better than at the familiar colleges. And I didn't know how *very* good until I spent a day here, talking to administrators, faculty, and students. It simply is first-rate, a warm, friendly place that exemplifies the ideal of learning together.

Millsaps is the only institution in Mississippi to have a chapter of Phi Beta Kappa, the scholastic honorary society. It is also one of only 16 colleges in the country, and one of three in the deep South, to have a Ford Foundation grant to prepare future college teachers. The other Southern schools are Eckerd, in St. Petersburg, and Morehouse, in Atlanta.

The great difference between a deep South school like Millsaps—or Hendrix in Arkansas, Birmingham–Southern in Alabama, or Rhodes in Memphis—and a prestige school in the Northeast is that the kids you nod to crossing the campus or interview between classes seem so friendly and unaffected while those at the Northern schools are so cool and self-satisfied. (As a client there told me, "It's hard to be humble at Amherst.")

At Millsaps, the level of expectation is high, the grading is tougher than at many a prestige school, and 40% of its seniors go on to graduate or professional school. A school of 1,300, it has 40 geology majors—an exceptional number—and 50 biology majors. Yet with all this there is no sense of competition or grade-grubbing; it is a collaborative learning adventure. Every student is actively involved; there is no way he can be a passive ear, as he would have to be at a university.

Millsaps takes 80% of its applicants, a third of them in the top tenth of their high school classes, about half in the top fifth, and 90% in the top half. Three-fourths of them have averages above 3.0 (B). The middle 50% have SAT scores around 1,070 to 1,280, which means the other half have scores above or below those figures.

What all those figures mean is that while Millsaps will take "B" students and maybe some in the C range, the message to them is clear: Don't come to Millsaps unless you're interested in getting an education, which means work.

Millsaps students are not as affluent as those at many Eastern schools; three-fourths of them are on financial aid. Nor are they as affected. They don't exhibit the world-is-my-oyster attitude of many Ivy Leaguers. Faculty members and administrators describe them as ambitious young people who are interested in their education. Not only do many of them go on to graduate and professional schools, but most of them leave the state for greener pastures after graduation. The feeling I got was that what they wanted was not riches but a broader range of opportunities than the state offered.

Fifty-four percent of the student body come from 30 other states and eight foreign countries, with Louisiana, Alabama, and Georgia providing most of the out-of-staters. Methodists, Baptists, and Catholics have nearly equal representation, trailed by Presbyterians and Episcopalians, with 15% of other faiths. Five percent are African-Americans, 1% Asian, and another 1% other groups. Whatever their religious faiths or ethnic origins, all the kids I talked to were glad they came; more than one said, "this is my kind of school; it's so friendly and open," or, "I've had opportunities here I wouldn't have had at other places." One fellow elaborated on this with, "You can get a Stanford education here at half the cost." I told him it was a lot better.

The able and enthusiastic faculty has national rather than regional roots. Its members not only earned their academic spurs in the nation's top universities but have also taught in them. But they prefer to teach at Millsaps, a conviction that comes through loud and clear in just about everything they say. Their sense of gratification and joy in their work is palpable; being on that campus is like a day in spring. (In fact, if visiting high school students have sense enough to see what lively intelligences and caring teachers these are, they'll look no further.) All this may sound a bit like hyperbole, but I've not been more persuaded by a school in many years.

As a former Brown faculty member said: "Here the difference is that I'm given every incentive to improve my teaching skills, and [scholarly] publication is a way to hone those skills for use in the classroom. Millsaps offers a much more intimate relationship between faculty and students. At Brown there was absolutely no incentive or pressure for me to work on my teaching. I'd go to my department chairman and say my class is getting too large and I need another one and he'd say what you need to do is to put such qualifications that you can keep it low; schedule it at eight o'clock in the morning and put in a foreign language requirement. His approach was to limit the class so I could get my publications out.

"At Brown the classroom was only there to give you some financial support so you could do your publishing. And that's why I'm happy here; it's an entirely different perspective. Here people love to teach; at Brown they're being forced to teach. There are people there who do research well but who cannot teach. That's why I enjoy it here.

"I see more growth here. Brown students are very highly motivated, but the lack of any structure (no required courses) affects development of a good program. They have good creativity when they come in, but, having been selected for an elite group [Brown occasionally has been the most selective of the Ivies], they have no incentive to move beyond that. But these kids by the time they finish have a very similar type of creativity."

That statement eloquently summarizes one crucial difference between the university, whether prestige or pedestrian, and these high-quality places; they increase and improve the talents of youth.

Another vital difference is, as a business professor said, "We not only address their intellectual development but we don't separate their development as a mature human being from the educational process. I do a lot of advising and I don't make a distinction between my function as an educator and my function as an adviser. And that makes a tremendous difference; they understand that actual development occurs in a lot of circumstances. In a university they come to class and they want you to pour it in and then they go out. My classes at Alabama were 300; they're 30 here. I know them here; I didn't at Alabama."

An impressive English professor added: "We're asked to do something critical and that's to evaluate a student's development, and there's no way under the sun you can do that with multiple-choice tests or by reading essays. I know more about my students than anybody at the University of Michigan, or the University of North Carolina, or the University of Alabama [all places where she has taught] would ever know about his."

There are two reasons why all this is true. One is the imaginative way the Millsaps curriculum probes the human experience, and the other is the collegial nature of the whole enterprise.

The goal of the curriculum, developed over two years by a faculty committee, is not the stuffing of young minds with facts but rather the development of abilities that are going to be needed the rest of their lives.

The new program, faculty members said, alters the model of liberal education. Instead of trying for coverage of history, philosophy, or some other subject with the narrative approach, it dissects a culture to help students see the big picture, to make connections, to use their imaginations and gray cells, to make the bold leaps—abilities they will especially need in the brave new world of unseen opportunities.

In four interdisciplinary, team-taught semester courses, freshmen and sophomores first take a topic of the ancient world, then of the pre-modern world, the modern world, and, finally the contemporary world. They may choose courses in religion, history, fine arts, or something else, but all will be team-taught. For example, if an ancient world topic is theater, professors in religion, philosophy, and art will also be involved.

The other reason Millsaps is such a comfortable and effective learning place is that the faculty members talk to and learn from each other a lot. This also provides an implicit model for the students; they see professors getting each other's views, reading each other's work—sharing—and they do the same. It makes learning collegial rather than competitive.

Every morning the faculty teams discuss problems and listen to each others' presentations. "We all have a sense of where we're going; we all agree on the issues, which is wonderful," said one. "We're doing a better job of looking at a culture—how does economics fit in, and so on. We can pull a culture apart and see what's going on."

Whether it's the new curriculum or the perceptive way the faculty attacks it, they all talk of their excitement in seeing in students so much growth—in intellect, in self-confidence, in the development of a philosophy of life or values. And the teachers feel privileged to be in on the magic.

One of them, Dr. Ed Schrader, a geologist who left industry to teach because he was tired of having to tell college graduates how to do things and because he believes the future of geology must be in environmental concerns, is a Pied Piper who was surrounded by students when I went to see him. He said all—100%—of Millsaps' geology majors are regularly placed in jobs or in graduate school, and this year one of them got *the* major award at the University of North Carolina.

A 29-year-old senior, who is married with two children and has his own telemarketing business, hadn't planned to major in geology until he took a class with Dr. Schrader. He said this professor not only has the ability to spot a student's interests but that you don't have to make an appointment to see him. The whole geology enterprise is "like a family."

The biology and chemistry teachers proudly displayed their new state-of-the-art laboratories and research facilities housed in an eye-catching structure that is architecturally distinguished and has a three-story rotunda grand enough for receptions. Any college would be happy to have either the building or the science evangelists within it, or both.

All science students get involved in research, though how much they do is pretty much up to the student. The opportunities are not only there but are being pushed in front of them. In the second year, everyone does a research paper, which is part of the school's heavy emphasis on writing. In the core curriculum, a paper is due every week. Each year, the Ford Foundation grant starts a dozen budding scholars on the path to becoming college professors. The college also invites students and faculty to apply for fellowships on which they work together for a year, both in the classroom and outside.

Many students echoed what a faculty member told me: "They are attracted to the college for one reason or another and they change. They get new ideas about what they think they want to do with their lives, and they change because of what they do and what they learn and what they hear."

Leaving his office, I chanced upon a heartwarming example of this. She was a senior, a French and biology major planning to work for the Peace Corps in French West Africa before becoming a teacher. She said Millsaps "has helped me see myself and has made me want to be a teacher rather than a doctor because we don't have enough good teachers." The standards and the whole intellectual experience at Millsaps had opened her eyes to a great need.

Another example was a senior biology major who said, "When I came to Millsaps I didn't know who I was, and I just kind of stumbled around. But then some of the exceptional people here took me under their wing, and I've ended up with opportunities I couldn't imagine getting at other colleges. I'm doing research in genetics and assisting in teaching three classes this year under a Ford fellowship. My faculty mentor and I are going to write a textbook next semester based on our work together."

Others had reasons equally important to them; a sophomore English major said, "Everyone here is so nice and friendly, and it's so easy to meet people and get involved. I sure don't know of many schools where I could be a copy editor for the college newspaper my first year and also work on the literary magazine."

And a junior English major agreed that Millsaps had given her opportunities to develop leadership skills and strengthen her self-confidence, as a resident assistant and president of the Black Student Association, among other things.

A clincher of sorts was provided by a budding intellectual, one of that rare breed, a classics major. Asked why he was at Millsaps, he replied, "It's my kind of school."

Every college has dissatisfied students and those who just shouldn't be there, but I didn't run into any at Millsaps. The ones I queried spoke with one voice, saying the same sorts of things the faculty members did; they liked it here and found it exciting, they talked to and learned from each other, it was so collegial it was familial, and if they had it to do over again they wouldn't be anywhere else.

Rhodes College
Memphis, Tennessee

I f its elegant, Oxford-like campus of lovely grounds and collegiate Gothic buildings with leaded glass windows were transported from a residential area in Memphis, Tennessee, to a town in New England, Rhodes College would be as selective as an Ivy school. But so long as it isn't it will have to be satisfied with being as good as, and in some important ways, better than an Ivy.

The catalog says beautiful architecture "inspires and broadens the mind, expands the consciousness to beauty and harmony and reminds the community of the history and breadth of learning, shapes the quality of education, and provides students with a constant vision of excellence." Or, as

Winston Churchill said, "First we shape our buildings, and then our buildings shape us."

Not only does the campus have an architectural unity that is probably unique, but every stone of its many buildings comes from the same quarry, because a long-ago president accepted the quarry in payment for a debt to the college. Fourteen of those buildings are in The National Register of Historic Places.

Rhodes is more selective than most of the colleges in this book; while it accepts about 70% of its applicants, 62% of them had grade point averages of 3.5 or better, and 56% were in the top 10% of their high school classes. Ninety percent had averages of 3.0 (B) or better, and 10% were below a B average.

The middle 50% had SAT verbals ranging from 590 to 700, and math scores from 600 to 690. Half of them had SAT totals under 1,280. But figures don't tell the whole story. As David J. Wottle, Dean of Admissions and Financial Aid, said, "No grouping of numbers can adequately convey the importance we place on the subjective criteria . . . counselor and teacher recommendations, a personal interview, the application essay, and extracurricular involvements. "We want, he said, "a very motivated and diverse group of talented students." About 90% return for the sophomore year and about 75% graduate in four years.

Most of the students come from the Southeast or Southwest but the college is seeking and getting more diversity. It has a little more than 5% African-Americans, 3% Asians, and about 3% foreign students. While Memphis has a large African-American population, the competition for its college-going teenagers is cutthroat; colleges across the country are bidding top dollar for every one of them.

Rhodes costs about $24,000 [1999] and nearly half the students get need-based financial aid averaging $16,650 a year and another third get merit-based aid averaging about $7,700 a year.

For decades the college was sunk in anonymity as one of 16

Southwesterns. Then in 1984 it broke out of the mold not only with a new name—honoring a former president—but with a campaign to let people know how good it was. The matter-of-fact, unprepossessing 1984 catalog says not a word about the beauty of the campus, the school's high mission, or its top quality. The 1999 catalog casts the old modesty aside to proclaim these virtues but, unlike most other colleges, it makes good on them. As a maverick prexy in the roaring '50s said, "If the Federal Trade Commission ever started prosecuting colleges for false and misleading advertising, there'd be more college than corporation presidents under cease and desist orders." The word about Rhodes is getting out because my clients here in the Washington, D.C., area now ask about it, a sign that teenagers are talking about it. They should be, for Rhodes has a lot more to offer them than most of the schools they talk about.

Many of Rhodes's students have the look of people accustomed to its expensive beauty. For one thing, the hair-dos and handbags are clues that fewer of these kids are on financial aid than at Millsaps or at many Midwestern colleges. The figure is just over 40%, or a little better than half that at Millsaps. However, Rhodes offers so many merit scholarships in which need is not a factor that the percentage getting some form of aid jumps to over 70%. This almost puts Rhodes in a class with that nonpareil men's college, Wabush, where half the students get merit scholarships and 93% get need-based aid. It makes Rhodes a prime prospect for high school seniors looking for merit scholarships.

Slightly more than half of the men and women belong to one of the six fraternities and seven sororities, but it is not necessary to be a Greek to be a big shot on campus or to have a good social life. One reason is the students do not live in the fraternity or sorority houses; everybody lives in the dorms. The student body is, as one faculty member said, "middle-of-the-road conservative." But on my first visit 20 years ago what had made an indelible impression was how accepting and friendly they were. At a time when black students on many campuses in the North were segregating themselves, the blacks at Southwestern told me they were contented members of a single social group.

A clue to the students' mostly middle-class origins is what faculty members say about them: "They expect to be cared for—a sense of entitlement," or, "they could work harder." Still another was the note I saw on a professor's door: "Dr. Haynes, I need to have a meeting ASAP. Please give me a call at 3204. Ralph." While such a note may convey a perhaps irritating sense of entitlement, it also suggests that faculty-student relations are close and easy. Just imagine a student daring to do that at any university you may yearn for.

Professor and former academic dean Marshall McMahon, who has won an outstanding-teacher award, said the fact that more Rhodes students have educated (and affluent) parents than at places like Rutgers or Florida, where he had taught, explains the sense of entitlement. He also made two important contrasts with the large schools: For one, the bottom one-third in ability at those universities don't get into Rhodes, so it can focus on the problems of the rest, "and they can't fall through the cracks." A student would have to hide, he said, to avoid getting help. The other is class size; they are 15 or 20 instead of 150 or 200. "So, this is a great place to learn; there's a lot more student contact. And you get kids who see the light come on."

Asked if he thought Rhodes had an impact on them he said, "Unquestionably. There is a community of scholarship among the students. Even in their social life it's hard to get away from their common purpose. When you're out on Saturday night you get conversational exposures to the ideas or problems discussed in class. Life is a learning experience. At Harvard, students are taught by students. Here they're taught by scholar-teachers. I repeat; this is a great place to learn."

But that is only part of the picture. A professor who gave up a rich research fiefdom and a larger income at the University of California at Los Angeles to come here "to teach and to talk to students," said:

"Here they're incredibly polite to each other and in class they help each other. They are remarkably honest. I've never been at a place where the honor code was as effective in bringing about the sense of values it was intended to, and it is student administered. In one case a student was exonerated, so it works very well; it's not just punitive. There was cheating at Gettysburg [where he also taught] on exams and plagiarizing of papers. There is a striking quality here and a high level of expectation. There is definitely more interest in learning here than at UCLA or at Gettysburg. At UCLA they were much more focused on what they wanted—the job or career. And there's a seriousness of purpose here that was lacking at Gettysburg."

The institution planned it that way. And here is where it bests an Ivy. It hires faculty members who believe in "lives of faith and service and that a liberal education is the best one for all of life." And it requires every student to take one of the two four-semester sequences intended to make them examine, and strengthen, their values and beliefs. One is "The Search for Values in the Light of Western History and Religion," an interdisciplinary exploration taught by profs from the religion, philosophy, history, political science, art, English, humanities, Spanish, and German departments. The other is "Life Then and Now," a study of the Hebrew-Christian tradition which is taught by members of the religion, philosophy, and English departments.

While Rhodes, like most private colleges, is church-affiliated (Presbyterian), its emphasis on an examined and moral life is the only clue a student would get. There is no denominational tinge, and people of all faiths or no faith feel equally at home.

Aside from the core courses, students have a panoply of

choices: traditional majors or interdisciplinary ones, internships in many different fields that may open career doors, and a variety of foreign study experiences—including, of course, a term at Oxford.

What Professor McMahon had said was spelled out in detail by a chemistry professor who had taught at the University of North Carolina and at the University of California at Irvine: "I know 400 students by name; I've got 30 kids coming to a Christmas party tonight. Seventy-five percent of the chemistry students do research, both in the academic year and in the summer. To be alone in a place like this you'd have to work at it. My own child is a senior here. The individual attention he gets, the quality of it, and the students' appreciation of it—I literally could not ask for more."

The psychologist who had left UCLA added testimony that is particularly relevant for preparing for a new and different world. He said the kind of education needed today is not possible at a place like UCLA because, "If you're going to make a career contribution you have to find out what your interests are; the ball has to be put in your court. That kind of interaction—dialogue, questions—is necessary, and I can do that now; I can talk to them here." In fact, it was a visit in which he saw what kind of learning community it was that sold him on chucking a research empire to teach at Rhodes.

A similar choice had been made by a business-economics professor. He'd had tenure at Vanderbilt, had quit to run the family's national petroleum business, then wanted to return to teaching. Asked why he didn't go back to Vanderbilt, he said, "The kids are the same at Vanderbilt and here, but you can go through Vanderbilt and never write a sentence or see a prof. I wanted contact with students. And that's precisely why I am here. And here they learn to write."

According to another economist who's been at Rhodes for 20 years, its students have changed a little bit. He perceives them as better students, more like good consumers, and there's a sense of community in spite of fraternities and sororities. But in the matter of community service he sees no change, because "We've had a long tradition of community service with an established program, and a large percentage of the students are involved."

He also said the honor system has a lot to do with a major objective: "We hope to make them responsible for their own actions." The way the economics-business faculty handles its internship program also has a lot to do with that objective. "We don't just send them out," he said, "they have to do résumés to show what they've done and what their objective is. There is lots of economic theory in our joint business-economics major, and every major has to do a research paper and present it to the class."

About 35% of Rhodes graduates go on to professional or graduate school, with medicine, business, and law accounting for a large share of them. The acceptance rates in all fields are near the ceiling. In the last ten years, Rhodes has had 16 Fulbright Scholars and six National Science Foundation Fellows. Since the prestigious Rhodes Scholars program was founded, the college has had six win that honor. Its literature boasts of being in the top 20% of all colleges and universities in the percentage of graduates who later get Ph.D.s in the humanities and social sciences, which puts it in good company if not in the top 50.

As at many other colleges, there are fewer business and more English majors these days. Theology, psychology, and letters divide up a quarter of the majors.

As at Millsaps, Birmingham–Southern, Guilford, and Eckerd, one gets an unmistakable sense of a quiet live-and-let-live atmosphere. A biology prof observed, "We are not venturesome. Southern educational systems don't put out the product others do. Our students often come not well prepared, but they have two years to overcome it." They tend, he said, to be bright, middle-of-the-road conservatives. Fifteen of them in his department are doing research with faculty members, and three of them were co-authors of an oral presentation at a national professional meeting.

Rhodes's students are also comfortable in the assurance they're in a top-notch school; they're not frustrated rejects in a fallback college. The editor of the school newspaper, for example, chose it over Bowdoin, Carleton, and Haverford, and he would do it again, even if he thinks that not enough of his peers are interested in the life of the mind. But then he's a philosophy major headed toward the academic life, and his reservations were the only ones I ran into.

The son of a faculty member said he had tried "an Eastern college" his freshman year and switched to Rhodes, even though his father was there. As at Millsaps, some said their Southern high schools had not prepared them for the rigors of a place like Rhodes. Everyone I talked to was glad he or she was at Rhodes and gave the impression that being there was a star in their crown.

The stately beauty of the campus and the smiles one gets walking from one imposing building to another convey a sense of stability and civility. The people are just as friendly as they were 20 years ago. It would be difficult to imagine a sit-in blocking the administration building, a mass protest, or graffiti on a wall, much less a revolution. The nature of things wouldn't stand for it.

First-rate, caring scholar-teachers are the hallmark of the colleges in this book, but I was especially impressed with the ones I talked with at Rhodes. The college awards rich monetary prizes each year for outstanding teaching, for research and creative activity, and for service to the school. It is one of those few colleges that gives what it proclaims in the catalog in full measure to its lucky customers.

St. Andrews Presbyterian College

Laurinburg, North Carolina

In the southeastern corner of North Carolina is 30-year-old St. Andrews Presbyterian, a college of nearly 800 students on a lovely 600-acre campus where a 70-acre lake scenically separates living and recreation areas from the academic ones. It is a design so logical and so attractive that it won major awards for architectural excellence.

The main academic buildings are on one side of the lake. Across a pedestrian-only causewalk are all the facilities for student housing, dining, recreation, and athletics. All buildings are barrier-free and air conditioned and many are equipped for audio-visual instruction. Behind all this are 300 more acres of woodland trails and riding paths and an equitation center with 40 horses. They are the mounts for a nationally ranked equestrian team, as well as for any student who wants to ride.

To walk into the science lab is a shock. It is the size of a soccer field—20,000 square feet. It is that size because it is interdisciplinary—one of the "bold experiments" that fits in with team teaching and making intellectual connections. There is also a state-of-the-art music lab that facilitates the study and performance of the music of many ethnic groups.

It is the only college in the country where every building has been designed and every amenity provided to make things easy for students with physical disabilities. Students in wheelchairs have no problems here.

It is also a financial bargain; in 1995 99% of the students received some form of financial aid.

St. Andrews is a college that has National Merit Scholars, but that also accepts and then empowers "C" and "C–" students to compete with the best. Although it is easy to get into, no one slides through. Students get involved in a community that encourages both participation and intellectual exploration. A business professor boasted, "We take kids who haven't done very well in high school, but we turn out people who compete with the Ivies. I'd put them up against the Ivies."

The business professor's claim was echoed by seniors I talked to. They had beaten out students from other schools for summer jobs or they had been in internships with them and could make comparisons, or they had been accepted to graduate or professional school programs where the competition was intense. At the very least, they considered themselves as well-prepared as those from much more selective schools; indeed, most of them thought they had an edge in their ability to perform.

The college takes pride in a near perfect record of medical school acceptances of the seniors it recommends. And echoing the business professor's boast, a St. Andrews alumnus in Emory University's MBA program was picked by Procter & Gamble out of 100 applicants for a special internship. The interviewers were particularly impressed by his ability to communicate easily with different kinds of people, something St. Andrews had taught him.

Another, more dramatic example was one of my young clients who had such a severe learning problem that his highest SAT verbal score was just over 300. He compiled 3.6 averages in three years at St. Andrews and again in two years at Georgia Tech, graduating magna cum laude in the 3–2 engineering program. In 1995, he was one of only 200 new engineers hired by a major corporation that had been laying off thousands of them. While he gives St. Andrews much credit for developing his skills and his ability to handle a brutally tough engineering program, his was another demonstration that students with learning disabilities always—repeat, always—succeed if they want to.

After their children have graduated, parents have written to me expressing their appreciation for having learned about the school. An Ivy alumnus was so pleased with his son's experience that he had no regrets that the boy hadn't followed him.

It is a beacon of hope for the thousands who fear that Cs and Ds on the report card and low SAT or ACT scores mean they won't have a chance at the springboard of a really good college experience, which St. Andrews provides. It can truly claim to be a value-added place. The track records of its graduates bear witness.

But that doesn't give the whole picture. St. Andrews also attracts a lot of very able students who've led their classes in high school. To keep them challenged it has an honors program for people in the top 15% of their entering class. They get special honors courses and do a public service project to challenge them to think critically on the moral, political, and religious foundations of public service, and to acquire the basic knowledge and skills needed for effective social action. In their junior year they write a paper that integrates the theme of their two years of honors seminars with the issues of their public-service project.

Writing is strong here for everyone, and is more than just a curricular emphasis. One member of the English department was a Pulitzer Prize nominee, and St. Andrews claims to be the only undergraduate college with its own press. Its weekly Writers' Forum brings in famous speakers, including Tom Wolfe, Barry Gifford, Clyde Edgerton, Daphne Athas, and James Dickey. As the co-editor, a junior from Atlanta, said, "There are great opportunities here. I just met the poet laureate of North Carolina and South Carolina, and Robert James Waller, whom we had as speakers. I love it here."

In addition to being one of the very few colleges that has buildings designed especially to accommodate those with physical limitations, it also provides special living facilities, which include nurses and therapists on 24-hour call. About 5% of the 700-odd students have some disability, and it is common to see a pair crossing the long campus bridge, one on foot and one in a wheelchair. It is the only such campus in the country and the only one where disabled students form such a sizable group that they feel they are part of the mainstream. Some of them are also millionaires, as the result of auto accident settlements.

This school was called "a bold experiment" at its birth 30 years ago, principally because of SAGE, an acronym for Saint Andrews General Education. Today, one would call its curriculum typical of the newest ones designed to make students aware of the world, of themselves, and of their responsibilities. Like those of several other colleges that have followed its lead, the program consists of six courses that emphasize writing and discussion—to develop critical thinking and communications skills—as it moves through great issues and achievements of major world cultures to a senior-year class in decision-making that stresses values.

There is a variety of foreign study programs around the world and more than half of the students take advantage of them. One is an exchange of both faculty and students with a university in El Salvador. In 1989, when the Chinese students staged their uprising in Tiananmen Square in Beijing, a group of St. Andrews students and their history professor were right there. They were spending that term at China Normal College.

Experiential education is also important here. There are internships in every department, and students are encouraged to share their experiences. Faculty members also go on internships. Corporate CEOs and other experts are brought in for a series of talks on management and other aspects of preparing for life in a changing world.

Such a breadth of experiences gives the St. Andrews graduates an edge in the job market; they're not narrowly focused. Furthermore, they can express themselves clearly—an ability that job market surveys have consistently found employers put at the top of the list.

SAGE broadens the faculty as well as the students, for any one course may involve faculty in science, the humanities, and social science. This has also sparked a lively examination of teaching methods. "We're in and out of each other's classes, everybody picks everybody else's brain, we sit here and plan team teaching, and a lot of viewpoints get examined." Also, all this active concern with the art of teaching tends to attract the right kind of faculty: scholars who are interested primarily in teaching.

Most of the faculty got their doctorates at Ivy or other prestige universities. But unlike their Ivy counterparts, they're primarily teachers because that's what they love to do, and they genuinely care for the well-being of the kids they teach. All it takes is a young mind and heart willing to respond and things cannot help happening.

The Assist Program is another bold experiment. Thirty students who have been referred by counselors or teachers are taken. Each has two advisers—one a faculty academic adviser and the other an Assist developmental adviser—who work with him or her on developing study skills and the best methods for remembering lectures and films, discussions, and readings. They also focus on time management, goal setting, and career planning. A continual assessment of learning styles helps the student make adjustments, and counseling on facing various assessment situations helps reduce test anxiety. There are writing and speaking courses, instruction on how to use the library and the computer, and how to cope with college life.

I found St. Andrews' students just as proud of their school as the faculty was. When I asked a group of upperclass students what kind of person should come to St. Andrews, they said, "if you want a first-rate education and want to be active, to participate, and to be a person, come here." All of them stressed the involvement, the openness, and the friendliness of the place. Two seniors, one black and one white, who had planned to go to the University of North Carolina but found it wanting, were happy they'd made the right choice. One of them is so enamored she will work in the admissions office upon graduation; the other said, "I got a job in competition with a hundred others, many of them MBAs."

Some talked about how college had affected their perspectives on religion. A senior girl said it best: "My faith has broadened so much at St. Andrews. Now I don't see just one rigid re-ligious path—I realize there are vast interstates and winding hiking trails that are equally spiritual."

The views most often expressed were ones like these:

- "You're a person here; it brought me out of myself."
- "Four years ago I never imagined I'd have the op-portunities I've had here. If you have an interest you can take it and run with it."
- "Because of the overseas exchanges, travel abroad, switching roles with international students, I now reach out to those people more than I would have. There's really something precious here. It's unbe-lievable. I wasn't involved in high school. I've blos-somed here."

Antioch College
Yellow Springs, Ohio

A ntioch is in a class by itself. There is no college or university in the country that makes a more profound difference in a young person's life, or that creates more effective adults. None of the Ivies, big or little, can match Antioch's ability to produce outstanding thinkers and doers. A handful of distinctive and distinguished colleges—also in this book—have equal but different effects.

For decades this yeast of American higher education in charming little Yellow Springs, Ohio, with a 1,000-acre nature preserve next to its 100-acre campus, has produced higher percentages of future scientists and scholars than any Ivy university except Princeton. When it comes to the country's top achievers listed in *Who's Who in America*, Antioch shows a higher percentage of alumni than some of the Ivies, most of the major research universities, and all of the Big Ten except Northwestern. It also has better medical and law school acceptance records; for a couple of years running its medical school acceptance rate was 100%. As a medical school dean years ago said, "Antioch students know how to think."

Yet you will not find the words "grades," "grading," or even "evaluation" in the catalog, nor a degree requirement section that says you need a 2.0 average to graduate. Students do get written evaluations from their instructors, which several valued because "they go beyond grades."

What makes this so impressive is that most of Antioch's 700 undergraduates couldn't get into the very selective schools. It accepts 80% or more of its applicants. The middle 50% have SATs ranging from 480 to 600 verbal and 450 to 580 math.

What makes little David so mighty? The central reason is that the power of an Antioch education focuses on the student rather than on the curriculum. It is entirely possible that no two students will have identical programs.

In the 1920s Antioch pioneered a challenging, maturing Outward Bound–like adventure of classes interspersed with real-life jobs. Today, each student spends six quarters in these co-ops. Other colleges have cooperative education programs, but they're simply not the same animal; they're just vocational internships. Here, most jobs, especially the freshman year, will be unrelated to majors, but students learn how to find their way in a new city or country, how to budget their salary to eat and pay the rent, how to fit into a group of workers. As one student said, "Classes involve ways of looking at the world, and co-ops involve ways of dealing with the world." The effect is powerfully synergistic; one complements the other and the result is magically greater than the parts.

Anyone who gets an Antioch diploma goes out into the world with the same conquering confidence that Sylvester Stallone had in the movie *Rocky* in his final triumphant training run up the steps of the Philadelphia Museum of Art. Twenty years ago and last year these kids were saying the same things: "I could survive, I could cope and meet the challenge anywhere or in any situation." Or, "A Princeton grad may have memorized more things, but I feel I can think better."

That's not surprising, for as undergraduates they are the most independent, uppity, tell-it-like-it-is student body on the face of the earth. Those brash qualities reflect an attitude toward truth, for they are without arrogance and their protests may be environmentally considerate. A feisty client of mine gave vent to her demands on the administration building sidewalk, but in chalk—the rain would wash it clean. They are friendly and without pretense. Their dress so testifies; it is unconventional, as one might expect in a family of individualists. They are not slobs and I saw no green hair, but a conservative Southern girl would know her lipstick was out of place here.

Antioch is a democratic community. Students have a voice—a strong one—in the governance of the college, and they exercise it. During a visit 20 years ago, I attended a meeting on cafeteria prices that might have drawn four or five students at other places, but that brought a hundred crowding into one room to hear the student chairman tell the cafeteria manager, "Now Jack, we're not asking for answers; we're demanding them." I must have talked to at least 50 students then, and every one of them had some criticism or suggestion for betterment. Implicit in them all was a possessive loyalty that brooked no excuse for imperfection.

Twenty years later, students were just as feisty and just as sure they were running the place. Antioch's now famous sex-conduct rules for dating, which requires permission to be asked for every touch or kiss, is an example of how different Antioch is from the world of other colleges in which speech and conduct codes are imposed from above. It is a student creation built on lessons they learned from an earlier, failed code of no-nos that was also their work. Then-president Al Guskin said, "I knew the first one—a policy of prohibitions—wouldn't work, but they had to live with it, find that out, and they changed it to one of mutual consent that would."

One measure of its effectiveness is that the dean of students says Antioch, of all places, is more at peace than any place she's worked. Another is that hundreds of other institutions searching for solutions, including Harvard, Yale, Stanford, and New York University, have been asking Antioch how they do it.

The reason it works is that at Antioch—as at Reed, Hampshire, and Marlboro, communities most people would consider far out—there is no peer pressure to conform. Every person is respected as an individual. Antioch was the first college to have open dorms 30 years ago, but when I first visited there, both girls and boys said they felt no sexual pressures whatever, and assured me that "anyone who's into drugs isn't going to hack it here."

In over a quarter-century of advising I've had the secret wish that everyone could have an Antioch-like experience, even though I know it wouldn't be possible. Usually it takes a person who is, or who has the potential to be, self-reliant, independent, and self-motivated. They should also have sharp antennae. Most adolescents don't fit those categories; as a physics prof friend said, "Most teenagers have a planning span of about ten hours." But they do tend to be adventurous, and as a long-time prof said, "Antioch is a wonderful place for people who are adventurous and willing to take charge of their lives, or who can become so."

Antioch's graduation requirements include courses giving the framework of a liberal education, a cross-cultural experience among their co-ops, and conversational mastery of another language. Otherwise there is great freedom for fashioning one's own program, as a course or a job experience changes him or her from an art to a psychology or a philosophy major.

Every other quarter working at a job is a maturing experience that makes Antioch classes unlike those anywhere else, even at Hampshire. "Antioch students will challenge you. They've had real jobs where they have been responsible for themselves," as one prof said, "and then they come back and want to see how what they're doing in class relates. So it's hard to walk into a class and say, 'Here's what happened.' They'll say, 'How do you know, what is your source?' And they'll do it all in perfectly good humor." A psychology prof added, "They really challenge you. I was interested in research but I can't get away from teaching here; it's too exciting."

A class may strike a visitor as some chance gathering of colleagues on a first-name basis, one where anything goes. On a

September day in a French class where everyone had a cold, and all were lounging on the carpeted levels of a tiny amphitheater with no chairs, one student went out and got a Coke, another left and came back with a roll of toilet paper, and the instructor was the first to ask for it so he could blow his nose. A boy started to ask a question of a girl who was asleep and the instructor said, "Oh, don't bother her; she probably didn't get enough sleep last night." And later a Belgian assistant demonstrated proper Parisian propriety and provincial slouchiness in the wearing of a beret. Unconventional, disorderly? Yes. Involved, happy, effective? Yes.

The co-op is one of Antioch's principal special ingredients. A staff of six faculty members helps students connect with jobs. Antioch has been doing this for 70 years, so its contacts are worldwide and growing. It also now uses the Internet in its placements. A job might be anywhere and involve doing anything, but it has to have specific duties: It has to be a real job. Later, jobs that are more sophisticated often lead to careers or to graduate school. The other side of the coin is that because learning is negative as well as positive, a job experience can show a student he or she is really not interested in this kind of career. The pay in 1993 ranged from $475 a week to room and board and $100 a month. Many work on low-paying jobs or on unpaid volunteer assignments because these idealists have their hearts in the missions.

After four weeks on the job, each student must write a report, partly for the benefit of others who might follow, and partly so he can think about what the experience is doing to or for him. Also, most majors require the student to complete at least one independent study course while away on a job. Such courses are designed to help make connections between theory and practice. An example might be studying moral decision-making while counseling in an abortion clinic, or child psychopathology while working in the juvenile ward of a state hospital.

What's more, classroom faculty are sent along with the co-op faculty to visit employers and students on the job, and, as psychology profs Patricia Linn and Katherine Jako reported in a study of the co-op program, the teacher may get an eye-opening appreciation of the student he didn't have in class. One, for example, watched a student who had been tentative and uncomfortable in class take command to restrain an emotionally disturbed child about to injure herself. At the start of each term, co-op faculty hold swap sessions for returning students to share experiences. Not only do classroom teachers often get to see their pupils in a new light, as effective doers, but the students' real-life job experiences often bring an immediacy and relevance to classroom discussions.

There is also the magic of serendipity. Even when students opt for jobs requiring physical labor or ordinary office skills, they often come back after only three months more self-aware, responsible, and mature youngsters. "And it's amazing how they've grown in wisdom," the psychologists said. "These subtle forms of integration of co-op and course work are hardest to describe, but they may be the most central to student development."

At Antioch, even the new president, alumnus Bob Devine, his Dean of Faculty, and half of the administrative officers teach. They want to keep in direct contact with students, and the college's educational mission. Also, 16 new tenure-track faculty members have been added, as well as a director of academic support services to provide assistance to students with learning disabilities and any others needing help. Also new as of 1999 is a four-week summer program, Accelerate into Antioch, to help entering students prepare for the challenge of a full academic load in the fall term.

The calendar is also being changed from semesters to trimesters, and the summer term will be on the block plan, three blocks of one course each. The idea is that some subjects, such as theater, will profit from this format. Distinguished guests will be brought in for the summer term. Under a new collaborative agreement with Wilberforce University, one of the nation's oldest historically black liberal arts colleges, Antioch and Wilberforce students can cross-register for classes, share co-op resources, and community activities.

Many faculty members at Antioch would refuse jobs elsewhere at more pay; indeed when the school was having a major financial crisis years ago and the job market was good, many stayed. All of them talked as if they were boasting about their own kids. One who stayed, Prof. Steve Schwerner, summed up their views of the students, "There is much diversity here. In one class I have a descendant of William Bradford [governor of Massachusetts Bay Colony in the 1620s] and a girl from Nigeria; whoever they are, they all challenge. Antioch prepares them for a new world. It gives them versatility, resourcefulness; they land on their feet no matter what happens. They also challenge each other, they take risks, they ask the difficult question, and out in the world they say, 'Why can't this be?' "

Every student I talked to was glad he or she had found Antioch, because they were sure there was nothing like it. For one girl the Antioch experience had been a full conversion. Reading about the college's record in producing Ph.D.s had attracted her originally, but on a visit she was deflated to learn it had none of the trappings of a "real college," such as football teams or fraternities. But now such things are not priorities for her.

Several seniors were headed for graduate school, some were going to take a year off and work before deciding. When they were asked what Antioch had contributed to their experience that they didn't think another place would have, they all said such things as:

- "I have the ability to adapt and thrive."
- "I know how to go into different situations and cope; and make it pay, take lessons from it, set my own goals, and be able to teach myself."
- "I have an integrated sense of where I fit in."
- "You can find yourself. It's a lot of excitement. You get out and get experiences and you say 'I'm on the

wrong track.' You're a participant in your own education. You're learning how to adapt in a situation
you've never been in."

- ▪ "You're learning how to become confident in your
own ability to take control of your experiences."
- ▪ "You go over to the professor's house for conversation, and a class is conversation. The professor is
on the same level. That's what I really like more
than the co-op."

The kind of person who should come to Antioch, they said,
is one who is open-minded about both ideas and experiences.

Years ago, when Antioch's administrators seemed to be doing
all the wrong things, the college was in financial crisis, and the
trustees even let one president operate absentee-fashion from
New York, clients would ask me whether it would still be in
business in four years. I'd tell them that if it really was life-
threatening, some foundation would come to the rescue, because this country could not afford not to have an Antioch. As
for leadership problems, many of the best colleges have sur-
vived ambitious or mistaken CEOs, and are doing so today.
They survive because the ethos of a place is what animates it.

However, Antioch was fortunate after that period in having
as president Al Guskin, a man of humor, vision, courage, and
candor. His analysis of what Antioch does was right on the
mark:

"The power of this education is that it creates an environment for profound student learning even when the components are not done very well by the college. For, and this is
humbling to an educator, the focus on student learning creates
such a strong force . . . that it overpowers the problems in the
program itself. I remain very impressed, as an educator and a
parent of a graduate, with the power of our graduates . . .

"My belief is that our education works so well because it develops a creative tension between structure and freedom, between the intellectual and the experiential, between learning

and doing. This balance or creative tension releases enormous energy within the students and allows them to feel a sense of effectiveness, competence, and personal power which permits them to learn about themselves in ways that previously they thought were unimaginable."

It is also important, as he points out, that Antioch "gives a shield of protection" to let them take risks; it gives them confidence. It is such a profound learning experience. And Antioch is more important in the 2000s than it was in the 1900s.

 Beloit College

Beloit, Wisconsin

In the 70-odd years since records have been kept, a group of about 50 liberal arts colleges has consistently produced high achievers and contributors to society out of all proportion to size or selectivity. Beloit is one of them.

Beloit also is one of the least selective of this group, which includes such schools as Amherst, Wesleyan, and Williams, yet like them, Beloit gets 94% to 97% of its freshmen back for the sophomore year. This devotion persists, for among all the 3,000 U.S. colleges and universities it ranks in the top 20 in percentage of alums who contribute financially. That is one consequence of Beloit's sense of community, which one student described to me as "so tight here it's tremendous," and which another called "incredible." While Beloit has fraternities, they do not Balkanize the community because only 11% belong.

In my visits, one nearly 20 years ago and one recently, I had trouble finding students with complaints. The first time, I met a few who disliked that era's "Beloit Plan" mandating an off-campus field term, because it interrupted friendships. On the most recent visit my sampling didn't turn up any real gripers; it is just one of those places that can be described as happy.

Sixty-three percent of graduates go on to get graduate or professional degrees, which puts the school among the top 50 in the country. And when it comes to producing future Ph.D.s in sociology, anthropology, geology, and foreign languages, it's in the top 15%. When *Who's Who* is used as an indicator of major contributors or achievers across the board, Beloit again appears among the top 50. Several years ago Standard & Poor did some digging to find out what colleges produced the highest percentage of corporate executives, and again Beloit was among the top 50 of that group. Only 21 colleges can claim to be in all three listings. (The others are Amherst, Bowdoin, Carleton, Colorado, Davidson, Denison, Grinnell, Hamilton, Haverford, Kenyon, Macalester, Middlebury, Oberlin, Occidental, Pomona, Swarthmore, Union, Wesleyan, Williams, and Wooster.)

What Beloit turns out is a better, more effective person, and one who tends to go on getting better. And it takes "B" and "C" students.

Dean Dave Burrows, a cognitive psychologist, says, "Our faculty are passionately devoted to students and will go the extra mile to engage students in the intellectual conversation that leads to true learning. Students and faculty get to know each other very well. You can hear the pride in a student's voice when she says her adviser made a special effort to attend a play she was in, or spent hours helping her refine a poster for her seminar presentation." Or, when a new student was told he'd been assigned Dr. Steven Wright as his adviser, he said, "Oh, I know Steve." Dr. Wright had seen the family on campus and had taken them to lunch.

Beloit has a program that creates a sense of belonging and that provides a way to help adolescents confront problems, air frustrations, and make choices at the critical periods of their first two years. It's more than a successful plan; it's palpable in the atmosphere, in the attitudes of faculty members and administrators, and in the way the students talk about their lives here. And while a statistician would say my sample is too small to be significant, over a 30-year period I have received some euphoric notes from freshmen excited by the diversity of their classmates and telling how wonderful their profs are. To me it's significant because it takes a lot to bestir a teenager to write.

Many colleges have tried various freshman orientation schemes preceding the fall term, and with varying degrees of success. Beloit's—as its retention figures show—has been a resounding triumph. What they call the First-Year Initiatives program begins ten days before classes, continues through the fall semester as a for-credit seminar, and becomes more of a social group for the spring semester. In the second year it does a sort of metamorphosis to combat a condition eternally endemic in the collegiate world: sophomore slump.

In the area of advising, where nearly every college, good or bad, falls on its face some or a lot of the time, Beloit has achieved the best kind of *in loco parentis,* supportive and thoughtful but not intrusive. But that is only half a program that gets students and teachers involved intellectually, with each other and in their various groups.

On arrival, each freshman chooses a seminar group of 15 that will explore some aspect of a common theme as his first intellectual adventure. One year it was "Continuity and Change," which suggested such questions as, What is the effect of the past on the present? Where do we adapt and where do we adopt? Do we own the past or does it own us? Each seminar is supposed to suggest two lines of inquiry: How the here and now affects the future; and a sense of cultural pluralism, and global awareness. While there are common tests or readings, each group has a leader who brings his particular expertise and viewpoint to the discussion, whether he be a physicist or a philosopher. The idea is to keep the seminars nondisciplinary; hence the leaders' fields are not identified, and prospective psychology or economics majors can't pick their particular specialists.

The term "leader" is used rather than teacher, instructor,

or professor, because it means just that; he or she is only the leader of a cooperative academic experience that stresses the sharing of ideas and acceptance of responsibility for mutual growth. It encourages students to engage actively in inquiry and analysis. It also stimulates the setting and pursuit of personal goals, self-reliance, and the taking of initiative in achieving worthy ends. Naturally, it seeks to introduce the satisfactions of the life of the mind.

The leader will also be that group's adviser for the next two years. Judging from what students proudly told me, as it has worked out, the label "adviser" doesn't cover the multifarious roles of confidant, counselor, and friend each leader fulfills.

As the seminar goes into the fall semester it is beefed up by out-of-class group assignments, such as community service projects, which help build on the sense of cooperation and tolerance fostered by the emphasis on group learning. There is also much writing, the seminar is the start of a strong writing program that features a drop-in writing house with talented instructors and provides the help that is often needed to back up the college's carefully planned program of writing-intensive courses.

In the third or fourth week of the spring semester each group has a social event, about mid-term there is a Great Lecture, in the 12th week a "reunion" meeting, and near the end of the semester a major "Rites/Rights of Spring" blast.

The sophomore year program, starting with a six-day preterm seminar, seeks to combat the affliction that causes many a youth to worry about lack of direction, to feel frustrated about having to make a decision about a major, and in some cases to wind up not doing well or withdrawing from school. Many colleges, in fact, have greater attrition after the sophomore than after the freshman year. The fact that one of Beloit's own deans had been a victim of sophomore slump and a dropout had a lot to do with Beloit's 911-type answer. A unique part of the sophomore year program is the Sophomore Retreat. Students and faculty spend an entire weekend discussing careers, aspirations, problems, choice of a major, and generally planning their futures.

Instead of getting so much nurturing, sophomores work more independently but with specific support from faculty and staff to confront such problems as committing themselves to a major, deciding whether they want an interdisciplinary minor, exploring off-campus study programs, internships, field experiences, or completing their Comprehensive Academic Plan. The CAP is just what it says: an outline of the student's general direction, including specific courses, internships, or special projects for the rest of his college career, and possibilities for life after graduation.

The sophomores' seminar is an intensive one titled "Crisis, Conflict, Consensus" that challenges their skills in research, analysis, and presentation. The specific topic is announced on the first day. Students work in groups of ten to attack the topic problem. Each group represents a region of the world. Faculty, staff, and invited guests serve as resource persons or in other helpful roles.

After the fall term begins there are Exploration Weeks during which the various departments hold informational meetings with outside speakers, symposia, and social events. Later comes a two-day retreat for more exploration with alumni and alumnae leading workshops on career directions and planning, with entertainment and social activities added. Still later comes Declaration of Major Day, when departments hold open houses to answer questions and to help the sophomores complete their comprehensive college plans (CAPs). I know of no public institution that displays such empathy, and the thought of any university showing such concern is beyond imagining. Beloit's caring may be one reason why complaints are so rare.

Beloit's charming campus is probably the only one in the country where several Indian burial mounds provide its distinctive decorative features. This is almost as if nature and fate had decided it, for Beloit's Logan Museum of Anthropology owns the largest archaeological and ethnographic collection of any college in the country, and much of its collection was provided by Beloit's own Roy Chapman Andrews, the most famous archaeological explorer of the 20th century. (Rumor has it that he was the model for the film character Indiana Jones.)

That helps explain why Beloit is an outstanding producer of people who go on to get Ph.D.s in anthropology. It doesn't explain why it is one of the top 50 in foreign languages and international studies. One of the reasons for that is its membership in the Associated Colleges of the Midwest, a group of 14 colleges that has pioneered study-abroad programs. The ACM has programs in London, Florence (one in art history, one in the humanities), Hong Kong, India, Japan, Russia, Costa Rica (one in Latin American culture, one in advanced field studies), and Zimbabwe. ACM also has a rich array of domestic off-campus programs to fulfill almost any interest, from nuclear science programs at Oak Ridge National Laboratory, to environmental and nature terms at their Wilderness Study Area at the headwaters of the Mississippi, to urban studies, to research programs in the humanities. In addition, Beloit has 17 study-abroad programs of its own. It is not surprising that by the time they graduate, more than half of Beloit's students have had some kind of off-campus study or internship, in this country or abroad. Also, over 80% of graduates have completed an independent study or special project.

Beloit is also a founding member of the International 50, a group of colleges distinctive in their interests and achievements in international studies. This group produces foreign service officers, ambassadors, and people who get doctorates in foreign languages and international studies at four to six times the rate of even the major research universities. In 1991, Beloit hosted a meeting of the 50 to exchange ideas and suggest plans for cooperation in furthering such studies.

As at other good colleges, Beloit's students are heavily involved in their own education. Each presents an individual project in open forum and submits to questions from other students, faculty, and staff. Some projects have been good enough to be accepted for academic professional meetings. I was there on a report day and at any one time there'd be at least half a dozen faculty and administrators (including the president) and 20 or 30 students, depending on the topic being presented, most of them eagerly asking questions.

Furthermore, all of the science students do undergraduate research, and the emphasis is on graduate rather than medical school, which means that it is scholarly rather than job-oriented. It is not unusual for students to be co-authors with faculty members of papers presented at professional meetings, and occasionally of a book. It would be unusual for an undergraduate to have this kind of excitement or get this kind of recognition at a university.

Beloit has always produced a disproportionate number of writers and one reason is the attention given to writing. When Dr. Steven Wright, a friendly English professor, hands back a paper the student gets not only marginal notes but a full page, single-spaced, of critique. "I walk them through it," he explains. At Beloit, the profs' first interest is teaching, not in their own publishing.

At many colleges and universities honor students find they can't get into honors courses—I've heard such complaints not only from prestige universities like Michigan, but from prestige colleges like Williams. At Beloit, teachers often give a tutorial to satisfy one student, or may arrange an independent study plan.

It would be easy to think the students were on the college's payroll with statements like these:

■ "In every class I've come out a better thinker, a better person, and a better writer. Beloit is open to letting you try new things."

■ "I've gone to lab at 10 p.m. and a prof helped me because he cares so much. Someone's always there."

■ "Students are on committees with faculty and they

listen; and they're on the Academic Affairs committee."

▪ "I've learned as much out of class as in class. The sense of community here is incredible."

▪ "If you want something to happen you can make it happen, and they'll go out of their way to help you."

Every last one of them would pick Beloit again and hope their kids would too.

For those who might long for privacy as well as diversity, Beloit is the right place. Dean Burrows calls it a place to develop a strong sense of identity.

Beloit reminds me of a long-ago billboard ad for Chevron gas that read, "Fits any size tank." I talked to whiz kids from magnet schools like the intellectual, science- and math-oriented Thomas Jefferson High School of Science and Technology in Fairfax County, Virginia, which are tough even for whiz kids to get into, and they felt as fulfilled as any of the others. And when one considers that Beloit takes most of its applicants, who represent a fairly wide range of academic ability, and out-produces very selective schools in graduates who make significant contributions and achievements, that testifies to what good teachers have always known: that a mix of abilities produces a good synergy; it also says something good is happening in and out of its classrooms.

Traci Kyle, a student who was dissatisfied at Wesleyan and decided to try Beloit, restates a forgotten verity that should comfort those who think that because an Ivy has more high-ability students it offers more learning or intellectual challenge than a good but less selective school. Here is what she has found:

"I was at Wesleyan three semesters and I liked the people a lot but I wasn't happy on a day-to-day basis. The professors were inaccessible and there wasn't much personal attention, so

I took a leave of absence to go to Beloit for a semester and I liked it, and then I took another, and I think I will stay.

"I didn't know what I was missing; the professors here are right there when I want them, and in abundance. They are open, they are friends, they are wonderful. The students here are more laid back and they care about more things. The Wesleyan students are incredibly bright. For the first time I didn't feel I was the smartest; I was just average and it scared me to death. But they tend to have tunnel vision; they don't realize there's more to life [than schoolwork]. At Beloit, students are developing in more ways. I didn't realize what I was missing; it was only when I got away that I realized it."

When I asked her if she felt the atmosphere at Wesleyan was more intellectual, if there was more discussion about what went on in class, she said, "At Wesleyan there are more conversations about what went on in class; at Beloit it depends on the group; you find your own niche."

Many professors I spoke to agreed that a mix of abilities produces a more intellectually stimulating class of students who are much more willing to ask questions. When I asked Traci if she would agree, she said, "That's definitely true. People are so open at Beloit, I don't feel embarrassed about asking questions. At Wesleyan it was stifling. I find I learn more at Beloit, even though it doesn't have the prestige."

Also, because Wesleyan has 3,400 students, freshman classes are large, with 100 or so students. There was not nearly as much writing required as at Beloit and not nearly as much personal attention. Papers, she said, would come back "with only a few comments and those the negatives—it was minimal. At Beloit, the professors give us 15- or 20-minute conferences every week and two- or three-paragraph write-ups telling us where to go."

At Wesleyan the sense of community "is not very strong; there is a concerted effort for everyone to be his individual self; there is no strong sense of place. Here, everyone is fiercely proud of Beloit. [As the Chevron ad said] it does fit any any size tank. You would have to work hard not to fit in at Beloit."

Cornell College
Mount Vernon, Iowa

With the Cornell University admissions director seated beside me, I once told a counselors convention, "Cornell College will give your advisees a better education than Cornell University. Its students will be actively involved in their own education, not passive ears. Its able professors are there because they love to teach, and their research keeps them on the cutting edge. In the university, the reverse is true; teaching helps fund the research that brings raises and promotions. Teaching undergraduates is an incidental nuisance and full professors do little of it."

The university official quite naturally passed it off as a joke, but it was true then and is still true today. Since Sputnik, the university has become a dollar-grabbing research institute in which the undergraduate is a second-class citizen who gets the short end of the stick. Simply put, he is cheated of his educational birthright.

The meeting was in the Midwest, and Cornell College in Mount Vernon, Iowa, was—and is—a prime example of how much more a good college does for young people than a university. Anyone parachuted down onto its lovely 129-acre campus with a lake and 41 buildings on a wooded hilltop in this beautiful rolling countryside 200 miles west of Chicago wouldn't guess it was Iowa.

It is the only entire campus in the country to be included in the National Register of Historic Places, and even some of its modern facilities, particularly the Life Sports Center, are breath-taking. That structure, which serves the community as well as the college, has five basketball courts with movable bleachers, a six-lane, 200-meter track, four tennis courts, five volleyball courts, four racquetball courts, golf and batting cages, weight training, wrestling and training rooms, as well as locker rooms. The 25-meter swimming pool has submerged observation windows in addition to seats for the spectators at swimming meets and water shows. And outdoors it has the football stadium, the baseball diamond, open practice fields, six tennis courts, and a six-lane, 400-yard crushed brick track.

This college of 1,200, with its distinguished history and an impressive present, takes four-fifths of its applicants, whose average SATs are 520 verbal and 560 math. Students come from 26 states and ten foreign countries and fewer than 30% are from Iowa. Three-fourths of its graduates go on to graduate or professional schools. Three-fourths of the students are on financial aid or have merit scholarships for being top students in high school.

Except during the college-going panic era of the '60s, Cornell has never been selective, yet only 44 other institutions have a higher percentage of graduates in *Who's Who in America*.

The Block Plan sets Cornell apart. Cornell and Colorado College are the only colleges using this intensive learning method. With this approach, a student takes one course full time for three and a half weeks, has a four-day break, and then takes another course. In each block he will do a semester's work. Over four years there will be nine such terms and a student's course work is completed in eight. So the college lets him or her take the ninth term tuition free, and he can take any courses he wishes.

A student spends between two and three hours in class each day, perhaps from 9 to 11 a.m., or from 1 to 3 p.m., Monday through Friday. A day might be divided into classroom time and conference time; lab time and lecture time; independent research and group project work; on-campus and off-campus learning. Like the students, the faculty teach one course at a time and switch courses every three and a half weeks. After 3 p.m. every day, everyone is out of class and free to pursue extracurricular interests.

Both students and faculty are enthusiastic about the decade-old Block Plan. It lets students concentrate on one thing at a time, makes possible more intensive contacts with teachers, and is conducive to group learning.

Cornell's first student, in 1853, was a woman, and it conferred the first college degree given a woman in Iowa. It was the first college or university west of the Mississippi to grant women the same rights and privileges as men. It also was the first in this country to give a woman a full professorship with a salary equal to that of her male colleagues. About that time it established a music conservatory, and many Metropolitan Opera stars have performed here. The first college literary society west of the Mississippi was established here and Cornell has always turned out a fair number of writers. It has also produced many scientists and educators, one of whom was Dr. Lee DuBridge, the physicist who helped develop radar, was science adviser to presidents Truman, Eisenhower, and Nixon, and served as long-time president of California Institute of Technology.

In the sound body department, no other college in the country has this record: Cornell had athletes in every one of the Olympic games from 1924 to 1964. Eight Cornellians were members of Olympic wrestling teams, 25 have won national championships, and in 1947 Cornell won both the AAU and the NCAA national championships in wrestling. And all this was done with genuinely amateur students.

Then why isn't Cornell better known? Developing either writers or wrestlers doesn't generate publicity, and like many other good colleges, Cornell did not exploit the admissions frenzies of the sixties and seventies to tell the country about its virtues.

Perhaps because he was educated by the university system—Michigan and Northwestern—Dean Damon Moore was full of superlatives about Cornell students and what the Cornell ethos does for them. (He had five job offers before he chose Cornell.)

I found Cornell students to be just plain nice kids. The dean described them as not well-prepared or independent when they come, "but they are willing and bright and they do good work" in a program that changes them powerfully. But lest his words give the wrong impression, he cautioned that Cornell is not a place for people with learning disabilities; the demands of the block plan are too rigorous.

Unlike those at many colleges, he said, students are not career-oriented; they are here for an education. Also important is the fact that for 90% of them Cornell was their first choice. That means there's no morale problem as there is where many students feel they're some other college's rejects. It also undergirds the sense of community, because this is the place they all want to be.

To give a sense of what the students are like, Dean Moore told of a block English course he gave for students who wanted to do more writing. Taking it was entirely voluntary and it was given off-time, but "every student turned in every paper. It was a true group momentum. These are nice, sweet, interested kids who put out."

Dean Moore was just as enthusiastic about the faculty, which he called "terrific." They are continually talking about teaching, he said. They attend brown bag lunches, which are not command performances, and may show how they conduct a class, as when one gave 35 other fascinated professors an art lesson. There are student evaluations as well. "The rewards for teaching here are great," he said.

Although adoption of the Block Plan at first caused a generational split in the faculty, as it did at Colorado, everyone now thinks it was the answer. The dean called it "total immersion, like a graduate experience." A political scientist, who has also taught at Grinnell and Princeton, summed up the enthusiasm of several others when he said:

"It engages like no place I've ever known. It has dramatically changed my classes and liberated them. I couldn't teach a semester class the same way. It's motivational magic. Attendance is very high. There are no long-term deadlines ten weeks off. This is their only course and it concentrates attention; every student in my class is a political scientist."

Another said, "The ethos here encourages questions; the students are very open, and where everyone in the class is concerned with only one subject for nearly a month, students just pull together. This plan helps the 'B' and 'C' students because they have time spent with them. And it's good for everybody because there's no place to hide."

There is not only much discussion in these long classes but also much writing. And like converts testifying to their new faith, these men and women from the country's greatest universities talked with pride about how well the graduates of this program and this college do in graduate school or in the corporate business world. They succeed because they have learned to think and to write clearly, and because they have learned to see and to tolerate other positions.

A psychologist educated at the universities of California and of Wisconsin said, "We need to protect the choice between the large and the small school." In other words, the consumer should know enough about himself and the real differences in the schools to make a fruitful choice.

All of the students I talked with, who were from many parts of the country, were no less enthusiastic than their teachers about their college, the Block Plan, the warmth, and their friends the teachers. Some used words like "terrific" to describe their professors; every one of them said if they came back years from now they'd have dinner or spend a night at a faculty member's home, often adding, "We have dinner with them now."

Another thread running through their comments was that Cornell had changed them by making them more open to the views of others and by making them examine their own beliefs and values.

For many of them the Block Plan and the welcoming attitude of Cornell students when they visited were the things that made them choose it over more selective colleges or universities. Typical was the answer of an African-American junior from Chicago, much courted by colleges as both a National Merit Scholar and a good football player. He said a visit showed him how friendly everyone was and how appealing the Block Plan was. It convinced him he could get involved, play football, and major in biology too.

What Dean Moore had said about Cornell being a first-choice school was borne out in student reactions; every person I talked with was glad he or she had come and wouldn't attend any other place. Some who'd had other offers chose it because they were made to feel welcome here, in contrast to what they called "a certain arrogance" at the very selective colleges.

A young client of a dozen years ago, whose father was a major newspaper executive in Los Angeles and who in his undemanding high school had been interested only in redoing old cars, went to Cornell. Four years later I got this telephone call from him:

"When I came to you four years ago I had no idea I could hack it in college, and the first year at Cornell I didn't like it, but every year I liked it more, and now I think there's nothing like it. I wanted you to know that I've just been accepted for a Ph.D. program in history."

That never would have, never could have, happened at Cornell or any other university, even if he had been able to get in. This is what Cornell College is doing for each next generation, and therefore, for society.

Denison University
Granville, Ohio

D enison's tree-lined spread in lovely Granville, Ohio, is a quintessentially beautiful college campus. But even more impressive than its beauty has been its transformation in the last decade into an exciting and very attractive new academic and social personality. Over ten years ago, Dr. Michele Tolela Myers became the catalytic president who made great changes that are being carried on and expanded by the current president Dr. Dale T. Knobel.

Since 1920, Denison has been 35th in the nation in the production of scientists, and from year to year it ranks between 12th and 20th in turning out future psychologists. But it also had the reputation of being a backup school for many Easterners. And fraternities and sororities long dominated the social scene. When I visited there in the late '70s, it was distinctly preppy, and nearly every African-American student I talked to expressed feelings of anger and alienation.

Today it is a different story. Faculty members affirm Denison is now a different place. In 1995, fraternities at Denison were made non-residential (sororities already were). To my surprise, fraternity members say their organizations are far less important to them today, and every black student I talked to was enthusiastic about what Denison had done or was doing for him or her, not just academically, but socially as well. "Ten years ago," said an English professor, "a fraternity man would slouch down in the back row, his baseball cap on backward with an I-dare-you-to-teach-me-something attitude—if he were awake. Now he sits in the front row and participates."

There are several reasons for the change. For one, Denison is offering rich scholarships to outstanding students, some for full tuition and some for half. Also, it has an honors program for them and for all others who qualify. The proportion of top students and the interest in honors work have been steadily increasing for six years. Now, more than one-third of the freshmen are in honors courses. Less serious students, who used to cause most of the problems in or out of the classroom, have been crowded out. There has been a surge in student-faculty research projects; more than 80 students spent a recent summer working with faculty members.

The newest of Denison's array of inventive new programs are a smashing new 350-acre biological reserve and Polly Anderson Field Station, providing a natural laboratory for its new environmental studies major, and one which has enabled it to attract outstanding faculty who otherwise might be lured to a large research university. This program promises to be something new and different, because in every division professors are interested in bringing their subject matter into it.

A new political science–philosophy–economics major will equip people to work intelligently in the global world of the 21st century. Students do a rigorous exploration of the interconnections of these three fields to help them understand the theoretical foundations of political and economic thought. Coursework in each of the three disciplines, plus a senior research project, require so much work that it is in effect a double major, and anyone in it may not take another major or a minor. But students who finish will be equipped to work for fellow alumni like Senator Richard Lugar of Indiana, or to become senators of broad understanding themselves.

If they'd rather seek their fortunes abroad, a new international studies major will fit them to work in many areas of Europe and Asia. But it won't be a snap; they'll have to study the languages as well as the histories, cultures, and economies of each. For the many who long for an off-campus study term in almost any field of interest, whether in this country or abroad, Denison offers an array of programs, several of them in cooperation with the other good colleges of the Great Lakes Colleges Association. Each year more than one-third of the junior class takes part in an off-campus study program.

Some academicians are fond of saying there's an underground at work in college selection, that certain kinds of students are attracted to certain kinds of schools. Now, they say, Denison attracts a more idealistic type. Thirty years ago Denison's students didn't worry about social issues; now they are much more sophisticated and aware. One instance is an innovative program—part of the coursework—of teaching illiterate workers in nearby Newark and getting something in return: "I'll teach you to read; you teach me how to fix my car." In chemistry there is a heavy involvement with nearby high schools. And there is much more volunteerism throughout the student body, they said.

One reason is that the new regime has abandoned the old laissez-faire attitude toward fraternities. They have been reined in and forced to accept responsibility. They are being held strictly accountable to the rules, something that didn't happen in the past. Besides, said the dean, to put things in perspective, there are only 10 fraternities (one of which is African-American) in a college of 2,100 students, compared with 32 for 4,000 students at Lehigh. The college has made great efforts to offer other social alternatives so that fraternity parties are no longer the only game in town.

Something is indeed happening when the college graduates 75% of its freshmen in four years, nearly double the national average, and 78% in five years. The percentage of freshmen returning for their sophomore years has risen to about 88%, and what is more telling, every one of the African-American freshmen returned. That probably wouldn't have happened 15 or 20 years ago.

The percentage of skeptics in a faculty usually is a good deal higher than in a school's general population, but among Denison's professors I found a general agreement with the things the dean had said about a changed Denison. One volunteered this estimate: "If there's a place where students and faculty work better together, I don't know where it is." Another, a Denison alumnus, asked, "Why should my child go here? Faculty attention; that's what changed my life. I want it to happen to every student; not just one here and there."

Faculty also are proud of the school's strength in the arts. Its drama department, they point out, has been the starting point for many careers on Broadway. They also brag about how good the departments of dance, music, art, and art history are, not forgetting the cinema major.

Some of the credit should go to the active concern for the art of teaching. There is a brown bag discussion group in which faculty talk about teaching problems and trade ideas. "We talk about learning all the time," said one, adding, "These are the kinds of kids I like to teach. This is a value-added school for the 'B' student. We are turning them into active learners."

The reactions I got to the same kinds of questions I'd asked years before were strikingly different. On fraternities, I got the same story from two different students. A senior from Cincinnati majoring in French area studies, who thinks he'll do a stint in the Peace Corps, said he was trying to get out of his fraternity, that it was not nearly as important as he'd thought it was as a freshman. Then it was a group to belong to; now he has friends outside it and the sense of community he feels at Denison today makes it an anachronism.

Without my asking, he added that a lot of other seniors feel the same way. Then he offered this testimonial: "I get in every class I want; my friends at Miami (enrollment 15,000) can't, and some are taking four and a half or five years to get their degrees. It's amazing how much I've grown here; in three years it seems I've grown about fifteen. I have so much contact with faculty members."

Later in the day a Sigma Chi senior who could legitimately be put in the preppy category because he'd gone to Hill school said he agreed. "As a freshman the fraternity gave me a sense of belonging and friends; now I look beyond the fraternity for friends. Also, the college is changing, the administration is more involved in student life now." He said he was more service-oriented than he'd been as a freshman, that he was going to take a year off "to work, and to think things over." He was grateful that Denison, because of its small size, "has given me a chance to get involved, to develop my leadership skills."

He would do it all over again, like everyone else I talked with, who each had his or her own reasons. Several freshman girls were still enamored of the college adventure, three black seniors from South Africa were full of praise for the helpful attitude of faculty members and their acceptance by the college community. A senior from Ethiopia said it had so opened him to new ideas that he was going to graduate school, something he never would have dreamt of otherwise.

The clincher was an African-American freshman from Bloomfield, New Jersey, a hard-nosed consumer. Because he was a good student, several other colleges had been courting him. He said, "I made four all-day visits here to be sure this was the place."

Was he happy with his choice?

"You bet!"

Ralph Waldo Emerson said an institution is the lengthened shadow of one man—or woman. What has happened and is happening at Denison proves it. The change in ambience and ethos is palpable. It is a place where good things are happening and a new spirit is in the air. The students feel it. It is a place where inner-city kids are as much a part of the community and feel as comfortable as the middle-class kids, and where distinctions seem to have faded. It is first rate.

Earlham College
Richmond, Indiana

If every college and university sharpened young minds and consciences as effectively as Earlham does, this country would approach utopia. People would tend to live by reason and the Golden Rule, they would vote by their convictions rather than by their pocketbooks, our capitalist society would be a caring one, and there would rarely be a Watergate, Iran-Contra, or Whitewater. But by itself Earlham has made great contributions and it quietly sets the standard.

Most of the colleges in this book are notable for their sense of community but none has more concern for others, their rights, their views, and their selves than Earlham. It is a community governed not just by democratic, majority decisions, but by Quaker consensus. Likewise, the learning environment is cooperative rather than competitive. Over all, the words "warm" and "caring" apply.

For its students, so do the words "earnest, intense, politically aware, and interested in studying." These students have a sense of stewardship about their lives. In fact, if you're not interested in studying, don't come. And if you're not open to exploration, don't come; this is a challenging place. To parents who have wanted their child to go to a college of their religious faith, I have said Earlham would be a better moral and intellectual influence. It has never been very selective, but since 1920 it ranks number 13 among all colleges in the percentages of future scientists and scholars it has turned out. Its seniors get accepted in graduate and professional schools at nearly perfect rates. The graduate admissions committees know about Earlham.

All this may sound overblown, but where do other college professors and educators send their own kids? To Ivy schools,

Berkeley, Chicago, Stanford, Michigan? No. Twenty-seven percent of Earlham's students are children of college and university professors and administrators, and half of them are children of educators. Many of these parents are in Ivy League schools and top universities like Stanford and Berkeley. Earlham administrators have reason to believe, from anecdotal evidence, that they have more Ivy League parents than any other institution, though it would be a costly handwork item to isolate them in the database (they're not that interested in bragging). Only the College of Wooster, which draws heavily from Great Lakes Colleges Association faculty families, can boast such hard currency of confidence from its own establishment.

The beautiful Earlham campus is an 800-acre world apart from the city of Richmond, Indiana. The front campus of 200 acres houses the academic buildings and playing fields; the back 600 are a mix of woods, creek, meadow, a natural laboratory for biology classes, paths for jogging or cross-country skiing, stables, and riding horses.

Earlham's endowment of $151 million puts it in the top rank of colleges, so it's not surprising its facilities range from very good to superb. Its Lilly Library, with more than 350,000 volumes, 90,000 units of microform, 25,000 art slides, 10,000 maps, and 1,400 periodicals and newspapers from all over the world, has for decades been recognized as the foremost undergraduate teaching library in the country. In the information age that means not only rich resources, all kinds of computer hookups and audio labs, a pleasant place in which to use them, and close collaboration with the faculty, it also means developing the student's ability to find, organize, and use the information.

Earlham's 1,200 students are a diverse lot. Only about 10% are Quakers—usually there are more Methodists, Jews, or Catholics than Quakers in the freshman class. About 15% come from Indiana, and more than half come from more than 500 miles away, from 40 states, and from 20 foreign countries. Fourteen percent are minorities, and they graduate at the same rate as the majority, 70% in four years, 80% in five. As at Harvard, 97% of the freshmen return for the sophomore year. Half the students receive financial aid.

In national surveys of freshmen attitudes, Earlham students are twice as interested as the national average in developing a meaningful philosophy of life, promoting racial understanding, keeping up to date with politics, or helping others in difficulty. They see themselves as well-rounded, high-spirited, hardworking, and down-to-earth. Here there are no fraternities or sororities, and no racial separatism; it is one community.

Earlham accepts nearly 75% of its applicants; 60% were in the top 40% of their class and 28% were unranked. The middle 50% had SAT verbal scores in the 480–600 range and math scores in the 500–630 range. But as with most of the other colleges in this book, statistics are only a part of the story. Earlham's admissions officers look at the human being and aren't afraid to follow their instincts.

All first-year students are hand-matched with veteran faculty to help them make sound course choices. And if someone needs help, he or she gets it. Supportive services and a learning center are available. But more important is a caring faculty. For example, professors will give students with dyslexia extra time on tests, or let them take exams orally or even tape-record their papers. There is also an August Academic Term for up to 25 students who need additional work in writing and critical reading.

For many, orientation begins with a small-group wilderness boating or mountaineering trip led by a faculty member. These expeditions build self-confidence, outdoor skills, and early friendships. It is no wonder Earlham loses so few freshmen.

Earlham students take three courses a term for three ten-week terms, a program faculty members think is more efficient than Cornell and Colorado colleges' block plans of one course at a time. They believe the level of intensity is as high. A student can't afford to get behind when there's so much work to do in so short a time.

Everybody takes a four-course humanities sequence. The first three are taken the freshman year, and they operate somewhat differently from other colleges' in that the students have to respond in writing to the texts they've been reading before there's any class discussion. Humanities IV may be taken at any time from then on, and it serves to make students apply what they have learned, and to make connections. All four courses stress the disciplined use of logic and imagination in the study of human civilization and its outcomes.

One of the college's distinctions is the way it emphasizes a global education. Nationally, about 1% of college students have an off-campus study experience. At Earlham, 70% of the students have at least one off-campus study term, and there is so much emphasis on international studies, with 28 programs in 20 countries, that 60% of the students have a foreign-study term.

The curriculum reflects both the interrelatedness of world issues, and the fact that international education is not just for the few specializing in international studies nor just for those studying off-campus, but for all who wish to be educated in the broadest sense for life in the 21st century. Hence, each foreign studies program is tied into the student's program so that one complements the other to make a cohesive whole. In Earlham's nationally recognized Peace and Global Studies program, for example, off-campus programs in Northern Ireland and Jerusalem expose students to the issues of peace and conflict.

Earlham is an excellent place to learn to speak Japanese or to prepare for a career involving Japanese culture. The college has had ties with Japan for more than a century, and for 30 years it has run study programs there and now has three, which are used by two college consortia. More than a quarter of the faculty have lived and taught in Japan and some use the language in their upper-level courses. Japanese students, scholars, and artists in residence spend time at Earlham, and everybody has to pass a couple of Japanese gardens en route to the book store.

Among the other programs are majors in International Studies in which the student works with a team of faculty advisers to ensure a broad coverage. The African/African-American Studies program likewise involves courses in many disciplines as well as study in Africa and prepares students for graduate school and for a variety of careers.

Students constantly coming and going in these programs give the Earlham community a cosmopolitan awareness and sophistication. The effect is to make one sensitive to the fact that no man is an island, and to the Quaker belief that everyone deserves respect.

To make these things work, everyone is required to become proficient in a foreign language, so there's a Super Languages Program—multiple-hour immersion courses in Japanese, German, Spanish, and French—which enables students to communicate in a relatively short time.

For all students, there are distribution requirements that provide the framework of a liberal education, and there are comprehensive exams in the major, which may be individually designed with the help of an adviser.

What makes Earlham what it is? My view is that any place staffed with the perceptive, caring people I've known at Earlham couldn't help exerting a lot of mental and moral torque. But here is how Dean Len Clark and several faculty members analyzed what happens to their students:

"Before they come here their culture has defined success by the percentile they're in and how much better than somebody else they are.

"From the first day their responsibility to learn from and with other students is stressed. That is a Quaker tenet and a part of the mission of the college. It takes new students by surprise but then liberates them. It takes some practice to listen to and learn from other students, and to build on ideas the other people have. That's a central focus of the humanities program the first year. They talk about the text and then they talk about one another's analysis of the text. There are lots of exercises throughout the curriculum in doing that, and that's of central importance to making students successful later, because almost nobody works by himself, in the college or in this new world."

All professors agreed that teaching at Earlham was more challenging and that students got more out of learning than at the universities where they had taught, which included Yale, Northwestern, North Carolina, Cornell, Purdue, and Delaware. When asked what Earlham did that Yale didn't, the answer was, "Earlham students work with faculty in a way that is enabling, that produces self-confidence, and that comes at a critical time when it can accelerate their career growth. I did not find that to this degree at Yale." (From what professors elsewhere have told me about minimal student-faculty contact at Yale, Dr. Clark may have wanted to be gentle.) A philosophy professor added, "It is much more intense here than at Northwestern. Also, status was very important there." One who had taught at Cornell and Purdue said the Earlham students were not only more interested and more challenging but much more politically aware.

A history professor who had taught at North Carolina said there was no comparison. "At UNC, kids wouldn't come to the office; I never had anyone show up. They were always out partying. In class here, they are not ashamed to ask questions. This is a real community of learning. It is also dangerous here because they find there are no satisfying, easy, comfortable assumptions they can take refuge in. They have to understand different points of view, that there is no particular argument that is right, and that they have to question, they have to confront."

I had a pretty good idea what the students would say even before I talked to any. Over the years, enough former clients or their parents have written to say how much Earlham had done that I expected only positive comments, and that was what I got.

Some came because of the atmosphere of acceptance and

tolerance, some because they'd heard of the close student-faculty relations or because it was so easy to get involved in research with faculty members, but whatever their reasons they wouldn't change schools. A senior honors student, one of the many university faculty members' sons who'd had offers from prestige colleges, said he had made the smartest choice, and other heads nodded in agreement.

Two frequent topics were how Earlham had affected their values and outlooks, and how it had pushed them intellectually. They said such things as:

- "I came from a conservative town, and Earlham gave me new ideas, made me think about my own values and made me change some of them."
- "It came as a shock to find out others had differing ideas and it made me think. It's great to intermix and to accept everyone and his or her ideas; it promotes tolerance."
- "A lot of different views opened up to me and there was no pressure to believe any one thing. When I go home I see that I've changed a lot compared to my old high school friends."
- "On race relations, there are some separate interests, but everybody is ready to accept everybody else. It's something we're taught. Consensus is acceptance of differences."

I often tell clients that Beloit, Earlham, and Wooster are remarkable, special places by reason of their strong sense of community. Beloit I rate as the happiest campus and Earlham the most serious. But don't get me wrong; this is not a convent and they're all healthy young animals. If it is your cup of tea, there simply is no better place.

Hiram College

Hiram, Ohio

Many years ago a curious administrator at Hiram College went through records to find out what had happened to students I had referred there. Of 40 he found, two had WDs (withdraws) after their names and two had less than C averages. All the rest were in good standing or had stayed to graduation. Only Harvard and Princeton have four-year retention rates as good as that sample's, so it says something about what students find at Hiram and what it does for them.

It also says that I think this attractive college of nearly 1000 —the panoramic view from its campus is stunning—in a pretty eastern Ohio village of the same name, is excellent. It's a well-kept secret. But in the fraternity it is known; the top honorary society, Phi Beta Kappa, has long had a chapter there. Since 35% of its seniors go to graduate or professional school right after graduation, and 60% go within five years, something is sparking, in the classroom and outside of it.

On weekends the population jumps to 1,300 because Hiram has a Weekend College for adults that not only offers them a variety of courses, but also provides overnight dorm facilities, not to mention cafeteria food, which I found to be pretty good.

Hiram hasn't been a household name nationally because three-quarters of its students are from in state. If quality determined selectivity, it would be mighty tough to get into. But as things are, provincialism is a greater influence on selectivity, and Hiram accepts more than 80% of its applicants, which means a lot of Bs and Cs are in those transcripts. Not quite half were in the top 10% of their high school classes and the mean SATs were 580 verbal and 560 math. It has done well in the competition for minority students, who make up 14% of the population (9% are black), and all the minority students I talked to thought they had made a smart choice.

Seventy-eight percent get need-based financial aid and 93% get some help. That number is high because Ohio gives residents grants of about $600 a year for tuition at the state's private colleges.

Whatever their past records, the kids at Hiram, especially the upperclass students, have a proud sense of ownership—a familiar theme in colleges that matter. For their part, faculty members—most of whom have taught at universities or other colleges—take equal pride in their young charges.

The results are good. Hiram has a long history of great success in medical and graduate school admission. In a far more competitive area, veterinary school, Hiram tops every college in Ohio State University's region in the number admitted, and by a ratio of three to one.

This is not surprising, a science student at Hiram has such a great wealth of resources beckoning him and such evangelistic teachers he gets excited and works hard. Students do hands-on learning and research and confront the critical issues in environmental protection at its wonderful Barrow Field Station. This is 360 acres of mature forest, streams and ponds, a two-mile interpretive nature trail, a lake with waterfowl observational building with teaching and student research areas, and a wetlands ecology teaching laboratory with a solar greenhouse. There is also a system of outdoor habitats for maintaining a collection of captive birds in semi-natural habitats. The animals and natural areas are maintained by students under faculty supervision.

The Northwoods Field Station, a camp in the Hiawatha National Forest in the Upper Peninsula of Michigan near Lake Superior, serves as the headquarters for field trips in the spring, summer, and fall. In the summer, Hiram students can take part in a marine biology program at the Shoals Marine Laboratory off the coast of New Hampshire under an arrangement with Cornell University. In addition, the college has opened a $6.1 million addition and updating of its science building. When elementary and secondary school teachers were a drug on the market several years ago, and teacher education majors in the state's other institutions couldn't find jobs, every one of Hiram's applicants was hired before graduation.

As at Beloit, freshmen get an orientation before the fall term starts that is much more than how to use the library. In a weeklong Freshman Institute, when they have the campus to themselves, they find out what college work is like. In seminar groups of 12 to 15 guided by a professor who will be their academic adviser, they start to grapple with such topics as The Quest for Justice, The Development of Scientific Ideas, or Studies in Self-Identity. They do readings, discuss them, and write essays about them. They attend and discuss lectures. They may take placement tests if they plan to major in mathematics or language. In the evening they may see a movie, go on a picnic, attend a dance, have an ice cream social, and in that week they also make new friends.

The bonding continues with the five-credit Freshman Colloquium in the fall term. Not only is there a list of topics to choose from but each is described in detail and includes a brief biographical sketch of the professor teaching that course. They do a lot more of what Freshman Institute foretold: read about great issues or ideas and then discuss them and write essays about them. Meeting every day in such intimate groups means everyone is encouraged to think straight and to write clearly.

These groups become little families. They may meet in the professor's home for dinner, drive to Cleveland to see a relevant film, or, as one group did last year, make a trip to Washington to listen to a Senate hearing on a Colloquium topic.

In the winter and spring terms everyone takes an Idea of the West sequence, which provides an introductory experience in Western thought and is taught by teams of professors from different disciplines. The class will examine a topic such as free-dom, in order to get an overview of the major ideas that have shaped the way we see the world.

Then, in one of the next three years, a Hiram student has to get it all together. He or she must take a collegium—an inte-grated three-course sequence diving into an issue—that may be molecular biology and its implications, gender and power, decision-making, or some other topic. The purpose is to ex-plore and appreciate the interconnectedness of knowledge. The collegia are interdisciplinary and taught by two or more professors from different fields. Again there is much discussion in small groups and much writing.

In addition to a major, which can be an individualized one, Hiram also has distribution requirements to ensure exposure to the fine arts, humanities, natural sciences, and social sciences.

For those afraid of language or who have problems with it, a skills requirement can be satisfied with computer science, cre-ative arts, or reasoning and analysis, which means two five-hour courses in philosophy or communications.

What do the students think about all this?

The most euphoric testimonial, from a junior girl majoring in English and French, also reflected a consensus: "Many cat-alytical things have happened to me. These are incredible peo-ple. They love to teach. We have a mentor relationship; they are always making cross connections from one area or disci-pline to another. They are always encouraging, pushing me to do better. There is so much pressure, so many responsibilities it forces you to keep going. They say 'this might be a publish-able paper.' One would like to come back here to teach—or to one like it." That reminded me of a letter from a client long ago who wrote (much to his amazement), "I've never had to work so hard in all my life; this place is great!"

A senior physics major added to the girl's comments that while "it's intensely stimulating intellectually, that doesn't mean you can't have fun." He said he had done research with a professor, as had a psychology major, who added, "It's so easy to get involved in research here."

Over half of Hiram's students have an off-campus experience, foreign or in this country. And, just as they do everywhere else, they think the experiences have changed them. For an African-American girl from the inner city in Cleveland, a junior sociology-anthropology major, it has been the blinding light. "Hiram has expanded my horizons, but my experience in Germany was the wonderful thing. It transformed me, made me a woman of the world and opened my eyes to possibilities that otherwise I wouldn't see."

Other students had these expressions of allegiance:

- "It has taught me how to write; there is so much writing and reading. One course was so interesting I changed my major."
- "It has taught me time management. I feel indebted to Hiram."
- "There is a wonderful sense of community. There is a sense of trust. It is very supportive. It is very confidence-building."
- "It's our school."
- "I look forward to coming here; I couldn't imagine studying in a city."

A faculty member may have put her finger on the key to the Hiram ethos when she said, "We teach students, rather than subjects. That's why we create a comfortable environment." In other words, the professor's concern is a young mind rather than the research that determines whether a university professor will keep his job.

Every faculty member I talked to took an obvious pleasure in teaching and being friends with the students. One observed, "We are sort of surrogate parents."

They preferred the kids at Hiram to those they'd taught elsewhere. At Carleton, said one, more students are from well-to-do families and "they come to college assured of success; they have no worries," whereas at Hiram, some are first-generation college students and many have not traveled widely or known what college is about. The result is that they tend to depend on their own resources and are hard workers.

They also made a point that is important to teenagers who do not feel as sure of themselves as they should. One professor said the fact that the college is not well-known "leads to a nice environment because students can find their own resources; they don't need to worry about keeping up." As a result, most tend to do very well. "They are a joy to work with," said another.

The Hiram faculty I talked to are happy to be there, and they work to improve their teaching on a daily basis: What are you trying today? Have you read this book? There are weeklong workshop retreats, and they find team teaching to be very effective.

One faculty couple's visit to their daughter's graduation at Williams tells a lot about their priorities. At a reception after commencement, the professor under whom their daughter had majored asked, "What are you going to do next year, Anna?" They were appalled, as they should well have been. The husband said, "I had to hold my wife; I thought she would spring at the woman."

My guess would be that any Hiram faculty member would have reacted as that couple had. Concern for the student's personal as well as academic welfare is one of the qualities that makes Hiram such a warm and happy place and such an exceptional college. It is one of the reasons why young people find their power and their confidence burgeoning and why they talk about realizing potentials they didn't know they had when they came there. More than a wonderful place, Hiram is a national asset.

Hope College

Holland, Michigan

Hope College, just a hop, skip, and a jump from Lake Michigan in pleasant Holland, Michigan, raises higher education's moral and intellectual level. It is a place where parents can send children of a wide range of abilities in the full expectation that their talents will be increased, vision broadened, and ethical acuity sharpened. They will also be actively involved in their own education and be prepared to prosper in a changed world. Those expectations will be fulfilled.

Its alumni often say Hope made them what they are. In fact, one of its black graduates from the inner city of Chicago kept urging me to consider it for this book. I already had a high opinion of it, for Hope has long been preeminent in science. It is third and sometimes second in the number of chemistry majors in the state, an amazing figure in the context of Michigan's array of mammoth universities.

Furthermore, Hope's reputation with state industries is so formidable that chemistry and physics interns often have built-in job offers by the time they graduate, if not before. But that is just part of the story. Hope is first-rate across the board, attracting students because of the reputations of its political science and economics departments and because its theater, dance, and music programs are outstanding. In many other schools they'd be bragging points.

Dr. Jacob Nyenhuis, the provost and a classics author of note as well as a spellbinder in front of a class, who has taught at Stanford and at Wayne State University in Detroit, said, "Hope provides a liberal arts education in the context of the Christian faith. We deal with ethical issues. We teach them to ask the right question, to have the right perspective. We nurture, but not in an intrusive way. We give them a sense of rootedness. We are distinctive. We achieve academic excellence; we have freedom of inquiry, a quest without boundaries. We value and will nurture a faith commitment; this means keeping a delicate balance. Service has been a long tradition. We do make a difference."

Founded by Dutch settlers 150 years ago, Hope is affiliated with but independent of the Reformed Church and has students of many religious faiths, including 137 who don't practice at all. It is like St. Olaf in this regard, rather than Wheaton, where one has to be a Christian of some kind in order to be accepted. At Hope students feel no pressure of any kind to conform to a set of beliefs, and there is no compulsory chapel. A Muslim girl from Pennsylvania is one of four non-Christians in the student body. Jewish students would be perfectly comfortable—if lonely—if they weren't orthodox; it is a very accepting place.

With 2,700 students it is about twice the size of most colleges. Three-quarters of them come from Michigan and the rest from 39 other states and 34 foreign countries.

Hope says that more than a third of its acceptees were in the top tenth of their high school classes and that their grade point average was 3.49. But don't let that scare you; most of those statistics come from small high schools. The key figures are that it accepts 87% of its applicants, and that the middle 50% have SAT totals in the 950–1150 range. In other words, not only "B" students, but "C" students who are ready to work are likely prospects.

When they come to Hope they'll have to work, but they must like it, and they must be interested, because they even work on weekends, which doesn't happen at a lot of places. All freshmen take a writing course, as well as a mathematics course. A core curriculum exposes them to their own and other cultures. In addition to a major, courses in the arts, humanities, sciences, social sciences, and religion are also required. And to wrap it up, a senior seminar course encourages them to reflect on their college experience.

There is a wide variety of off-campus programs, partly because Hope is a member of that consortium of excellent programs, the Great Lakes Colleges Association. A large portion of the student body spends at least one term in Africa, Europe, Scotland, Japan, Hong Kong, Russia, Nepal, China, or India. They may also spend a term in the Philadelphia Center in urban studies, or opt for a New York Arts semester.

All these riches add to the latitude students have in fashioning their college experiences. In the process they will get all the help and nurture they need. They won't feel driven to compete; students work together, often as teams, and they also work with their teachers. At Hope learning is a communal enterprise to which all contribute.

Dr. William Mungall, a remarkable chemistry professor, said, "We don't take attendance. We don't grade on a curve; the grading is absolute. I tell every class at the start how it will be, and if they do poorly on one test they can use the final to neutralize it. The students help each other and the teacher helps them."

Student-faculty research projects are common among the colleges in this book, but probably no college has more of this than Hope; the faculty encourages it both to get students involved in their own education and to promote collaborative learning. Chemistry and physics students even get the thrill of working in some of Michigan's major industries—including Parke Davis pharmaceuticals and Donnelly rear-view mirrors—because Dr. Mungall and a couple of his colleagues have consulting contracts with them.

Because some of these firms use Hope's lab equipment, students get to work on real-life problems instead of textbook ones. They also get to work in the various companies' labs on some problem or project for a product.

Back at school, it's easy to collaborate on these problems or projects; adjoining each lab is a study room where students can work together, and the faculty offices are right next door. These teachers like to work with students; any who don't are weeded out in the hiring process when they get grilled in interviews with students.

"Here," the chemistry professor said, "we use research as a vehicle to teach. Students participate in it and it makes things more exciting; it gives them an exposure to what science is all about. Research is why we graduate so many chemistry majors."

These professors, who have taught at most of the leading universities, are giving a most important message of assurance that teenagers and their parents would be foolish to miss. They testify emphatically that their senior students are equal in ability and performance to any students anywhere. Here is how some of them at Hope put it:

"I have taught at Stanford and at MIT; the students here are just as good; they're comparable in every way to MIT's. I had the same problems there; bright students have problems with chemistry because they've never had to work. I have to help them more, especially on study skills. We are getting a lot of kids with underdeveloped study skills. Kids who need encouragement and nurturing get it here. Talented kids blossom here. Hope develops confidence, broadens perspectives, gets them involved."

A religion professor who had taught at Wisconsin and Harvard said: "There is a great diversity of abilities here. They are universally interested and willing to work; they carry a heavy load—five courses—with a lot of assignments. It's a wonderful group and I have tremendous respect for them. They know the faculty is eager for their well-being. I want to treat my students like I want my own kids treated. There are a lot of people achieving things they never thought they could; for example, this kind of nurturing even produced a poet. They are reaching their potential. At Madison [University of Wisconsin] there are a lot of people with great ability going nowhere."

A communications professor who had taught at the universities of California and Wisconsin said: "Four years at Hope changes a student, there is such an emphasis on writing, speaking, and thinking skills. A Western Michigan graduate I know did not write a paper in four years. Here they achieve; they learn to be critical-minded; they're asked to engage moral issues, and after four years here they say values are important."

An economics professor who turns down offers from universities because he thinks what he's doing here is more important says: "Here students spend time with their profs. They get ready for the new world. They get confidence. At Harvard they're talented when they come in, but what happens to them there? I wouldn't leave Hope to teach at Harvard. The Harvard faculty's principal goal is to get research published. Here I teach and do community service. Most of the faculty could be making more money elsewhere, but they have a commitment to people, and it's not self-serving."

A most important point for anyone trying to decide between a good small college and a mighty university was made by Dr. Robert Ritsema, who heads the Music Department: "When a prospective student asks why she should come here rather than go to the University of Michigan, I say you'll play in a better orchestra there because they can choose from several performers, but here you'll get more playing time. The remarkable thing here is that we're all performers; we can't teach if we're not. And we're right there all the time, at night too, when the students need us."

What's more, he went on, "the level of inquiry is high here, of inquisitiveness; there's a work ethic here, and they blossom. We really do affect values. The students feel nurtured. The alumni all talk about how Hope shaped them, whenever and wherever I meet them on tours."

The students aren't the only ones affected. One professor after another talked with feeling about the atmosphere of mutual respect among the faculty. Even over issues that may be very divisive they said there are no fights. People like and respect one another, otherwise there couldn't be the sense of common enterprise and collaboration that is one of the virtues of Hope and colleges like it.

Most of the freshmen I talked to had been attracted by Hope's reputation. As one of them said, "I knew this was a first-rate school." Some pointed to its reputation in chemistry, or its 97% rate of medical school acceptances, or the fact that its seniors were in the top percentile in the national organic chemistry test. Still others talked about the economics, political, and music departments as their lures.

Students who had been there longer talked about other things. A junior girl from New Jersey said Hope is "a very friendly place, a great sense of community, people are nice, and the profs couldn't be more helpful." The sense of community was a common theme, along with how interested the professors were in students' personal as well as academic welfare. A senior talked about opportunities "I just wouldn't have had anywhere else" to work in a company's laboratory on "a real live industrial problem." Similarly, getting involved in a research project with a professor was something a couple of others had never dreamed of doing.

No one I talked to felt negatively influenced or burdened by the college's Christian commitment. The intellectual caliber of the religion courses is as high as those anywhere, "a quest without boundaries," as Dr. Nyenhuis said. The fact that there's no required chapel (as there once was in church-affiliated colleges) may have been a factor in their answers. Those who didn't go to church felt no pressure to go, and unlike Wheaton's students, many didn't go. They did, however, feel that Hope was a good place of good people. Every time I asked my stock question about having dinner or spending a night at a faculty member's home five years from now the answer often was, "We're doing that now," or "I'd have trouble choosing." And one fellow asked, "Do you include coaches?"

The affection continues beyond commencement. The black alumna who wanted me to see for myself about Hope credits her experience there with making her a successful newspaper-woman. She is right. I can now, with more informed enthusiasm, tell more people what a great place Hope is for students who want the kind of educational experience that will develop them into people who can be happy with themselves because they lead the examined and productive life.

Kalamazoo College
Kalamazoo, Michigan

Kalamazoo is more than a distinctive college; it is unique. Other colleges offer some of its features but none provides the same combination of a career development internship term, two foreign study terms, and a senior individualized project, which they call the K Plan.

The sense of community is strong because everybody lives on campus and everybody eats together in the big dining hall, often with faculty members. This means the entire community is able to gather to celebrate joyous occasions or to offer comfort in times of sorrow. Every Friday a voluntary ecumenical chapel planned by students and faculty brings in guests from a variety of religious backgrounds and affiliations. The Liberal Arts Colloquium, also operated by a student-faculty committee, brings in about 100 educational and cultural events each year to enhance the educational experience. A student must attend at least 25 of these events as part of the degree requirement. At no Ivy institution are the students so deeply engaged, so broadly prepared, or so heavily invested in a sense of community as at Kalamazoo. In short, no Ivy school is likely to have as much impact on a youth's development. Two faculty members who went to Ivy universities said they wished they'd gone to Kalamazoo.

Years ago, the psychology department chairman at a very selective college spent a day checking out Kalamazoo when I rec-
ommended it for his son and came back with the verdict,
"That's a good place!" His own school lost a good kid.

Kalamazoo's program appeals to the inquiring mind and adventurous spirit, and the timid learn by example to become
risk-takers. In that regard it has the appeal of Antioch, Hampshire, or Marlboro. It is a happy campus where the kids are excited about what they're doing. The atmosphere is one of trust
in a student-run honor system. In sports, the Kalamazoo tennis
team is the only one ever to win three national championships.

On a recent visit, my second in a dozen years, the reports of
a half-dozen foreign-term returnees made for a rousing dinner
hour, and not just for students. I saw faculty, administrators,
and staff scattered through the hall. The students who'd been
in Paris had complained about a lack of creature comforts,
while those in Senegal had been euphoric about their hardship-
induced adventures. An African-American girl back from Sierra
Leone was so excited about her experience her words gushed
out in a torrent. All were enthusiastically testifying to what a
watershed experience it had been, how their eyes and minds
had been opened, how they had grown in self-understanding.

For its part, the sophisticated and attractive city of Kalamazoo, population 200,000, is also special. It was the first city in
the nation to have a pedestrian mall. It supports a symphony, a
chamber music society, an art institute, a professional hockey
team, men's and women's professional soccer teams, a nature
center, and several live theaters, among other things. It is also
in a class by itself for distinguished residential architecture.
There are many homes by Frank Lloyd Wright, Alden Dow,
and Norman Carver in an area nature endowed with wooded
hills and lakes.

The college's 60-acre campus on a hill has the charm of a
grassy quadrangle shaded by great trees, some of which seem
to date from the college's founding year of 1833. The buildings
even seem to have sprung from the earth here; even the big

state-of-the-art Dow Science Center fits in comfortably. Like Allegheny's it was planned by the science faculty and boasts study and lounge areas scattered among the labs and offices for the very accessible faculty.

A more important feature I've not seen elsewhere—and that no Ivy institution can boast of—is another scattering of small labs for student-faculty research. Indeed, research is a way of teaching at Kalamazoo.

The 1,350 students come from 41 states and a dozen foreign countries, half of them from the top 10% of their classes and nearly half with SAT verbal scores of more than 600 and 70% with math scores of more than 600. But because it accepts nearly 75% of its applicants, it takes "B" students. Like other colleges in this book, it then makes grade-A adults of them. More than half get need-based financial aid and nearly half get merit scholarships that average $7,000 a year.

Like St. Olaf, Kalamazoo is preparing its students to prosper in a one-world economy by giving them a global perspective with its two foreign study terms. A leader in this field for 40 years, Kalamazoo has had study centers at almost 30 places around the world. As a member of the Great Lakes Colleges Association it also offers the consortium's many programs. These terms become an integral part of the course work because one's experiences often lend relevance to a class discussion, whether it be economics, sociology, or philosophy.

The career development internships offer 2000 different jobs in 35 states and a dozen foreign countries. They include positions at major corporations and publications such as *The New York Times,* and all manner of overseas opportunities. So it is no wonder that 85% of Kalamazoo's students spend one or two terms studying abroad, and that 80% of them complete at least one internship.

Every student takes a freshman seminar where one's writing has to pass muster to get a passing grade. The major may be a conventional one or self-designed in consultation with a faculty adviser, and everyone does a Senior Individualized Project, also designed in consultation with the adviser and which occupies most of the senior year. The completed project must be defended in an open forum of peers and faculty.

The school year is divided into 3 terms, and a freshman normally spends fall, winter, and spring on campus, and takes a summer vacation. Internships are typically scheduled during the summer following the sophomore year. Two foreign study terms usually come in the junior year.

This is the K Plan. Testimony to its appeal is that its three terms off campus enhance rather than dilute the sense of community. Thirty years ago, Beloit students had to have a field term off campus in mid-career but it was abandoned partly because students complained it broke up friendships. At Kalamazoo, as the dinner hour hinted, there is a sense of excitement and cross-fertilization when the kids come back and share the experiences others will soon have, or have had. They come back to classes with a broader outlook and a greater sensitivity and receptiveness. The faculty, who might be expected to deplore the interruptions, find their students born again, full of a new interest and zest; their courses have become relevant.

A former provost and chemistry professor who went to Michigan and got his doctorate at Princeton is another of those who wishes he'd had the Kalamazoo experience. "At Michigan I got into chemistry by accident," he said. "Otherwise my experience there would have been disastrous. In my third year a graduate student needed a research assistant. For the next two years, working closely with him I gained more knowledge, insight, and enthusiasm than courses alone could ever have imparted. That experience had such a powerful impact on me that I decided I wanted to teach at a place where close student-professor contact was the norm rather than the exception. K College is just such a place. Here what happened to me would have been by design rather than by accident."

Students at Kalamazoo, he went on, tend to be more first-generation college, while at Princeton they may be fourth generation. Kalamazoo's students have more motivation, more humility, and more sense of purpose than Princeton's, he said, where many sons and daughters of well-known parents "don't quite know why they're there."

He responded to the question "What does Kalamazoo do?"

"We produce creative people. They change more in four years than in conventional programs. The freshman seminar, the foreign study, and the Senior Individualized Project all contribute to a progression in responsibility. After the foreign experiences they come back more analytical, more comfortable with complexities and uncertainties, more understanding of the views of other countries, and more tolerant. They have more self-awareness and more self-confidence.

"The K Plan is complex to administer. It creates a campus community. Everyone has an 'outward bound' experience or two, and there is a great bonding within a class. It is a developmental model in undergraduate education."

Kalamazoo seniors get into all the best graduate schools. Eighty-five to ninety-five percent of its medical and law school applicants are accepted, and in that much more competitive area—veterinary school—ninety-nine percent are accepted.

Further proof is the kind of achieving adults the college produces. Kalamazoo outranks most of the Ivies in producing people who go on to get doctorates in all fields. It ranks 13th among all 2,000 colleges and universities in the country. It is 4th in business and management, 7th in physical science, 11th in life sciences, 14th in engineering and science, and 20th in math and computer science.

Testifying to the strength of its international studies and economics programs is the fact that at least four Kalamazoo alumni are economists at the World Bank, three are with the International Monetary Fund, and two have served on the staff of the President's Council of Economic Advisers. It is unlikely that another college can match that record.

The faculty members I talked with were no less enthusiastic than the provost. Whether it was in art or in English or in science, they all said Kalamazoo's preparation was far superior to that of the professional school or the university, the kinds of places they'd been trained. An art professor said, "At the professional art schools they're technicians who don't have a whole lot to say. They're concentrating on copying this or doing that traditional thing. In any art it is essential to have something to say. Here we're helping them express themselves aesthetically."

An English professor said that teaching classes of 75 or more at UCLA and Vanderbilt had kept things pretty impersonal. "Here, I am much more involved with students. We have collaborative learning. Students are teachers of others on campus and tutors off campus. It is interactive, sharing, one of the ways we prepare them to go out into the world."

A chemistry professor underscored a point others had made. "University professors consumed with research aren't good teachers."

As if there's some ESP at work, these teachers echoed what their peers at other colleges often said, that "It's not the top student who's most changed; it's the next group."

Or, "Alums often say, 'bet you didn't think I could do it.' Yes, I did; you didn't. Those are the kids who go out and stomp on the accelerator. They're the ones who come back and tell us. It comes down to having someone believing in them."

Or, "The difference about K students is a manic dynamism. We attract adventurous and we attract those around the edge who want to jump in." And they do jump in. She told of a painfully shy girl who had her first foreign term in Scotland where there'd be no language barrier. This gave her enough confidence to go to Senegal on her next one, and the two terms gave her a new maturity and self-confidence.

Every student I talked to would do it again, emphatically. One senior said it had shaken her Catholic faith and—as several others said—made her examine herself. She had changed her major four times and was unsure whether she'd go to seminary or graduate school. Another senior, who had come because of the K Plan, already had a job with a major consulting firm. Another, who'd been worried about getting into at least one graduate school, had been told by her adviser, "Don't worry, you'll get into all of them." And she did.

An African-American junior from New York City who'd come because of the K Plan said that a term in South Korea "transformed me. Now I really appreciate the U.S." She added: "I would want my own children to have this experience."

A strikingly handsome black junior from Detroit said he'd planned to go to the University of Michigan until he visited Kalamazoo. He was amazed to see faculty members playing with students in a basketball game. He said, "A sweaty guy, a prof, came over and shook my hand and said, 'Hi. I'm Dave Winch.' Right then I thought, I've got to come here." Much as he was taken with Dave Winch, the young man did not follow him into physics. He's a biology and music major, with a minor in German as a result of a foreign study term. "Speaking another language," he said, "makes you think more about your own."

Others said such things as these:

- "Four years here have given me a new life plan. They have forced me to be an aware person and to think more clearly."
- "I am going to seminary. It has changed my faith. The foreign programs have helped me develop more as a person; they've given me self-confidence. It was quite a challenge to live in a different culture."
- "The discontinuity here forces you to make new friends. It increases the sense of community."
- "It helped me find my capabilities. It did a great deal for my self-awareness. When you find yourself in a foreign environment, finding your way around develops you. I had worried about my independence in going to a small college; that's why I was thinking about Michigan, but I find I've gained independence. The curriculum, the Career Development programs, the foreign study, all were

important contributions to my development. Also,
the teachers are wonderful. The short terms (ten
weeks) make it intense, and I had to learn to manage my time."

The most dramatic testimony came from an English professor who had gone to Northwestern and the University of Virginia. She said: "I guess the best thing I can say about
Kalamazoo is that I went to two excellent universities and I really wish I'd gone to school here. I'm constantly struck by the
amazing changes Kalamazoo College is able to bring about in
young people and I wonder what might have happened to me
at this place. Partially it is the workings of the famous and
unique K Plan. As I watch my students rise to the challenges
posed by the Plan, becoming surer of themselves, their abilities, their choices, their goals, and accumulating an array of
experiences that were beyond my imagination as an undergraduate, I find myself deeply envious."

Kalamazoo's students share her enthusiasm. It is one of
those rare places where everyone is excited about what he is
doing and in love with the community of which he is a part. It
rubs off on a visitor and it becomes a part of the participant's
being and improves the quality of his life. Those who choose it
have made a choice they could not improve upon.

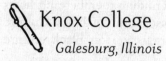

Knox College
Galesburg, Illinois

On my first visit to Knox in Galesburg, Illinois, 20
years ago I thought, "what a wonderful, charming
place to spend four such important years of a young person's
life." I was impressed by the faculty, the students, and the

cloistered tranquility of a campus of large lawns and great trees. The centerpiece is Old Main, an architectural gem. It is where Abraham Lincoln had to crawl through a window to get to his debate with Stephen Douglas because the speakers' stand had been built too close to the door. He then announced he had been through college.

Another jewel among Knox's many buildings is an oak-paneled library of such charm and grace that one student said it was a major factor in her decision to come to Knox. Except for a large reading room that looks as if it had come straight out of Oxford or Cambridge, the ceilings are low, and the rare book room, which houses the Finley collection of every important source on the history of the midwest printed since 1820, is a cozy place that brings to mind art historian Kenneth Clark's comment that "no great thought was ever conceived in an enormous room." (John Huston Finley, who was president of Knox around the turn of the century, was later editor of *The New York Times.*)

At the time of my first visit African-American students elsewhere were segregating themselves, even at egalitarian Oberlin, but at Knox they told me they were part of one happy family. This is not surprising; Knox was founded in 1837 by abolitionist Congregationalists and Presbyterians and was a station on the Underground Railroad by which slaves fled to freedom. In 1870, the first black in Illinois to get a college degree, Barnabas Root, was a Knox graduate, as was the first black senator from Illinois, Hiram Revels. Knox not only offers a major in Black Studies but is a founding member and hosts the national headquarters of the Association of Black Culture Centers, which leads academic discussion on black culture through its journal.

Knox has always admitted blacks and women, and today its 1,200 students come from 45 states and 37 countries. Twelve percent are American minorities and 11% are international students. Grinnell in Iowa is the only other good college so far from a major city able to boast of such diversity.

When I made my recent second visit, it became clear that of the many powerful attractions of Knox, one is that there is no better college in the country for developing a young mind and character; another is that no college offers more guaranteed entrées to top professional schools, whether in architecture, business, engineering, environmental management, forestry, law, medicine, nursing, or social work.

For the budding scientist or scholar, acceptance at graduate school is just as certain, for Knox is in the top 2% of all institutions in the production of men and women who achieve Ph.D. degrees, and it ranks number 11 in mathematics and the sciences. That too is not surprising; 65% of Knox graduates do post-graduate study within five years.

Knox offers so much aid, both need- and merit-based, that only 10% of the parents pay the full tab. Eighty percent of them get need-based aid ranging from $6,000 to $25,846. Another 10% get scholarships ranging from $1,000 to $9,500 a year, and six outstanding freshmen get full tuition scholarships.

Knox also awards scholarships to outstanding mathematics and chemistry students, to National Merit Scholars, to students with special abilities in the creative arts of writing, music, theater, and visual art, to American Field Service returnees, to junior college graduates, and—courtesy of Colorado alumni—to residents of Colorado.

In addition, 20 juniors each year are chosen as Ford Foundation Research Fellows and get support for independent research projects. Knox was one of only 16 colleges in the country chosen for this program to develop future college professors. The program has been so successful that the college has expanded it so that as many as 50 juniors now can undertake summer research projects with a faculty mentor.

What makes Knox such a desirable place is very much what makes other colleges in this book the best preparation. This college is educating—not training—people who can think clearly and independently, who have moral compasses, and who can live fully and courageously.

It does this in many ways. First, a sense of high mission is palpable. It is a family in which the teachers acting as parents encourage, push, and support their children. For example, Dr. Ivan Davidson, chairman of Knox's first-rate theater department, told of a girl who came to a dramatics class believing she wouldn't have to think but who discovered otherwise, and of casting in a lead role another who'd always been told she couldn't do that sort of thing; she discovered that she could. Dr. Davidson had the courage to cast her because he believes that putting people in roles allows them to learn and to grow. "We develop kids," he explained.

Dr. Robert Hellenga, English department chairman and author of two best-selling novels, "Sixteen Pleasures" and "Fall of the Sparrow," added, "We value the ones who blossom, who shift into a different gear."

Others told stories of a black student from the inner city who became a campus leader and is now a sociologist, and of a small-town boy who is now getting his Ph.D. but who probably would have fallen through the cracks at a university. Dr. Brenda Fineberg, author of a praised classics text, said that her going to graduate school after graduating from the University of Chicago had been accidental but, "at Knox, it wouldn't have been accidental."

There is equal concern at the other end of the performance spectrum. Failure is not the end. "We work with the students," said Dr. Hellenga, "we explore ways in which they can help themselves—also, eight or ten students have thanked me for kicking them in the ass."

A student cannot fade into the woodwork because he or she has to be involved, Dr. Davidson added. "At Knox we have a mission and we demonstrate it. We expect students to participate. They can't sit in the back of the class and not participate." Dr. Mark Brodl, a chemist who was one of three outstanding young scientists chosen as a Presidential Young Investigator in 1991, said, "My success has been due to the involvement of the students. At Drake and at Ohio State I met one undergraduate."

One faculty member who had taught at Trinity in Connecticut said there is much more discussion at Knox because "there's a better mix here. The minorities are not at the bottom here as they were at Trinity. At Trinity there was no discussion because of the social differences. The students are much more involved in their own education here. At Knox there is no room for pretense, either academically or socially."

A sure test of what faculty and administrators are saying about their college is what the students say, and at Knox they're saying the same things. I talked with students from Spain, Mexico, China, and with black and white students from diverse backgrounds, and while it may tax credulity, I didn't hear a single discouraging word about the college they had chosen. They all regarded their teachers as their friends and responded with such certainties as "of course!" when I asked if they might have dinner or spend a night at a faculty member's home if they came back in five or ten years. A black student said "the professors have an interest in you, and they don't at Morgan State (an all-black institution in Maryland), where some of my friends go."

Knox also affected their values. A black girl from Chicago said "it broadened my views; the diversity here gave me an appreciation of others." The girl from Mexico called it "a melting-pot experience that makes me more aware and more tolerant." A junior from St. Paul who had one of the research stipends said, "I was so closed-minded when I came, but the experience here and the foreign study programs have changed all that." A senior history major said of the learning environment, "I look back four years and I can't believe what happened." A sophomore from an all-black high school in a Maryland suburb near Washington, D.C., who plans to go to law school said he'd had a hard time realizing that there could be so much diversity and so much warmth and acceptance.

The fact that Knox operates under an honor code seemed to these students a most natural thing. How could it be otherwise?

The foreign students dwelt on how different Knox was from their universities. The sophomore girl from Mexico nodded as the boy from Barcelona, a senior major in international relations, said; "Here you are challenged and you can excel. At the University of Barcelona you're just a number and all you do is memorize. Here you grow intellectually a lot; you have to do critical thinking; you get a well-rounded view of what the world is like." To which the Mexican girl added that the one-on-one relationships with faculty members is unknown at home, and that there the emphasis is on technology rather than on getting an education.

A Chinese-American senior from Chicago, a chemistry and art history major, said he had picked Knox in the first place because of its strong sense of community—"and I had to feel I was part of the community"—the interaction among students and between students and faculty, and the fact that unlike the universities he visited, Knox would let him have full use of all the scientific equipment. "Knox," he says, "is very conducive to allowing students to pick and choose. You are responsible for what you do and liable for what you don't."

The Knox curriculum, like those at Allegheny, Beloit, and Eckerd, requires two shared intellectual experiences, a first-year preceptorial and another in the junior or senior year, that examine fundamental questions about human knowledge, human values, and human society. Both are interdisciplinary and are team-taught. For example, a classics and a physics professor might offer what their respective disciplines have to say on an issue. The intense discussion of political and moral problems makes students examine their own and society's value systems. There is also much writing to develop critical thinking. Students are challenged to analyze, develop, and express ideas logically, clearly, and with style.

Aside from these preceptorials and the distribution requirements, there is much latitude for students to design their own
majors with faculty guidance, to do independent study, or to do
honors work that requires producing a major piece of research
or creative work. Currently, 20% of the senior class is doing
honors work and the college plans to expand it greatly. Honors
students get financial help for summer work on their projects.

More than 30 off-campus programs are available to Knox
students, in Asia, Southeast Asia, Europe, and South America,
and in this country there are programs that cover just about
every student interest, whether in the humanities, the arts,
classics, environment, science, or politics (in a Washington
seminar). More than a fourth of Knox students spend from a
term to a year in one or more of these projects.

Closer to home, 20 miles from the campus, Knox has something few colleges do, a 760-acre biological field station where
the Illinois prairie has been restored to its original state. Slen-
der buffalo grass six feet tall cuts off so little sun that near the
ground there's a whole lower tier of flowers and other plants up
to a foot high. It makes believable the western historians' ac-
counts of riders having to stand up in their stirrups to see
across the sea of grass.

At every college I try to talk to a sociologist and a psychologist, because as people-watchers they often have insights that
are a little different. At Knox the sociologist was Dr. Jack
Fitzgerald, who went to Harvard as an undergraduate and who
got his Ph.D. at Iowa. Although a publishing scholar he said, "I
was a deviate because I wanted primarily to teach. First I
taught at Miles College in Mississippi [a black college desper-
ately in need of help in the civil rights days]. I chose Knox over
other offers in 1968, because I liked the atmosphere. It was informal, not snobbish, and it had more diversity than most.

"You can get as high a quality education here," he went on,
"as you can at Harvard. And it is much more personal. The
quality of teaching is every bit as good. There is a fairly broad

range of abilities at Knox. The students are eager and motivated. Harvard may have more 'A' students but most of the world's work is done by the 'B' and 'C' students."

What does Knox do?

"Science preparation here," he replied, "is top-notch. Students have more access to equipment than they do at universities or at most other places. Students express themselves. They understand cultural diversity. The many extracurricular activities spring from the students. They have values; they challenge. The preceptorials turn on value perspectives. Knox has an impact."

Lawrence University

Appleton, Wisconsin

I f an omniscient being were to describe the vital difference between Lawrence University in Appleton, Wisconsin, and one of the Ivies in New England, she or he would say that Lawrence is a growth hormone that raises kids' trajectories and instills the power to soar. The Ivies take in fast-track kids and turn out fast-track graduates not much changed.

A former Japanese ambassador to the United States said of his experience at Lawrence that it "remains in my heart as the most rewarding. It made a deep and lasting imprint on my life. . . . It shaped my outlook. . . . Without it I would not be where I am today. I am very grateful for the education I received at Lawrence; it is one of the best colleges in the United States." He had also spent a year at Amherst. Grammy-award-winning opera star Dale Duesing said Lawrence "transformed my life." Another alumnus said, "Lawrence cared about my education even when I didn't."

If people weren't provincial and if they were concerned only with quality, Lawrence would be considered as selective as any school. But until things change, there is no greater educational bargain in the country.

The educational establishment, however, is in on the secret. Three of its presidents have subsequently headed Harvard, Brown, and Duke. Nathan Pusey developed Lawrence's powerful Freshman Studies sequence before Harvard took him. Dr. Richard Warch, Lawrence's current president, one of the few in that role who make a difference, is both a Yale Ph.D. (divinity) and a former Yale professor (American studies) and dean.

Lawrence's faculty, the equal of any with its credentials, has few peers as mentors and friends who motivate young people and equip them to cope in a new kind of world. (Most of those peers are in this book.)

Lawrence has had seven Rhodes Scholars and it ranks in the top 20 colleges in turning out future Ph.D.s in the humanities and in all other non-science fields. It is a first-rate entrée into graduate and professional schools. President Warch says "Lawrence kids are better than they think. Yale kids think they're better than they are. Lawrence kids are less broad at first but as broad or broader at the finish. It is less competitive here than at Yale and there is more joy."

Lawrence is called a university because it has a music conservatory, a superb one that is most unusual. It not only has music for the non-music majors, but the music majors are ensured a liberal education. Furthermore, if someone wants to do a double major, say in government and music, as one fellow was doing when I visited, it's no problem. The music department would love to have everyone exposed to music courses or doing double majors.

"Here everyone participates," a piano teacher said. "Students are coddled; I go to hear every student's recital. At Oberlin nobody on the faculty came to hear mine. We have music for all. We work so hard for them. A course a girl wanted wasn't offered so I did it one on one."

Lawrence's 1,200 students come from 45 states with the

Midwest most heavily represented. Its percentage of minorities has climbed to nearly 10%, partly because of a program of internships with major corporations in the area, such as Kimberly Clark, which often lead to good jobs for these students after graduation. Eleven percent are international students from 40 countries. Lawrence accepts three-fourths of its applicants, about half of them in the top tenth of their high school classes. But here again, many of those were small rural schools. The average SAT scores were 630 verbal and 630 math. In other words, there are plenty of "B," "B−", and maybe "C" admittees, but they have shown that they mean business.

About two-thirds of the students get financial aid, which in 1999 averaged $18,700 a year for the need-based recipients, and about $8,000 for the aid given on a merit basis.

In the perspective of a young British art professor, Lawrence is "a conservative college where kids work. Its location increases student-faculty contact because they are thrown together, unlike in a big city [he went to University College London]. They are very friendly. There is a lot of volunteer work."

Lawrence's faculty could be labeled cosmopolitan, liberal, and caring. The freshmen are mainstream teenagers unlikely to have considered either conservative, religious schools like Wheaton or very liberal, do-it-yourself places like Antioch, Hampshire, or Marlboro. But four years later it's a different story; they have become critical-thinking do-it-yourselfers.

The attractive campus is on a bluff overlooking the Fox River, which flows into Lake Winnebago, so Lawrence has crew as well as a full lineup of other intercollegiate sports. It also has a 405-acre estate on Lake Michigan that provides recreational as well as study facilities.

The centerpiece of the Lawrence experience, the two-semester Freshman Studies course, was designed by President Pusey as a kind of intellectual culture shock to introduce students to the fundamental character of liberal learning. By reading, discussing, and writing about what some of the great thinkers have written, they grapple with questions of abiding concern: Why am I here? How should I conduct my life? Why do bad things happen? What things are worth knowing? They build intellectual foundations that serve them during their college years and beyond.

Faculty from all departments teach the classes. To give different perspectives, instructors are changed in the middle of a term. It is often a collaborative learning experience. A chemistry or a biology professor leading the discussions on Plato's *Republic* and grading the papers may be struggling and learning right along with the students.

A freshman may write five or more papers each term, often for different instructors who don't do or see things the same way. But help is provided. For one thing, the staff meets at lunch once a week to compare notes on interpretation of their texts and teaching methods, and just to try to keep everybody on the same track.

For another, Lawrence provides a magical little booklet every college ought to emulate. *The Freshman Studies Book* explains what the system is trying to do and how to beat it. It tells how to "use" your instructors, making the points that not only are they good sources of information, both practical and scholarly, but also that they too may be struggling with the text, and furthermore, that they will enjoy the chance to chat about problems.

A section that students everywhere should read, "what your instructor wants," says that what he wants is for students to "stop asking what your instructor wants and to start asking some more fruitful and self-liberating questions. . . . He wants you to think more deeply and more clearly, to examine and test your ideas, and to express them more lucidly and completely."

There are excellent sections on how to study the readings, how to be effective in discussion, and how to write a paper—with good and bad examples, plus tips on good usage. It even has some sample quiz questions. Any freshman who uses this 60-page booklet will have it made, and not just in the Freshman Studies course.

The Freshman Studies courses do indeed engage students in their own education. By the time they're seniors, 90% of the students are doing some independent study and half of them have had a foreign study term abroad. All of the science students get involved in undergraduate research; in biology 17 out of 30 seniors are doing independent research. One professor said, "Kids blossom here. At Oberlin I didn't have the faculty contact kids do here. My students have produced a dozen articles in six years. They develop critical thinking skills." In history, students have co-authored two papers this year, and one student is lead author on another.

Lawrence students are much better off than those at Wisconsin or at Brown, said professors who had taught in those places. At Lawrence they have many more opportunities in the way of independent research, and they get better recommendations. "We give good recommendations," said a biology professor, "because we know them. I know what my students' aspirations are. We find them summer internships, which they don't in universities, and parents aren't aware of this. Faculty members here are in academia because they want to teach. At Brown they're not interested in teaching."

The academic dean, who had taught at Princeton before coming to Lawrence in 1993, took a longer view. "This kind of place is the cutting edge of higher education. I didn't think so when I was at a research university. We're teaching them to think for coping in a fast-changing world. Now the Ivies are emulating us."

The students will buy that, and then some. A senior had heads nodding when he said, "I have gained a lot of self-confidence; I've been recognized for what I've done. My professors are all from the best schools. They're interested in trying to help you find your way. I feel I've gotten a lot of individual attention, one on one, with professors. You can make it what you want to make it, which you can't at a university, and it's kind of a good feeling to be a big fish in a small pond. Everyone here is concerned about academics but it's not an atmosphere in which you're racking your brains worrying about competing."

Another chimed in with, "Lawrence's Honor Code opens a lot of opportunities. I took a test at home. It's great; you can take a test wherever you want to take it. The professor puts the test on the board and walks out. They really treat you like adults. I think everyone obeys the Honor Code; people can leave their backpacks when they go into the cafeteria."

Other very prominent themes were that they had learned to analyze, to read and think critically, to question things, and emphatically, they were better writers. They said there was much discussion out of class about what went on in class: "It's something all of us do." The Freshman Studies course got much credit here.

"In high school," a senior added, "I could avoid thinking about things that are really important, analyzing what my life was about. College gave me an opportunity to consider who I really am. My head would be burning about things we'll never find the answers to. Lawrence gave me the opportunity to grow intellectually. It encouraged me with all the personal attention. The Music Department is incredible. I wanted a course but couldn't fit it into my schedule, so the prof gave it to me as a tutorial."

Several seniors headed for graduate or professional schools thought they had a decided edge because of research opportunities, independent study, or the quality of the learning. One of the aspiring lawyers said, "I did quite a bit better on my LSATs than those from the University [of Wisconsin]." A future geologist said, "Here we have small classes and we get to use the equipment. I really like it; it seems like home."

However, Lawrence has a good deal more diversity than home. There were so many international students on campus now that many felt it was "a microcosm of the United States and the world." Also, as already noted, half of the students take at least one of the college's array of 23 foreign programs.

But what was consistent was the enthusiasm for their school. A number of non-music majors used terms like "phenomenal" or "incredible" to describe the conservatory and the performances it brings to the campus. They also praised the overall quality of imported attractions such as plays and lectures. Several athletes were glad that they had been able to compete successfully at a smaller school like Lawrence, and be at least some kind of visible fish in the pond. Even more unusual was the number of students who volunteered that Lawrence was generous with financial aid. (About two-thirds get aid.)

The sophomore with a double major in government and music had been accepted by a couple of Ivies but chose Lawrence after spending a day at each. His verdict was, "Here it felt like home; there were more options; it was more laid back and relaxed, not competitive. At Yale you have the feeling you're lucky to be there; here they thanked me for coming. Here you can do graduate-level research. You can go as far and as fast as you want. Faculty, staff, and administration are all here to help you."

Alumna and successful novelist Susan Engberg had been an art major who loved words and took a creative writing course. She wrote in the alumni magazine: "If the course description had had a secret text, visible only to me, it would have read, 'Dive in Susan, do the work with your whole heart, let the pleasure of working do its work on you, trust the teacher, and by mid-winter you will emerge with the seed of your future in mind.'" She did and she was hooked on writing. What had happened? "These are the people who help us turn into ourselves."

If the undergraduates were as skilled with words as Susan Engberg, they would be saying much the same thing. Lawrence is a place that helps young people find themselves and then make the best of what they find.

Ohio Wesleyan University

Delaware, Ohio

O n many counts, Ohio Wesleyan is one of the best academic bargains in the country. A chemistry professor voiced a prevailing faculty attitude when he said, "Regardless of where a kid comes from, we can take him somewhere."

As every college and university did before the college-going rush after World War II, Ohio Wesleyan accepts a wide range of students, from C to A. It makes a special effort to help those with learning disabilities, and it has honors programs for the very talented or the very motivated.

Ohio Wesleyan is likely to be a financial as well as academic bargain, for over 90% of its students get some type of financial aid and about 70% get some form of merit aid. The average SAT score in 1999 was 1210, and the average GPA of enrolled freshmen was 3.25, about a quarter of whom get into the honors program. The school accepts just over 80% of its applicants, most of whom come from outside of Ohio. It is a diversified group, from 42 other states and 60 countries.

An important morale consideration is that 70% of the students accepted considered Ohio Wesleyan their first choice, another 20% listed it as their second choice. That bespeaks "a happy-band-of-brothers" esprit that may have something to do with why, across the board, it has a long history of helping them become achievers. A young client who'd been the despair of his parents in high school has done so well at Ohio Wesleyan that as a junior he won a summer internship with CNN news. Another, who'd wanted to drop out of high school, now has a doctorate in geology. Like Denison, Ohio Wesleyan is not the same place it was 25 or even 15 years ago, thanks in large measure to the efforts of its recently resigned president, Dr.

David Warren. There has been, in the words of one long-time professor, "a massive change in the student body and in the college." A $100 million fund campaign has raised $76 million so far and is enabling it to hire the best faculty available, offer more merit scholarships to good students, and complete a student center that rivals a shopping mall for attractions. The recruiting of honors students has been most effective in changing more than just the profile of the student body in ten years. It has changed the retention rate and the level of enthusiasm in the classroom.

Today, the professor said, "there is much one-on-one with eager students," an assessment others not only agreed with but enlarged on with such comments about their departments as:

- "Half our history majors are converts after taking a freshman course."
- "Our new Latin American Studies program is strong and many go on to graduate school."
- "Our fine arts program is unique and it is tops. It is strong throughout. We are one of the few to offer both the Bachelor of Fine Arts and the Bachelor of Arts degrees. We have the widest offerings of any of the 12 in the Great Lakes Colleges Association (GLCA) and one of the widest in the country. We are less career-oriented; we require writing in the art program as part of a liberal education."
- "We have the most comprehensive teacher education program of any GLCA college and one of the most comprehensive in the country, and we require a 2.6 average to get into the program."
- "Psychology majors have co-authored 11 research papers in the last few years. Another 15 are doing independent research, and five have apprenticeships."
- "Our faculty's research citations in scholarly publications rank number two among the top colleges."

- "Several chemistry majors have co-authored papers given at professional meetings, and we want to get more and more students engaged in research with faculty."
- "The honors program has a special curriculum and tutorials."

They kept saying things like "we nurture students; they are being taught how to think; there's writing across the curriculum—even in art. They are more eager students; they are more service-oriented."

In fact, every faculty member I talked to had the same kind of lively interest in his or her students I found at other campuses reviewed for this book. Some of it may have rubbed off from the chemistry professor, who was as passionate about getting students involved as any teacher I've ever talked to. He said he'd originally been headed for a seminary and the ministry. I told him he was still in religion.

There is, as at other colleges, a new interest in public affairs and in public service. Acting President William Louthan said, "There's something about this institution that does attract students interested in global and public issues and we can claim to be distinctive in that area." For ten years Ohio Wesleyan has put on a major lecture-discussion series called The National Colloquium to explore some public issue. The program brings in noted speakers for talks on various aspects of a given issue. They are followed by workshops and discussion groups with the speaker, and for students wishing to get academic credit, there is more intensive work. In 1993, Terry Anderson, the news correspondent held prisoner in Beirut, was the first of a series of speakers on "Waging War, Waging Peace." The colloquia are heavily promoted; they are discussed in classes, and it would be difficult to avoid a poster or a reminder of the next event in the popular campus center. They draw large turnouts, unlike some places like the University of Richmond where faculty have to give credit to get students to listen to such stars as the famed paleontologist and geologist Stephen Jay Gould.

Every bit as important is what Ohio Wesleyan is doing to give a hand to those with learning problems. Thousands of college students have learning problems but their schools give them no help. Freshmen with the lowest academic credentials often need a helping hand, too. Many institutions list services for them but most are on paper only, especially in universities. Ohio Wesleyan delivers with orchestrated help.

A student's academic adviser is the first, and confidential, source of help. The adviser will arrange any accommodations needed, such as choice of courses. A counseling center gives workshops on test anxiety, time management, or psychological counseling. A writing center helps those with problems in that area. A psychologist advises those with learning disabilities and offers strategies for dealing with them. Teachers, advisers, and the resource people all work together to meet the student's needs. They may even waive the foreign language requirement for graduation or permit a reduced course load. This is a far cry from the experience a student would have at a big university. Whatever help we can provide, the college well notes, the best help is still a caring faculty.

Often when talking to students at these colleges I wonder whether I'd have gotten the same answers 15 or 20 years ago and had the same reaction to them. I don't think so. Kids at these colleges feel they're getting a better deal than their friends who went to prestige schools. Ohio Wesleyan students say they have to work hard, that the demands are great, and the level of expectation is high. They say the professors are first-rate and they count them as friends interested in their success, and that they often have dinner, dessert, or coffee at faculty homes. Those going to graduate or professional school are looking forward to getting recommendations that not only will be good but that will mean something because the professor knows them well and can be specific about their virtues.

Several of them confirmed the faculty claim that they were having to learn to think. One fellow responded, when asked if the college had affected his values, that he wasn't sure whether that was the input of his home life or the college but that he and his friends thought they were much more reasoned in their attitudes and beliefs now.

Several upperclass students said they were able to get much more involved and have more satisfying and important roles in their schools than did their friends at universities. A California girl, a top student who had come on a merit scholarship, said that after a visit she would have come without a scholarship, even though several other schools were bidding for her with big grants.

An obvious change at Ohio Wesleyan, as at Denison, is the diminished importance of fraternities and sororities. A senior girl said she dropped out of her sorority because they're not necessary for campus involvement, there's such a strong sense of community at the school. There's also a great deal of social service work now, and (perhaps as a consequence?) a lot less drinking. A senior boy said his fraternity was heavily involved in service projects, something that was rare a decade ago.

Eight percent of Ohio Wesleyan's 1,900 students are African-American, and 12% of the 1999 freshmen were international students. As was the case when I visited there a dozen or so years ago, the ones I talked to all said they felt they belonged, that it was one community and not a lot of separate groups.

Among the things that helps the sense of cohesion is one of the most stunning campus centers anywhere. A very large and imposing $12 million building, it is a good deal more than a student union. In addition to the usual facilities for student activities are counseling, advising, and career placement centers; a variety of snack shops, dining nooks and terraces; a full scale—and very popular—bakery; meeting rooms; private dining rooms; and of course, other shops. Just one of the publications is a four-page daily bulletin that tells everything that is or soon will be going on. When I was there it seemed like the busiest place on the campus.

Since its founding in 1842, Ohio Wesleyan has had a distinguished history, albeit with some ups and downs. Now it is clearly a very effective force that is helping students of a wide range of academic abilities and home backgrounds. A first-rate faculty and administration share an enthusiastic commitment to making good on the boast of the chemistry professor that "regardless of where the kid comes from, we can take him somewhere."

St. Olaf College
Northfield, Minnesota

What strikes visitors as they drive around and up the curving hill of the St. Olaf campus is the beauty of the place, with its impressive light gray limestone-and-glass buildings, grassy expanses, emphatic shrubbery, and stately trees. The architecture might be called Norwegian modern, as could the mostly blond-and brown-haired students, looking as attractive as the buildings. Aesthetically and academically it is Camelot. If it were on the East Coast it would be as selective as any Ivy. But it will just have to be satisfied with being better in important ways.

It looks clean and wholesome and that's exactly what it is, through and through. An anxious father can send his daughter here as safely as to any other college that is not a fundamentalist detention center. St. Olaf is one of the few mainstream colleges with a religious commitment and a commitment to the life of the mind. Not many other colleges have the same sense of common purpose. President Mark U. Edwards says, "St.

Olaf is committed to helping students discover their calling. We firmly believe that our mission as a liberal arts college of the church is to help students develop lives of worth and service."

St. Olaf is a place of friendliness and trust as well as of high expectations. There are no locks on the mailboxes in the campus post office. Indeed, most of them sit open, and at strategic walkway crossings lie bags, briefcases, jackets, and other possessions waiting for their owners to pick them up after class. Not one, I was told, has ever been missing.

The college is Lutheran but its commitment is to character, not to denomination or creed. And it is a place that has an impact. Random interviews the college conducts with seniors reveal that their values have changed. They are more interested in service and less interested in wealth, and they emphasized, among other things, the effect of worship services and the international programs. On my first visit to St. Olaf a dozen or so years ago, I went to church on Sunday out of curiosity and found at least 1,000 of the college's 3,000 students were there.

St. Olaf bans cars for any students living within 250 miles, as well as alcohol, and visitation in the coed dorms after midnight (1 a.m. on weekends), but if many kids had complaints, they weren't very vocal.

The student body is a healthy mix, and the administration is trying to increase the diversity. A little more than 40% are Lutherans, nearly 20% are Catholics, with Methodists and Presbyterians trailing. Nearly 50% are from Minnesota but 42 other states are represented. About 10% are Asian, Asian-American, European, or African-American. I asked a junior from Jamaica how she liked the Minnesota weather and she said, "By now I like it, and I have a job with 3M lined up in Minneapolis when I graduate."

St. Olaf accepts about three-fourths of its applicants, over 90% of whom are in the top half of their high school classes, so plenty of "B" students and a few strong "Cs" are in the mix. The median SAT scores are 630 verbal and 630 math. The median ACT score is 27. Forty-three percent of the acceptees enroll. And they like it; a phenomenal 91% return for the sophomore year and 75% graduate in four years. Three-fourths of them have college-educated parents; two-thirds are on financial aid. In addition, to attract more outstanding students, the college offers a number of merit scholarships, as well as Lutheran Leadership and Community Service Scholarships.

St. Olaf is best known for its famous orchestra and choir. Both have performed in all the major U.S. cities. The choir sang at the 1988 Summer Olympics and is the only college choir ever to sing in the Sistine Chapel in the Vatican.

It is equally respected in the academic world. It has always been a prolific producer of the country's scholars and scientists, out of all proportion to its size or selectivity. Its faculty is superb across the board and works closely with their students. The student-faculty ratio is 12 to 1. An average of 45 chemistry majors a year puts it at the top of all colleges, and its nonpareil math department attracts 70 majors or more each year. Only biology, with 70 to 90 majors, and English, with 80 to 100 a year, have more.

There is a core curriculum to ensure that everyone shares a common understanding of the Western heritage in science, humanities, the arts, religion, and languages, as well as some non-Western culture or minority cultures of North America. But, with faculty help, students may fashion this experience in their own way. Students may take regular course sequences and distributions, or they may develop their own programs in consultation with an adviser. They may also have all the freedom they could possibly conceive of in the way of individualized majors. The Center for Integrated Studies, a new initiative, provides support for students who want to pursue individualized majors that are interdisciplinary or that combine diverse methods, learning styles, experiences, off-campus resources, you name it.

St. Olaf operates on a 4-1-4 program augmented by two summer sessions. A student takes four courses during each 14-

week semester (fall and spring) and one intensive course in a January term. He may use the summer sessions to graduate in three years or to go further and deeper in four years. The January term is no goof-off period: A student is expected to work 40 hours a week between class time and studying.

The opportunities for independent study, off-campus internships, or study almost anywhere around the globe are very nearly without limit. The catalog lists 30 programs, and some include study at several different locations. The Global Semester, for instance, takes students to Hong Kong to study the arts of China, to Cairo for themes in ancient Greco-Roman and Islamic-Egyptian history, to Bangalore for Indian political economy, and to Kyoto for the religions of Japan. I don't know of another college that has such a wealth of foreign programs.

In conjunction with the other 13 members of the Associated Colleges of the Midwest, St. Olaf also has a rich variety of programs in this country, in the arts, urban studies, science, the environment, and humanities. Just about any interest a student has can be served, and some new ones might be discovered.

Whatever their fields, the faculty members I talked to both on my recent visit and a dozen years ago thought the years at St. Olaf affected students' values. Some are attracted to St. Olaf, said an English professor, who had gone to Holy Cross and then to Harvard for his doctorate, by religion, but everyone feels welcome, and there is a strong sense of community. Also, the college is carrying forward its plans for more diversity. "The kids here are wholesome; they're delightful to teach. They're capable and committed; overachievers." Asked if relations with the students were close, he spoke for many other professors when he said, "That's easy; the faculty here are committed to the undergraduates. The whole system undergirds that. The faculty are active scholars, but to get tenure or to be promoted, St. Olaf has a different philosophy: A decision about tenure is promise; a decision about promotion is performance." In other words, a professor doesn't have to have a long list of books and articles to get tenure, but he has to be a stimulating and caring teacher as well as an active scholar to be promoted. One professor has won a national teaching award and a math department professor has been a national leader in shaping college math curriculums and has been president of the national professional association of mathematicians.

Several faculty members emphasized what one called, "a tremendous feeling that people ought to do things of service" that runs through the place. "There is a moral element here, no question," said one. "Students have the chance to be confronted with their values, but there are no religious requirements and we expect them to be comfortable in talking about religious views." Unlike most other schools, every faculty member I have talked with at St. Olaf believes that college has an impact on the development of values as well as giving students a broad outlook as a result of the Global Perspective element in the curriculum. After the foreign experiences, the kids come back "changed," which is just what faculty members have said at every college that has an active foreign study program.

As at the other colleges in this book, the students and faculty have a mutual admiration society. Comments I heard often were, "the teachers know me; the attention I get is wonderful," "I'm very close to my adviser," "when the profs write recommendations, they know me," "these teachers are my good friends," "the sense of respect is very strong." My sampling did not find a single malcontent in this area.

The president of the student council said, "There's a kind of energy here that's not found elsewhere. St. Olaf is inclusive, friendly, and is becoming more diverse politically. It is definitely a place of people who care. It builds a strong sense of community." And in a comment that may surprise teenagers, she added, "No cars is a help." Incidentally, I did not get a single gripe from any student about not having a car. One reason is that if you want to do something there's always a way.

A girl who had already paid her deposit at the University of Chicago when she visited St. Olaf was so enamored of the way it allows the student to participate in her own education, unlike the university, that she switched.

St. Olaf is lovingly regarded as a place, as one boy said, like Outward Bound: It challenges and tests you, supports you, and pushes your bounds outward and upward.

Whether the rest of the country rediscovers values in the next 20 years or not, St. Olaf will continue to offer unequalled preparation for a full life and for being a winner and a contributor in a new world. It is enlightened, forward-looking, and innovative, the teachers are caring human beings, and the welfare of the student takes priority. Whether you're Muslim, Jew, Unitarian, agnostic, or atheist, at St. Olaf you will not only be comfortable, you will be respected, and people will be interested in your views and beliefs.

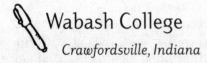

Wabash College
Crawfordsville, Indiana

Wabash is a happy band of 850 brothers, fraternity brothers, mostly. But it is a place like no other. Not only do these young men take pride in working hard, their fraternities see to it that they do. Students are proud of their faculty and faculty take pride in them. All are proud of their school. Wabash has no church connection, but its religion department draws even skeptics as majors. On this lovely campus 45 miles from Indianapolis, Wabash comes first.

This is a clan with élan. Not a single student I talked to would be anywhere else. Wabash was their first choice, and one reason was they'd been told, "It won't be easy, but it will be worth it." And if as a teenager long ago I'd known the luxury of comparison shopping, I'd have been one of them.

Not surprisingly, it is a place that turns young males with great, medium, and even mediocre high school records into clear-thinking men who lead the life of the mind and who have the confidence to take risks. And they go on to become high achievers and contributors to society at a rate that puts very selective and famous colleges to shame.

This is an academically serious place. As more than one faculty member pointed out, "there is a lust for learning" for learning's sake, and, "The quality of conversation here is as good as any place I've been. We discuss big issues." Or from an alumnus, "I read as much here as in graduate school." It is rigorous but not overly intellectual. "Everyone takes pride in working hard. It is competitive for achieving excellence, but the competition is with oneself."

The goal of every fraternity house and dorm is to have the highest grade point average on campus. "They push each other," explained a former Greek now on the faculty. "Peer pressure will bug him to get his work done."

Professors took pride in boasting, "Our students almost never miss class." Or, "Even when they bring their girlfriends to campus, they don't cut class; they bring their dates." And girls are not in short supply. DePauw, with 1,300, and Purdue with 13,000, are only 30 miles away. A bit farther is the cluster of universities in Indianapolis with thousands more. President Andrew Ford says that when prexies of former men's colleges ask him why Wabash is still single-sex, his answer is, "You're asking the wrong question. The question is, why did you go coed?" And everybody on this campus feels the same way.

Unlike any other college I know of, this is a collaborative community of learning because of the fraternity, not in spite of it. It is a distinctive thing about the Greek system at Wabash. Indeed, so far as I know it's unique. The sense of community is so palpable, it's as much a part of the atmosphere as the great trees and lawns or the New England feel of its lovely quadrangle. I can't remember ever having been at a place where I heard the pronoun "we" so frequently, even more than "I" (except perhaps at Agnes Scott).

Where else would a fraternity man say, "I have a hundred times more pride in being a Wabash Beta (Beta Theta Pi) than in being a Beta. We have a concern for each other and that the house have a concern for the school. When high school visitors come to the campus, you talk about Wabash first and the fraternity second."

A Delta Tau Delta added, "At the Delt conferences, other chapters don't understand what we do. Each house has pride. No other Delt chapter has the pride in its school that we do. In our Greek system we work together for the good of the school."

As befits surrogate parents, the teachers are no less committed. A young professor of English, Dr. Joy Castro said, "I have two classes of twelve each. If one of them misses a class, I inquire. If one fails to make eye contact, I inquire."

Historian Dr. Peter Frederick added, "I have sixty in one class and if someone misses he'll be embarrassed because at some point during the day we'll meet."

Another young professor, economist Dr. Kealoha Widdows, summed it up with, "They can't get away from us," and then proudly pointed out that unlike the Eastern school where she'd previously taught, "Here they don't become business majors; they're economics majors."

There is no doubt about how pervasive is the attitude of "It-won't-be-easy-but-it-will-be-worth-it" when that's what the head football coach talks about. Greg Carlson not only has faculty rank but has been there since 1980. In our chat he never once mentioned won-lost records or outstanding athletes. He said, "It's a joy to watch these kids blossom and become self-starters, and to have them leave here with a real confidence. A special young man wants to come here who knows the value of a difficult, tough row."

That kind of concern is not lost. Later in the day, a football player who'd been recruited by other schools explained, "The way the football coach talked about the school, you could feel the pride and tradition. It has far surpassed my expectations. As for jobs, the networking of Wabash alumni opens doors."

Two other distinctive things about this community are its freedom and the responsibility that goes with it. Wabash has only one rule, The Gentleman's Rule. It says, "The student shall live both on and off campus as a gentleman and a responsible citizen."

A Wabash man has the freedom, as one professor put it, "to be who you are. You are free to slump and recover. You accept the consequences. You can't hide." He can even fail and pick himself up and start over. He won't get kicked out. Dealing with such responsibility is important to a young person's development. As in other colleges in this book, cheating is virtually unknown.

Several students expressed variants on, "Coming to school here makes you a man." A black senior said, "I decided to go here to be a better man. Wabash could take me somewhere. Tradition and pride go into being a Wabash man. The other schools I looked at, they weren't that good."

Even those who were second- or third-generation Wabash men had their own definite reasons, such as the rapport between students and faculty, "the integrity of the school," or "Wabash overshadowed all the other schools I looked at. The camaraderie here is just great; it's wonderful! It's a good place to study, and the involvement is really important."

Among the many notes of pride in the faculty, one senior said, "Wabash's religion department is unparalleled in the U.S., but I didn't come here to be a religion major." It is so good, he said, that students who have no interest in the ministry, even skeptics, major in religion. They have a wide range of choices: Jewish, Muslim, Christian, or one of the Asian faiths, an area of particular strength.

A senior psychology major warned that Wabash is not for everybody. He'd been drawn to the school by the quality of its faculty and its liberal arts curriculum. "Wabash," he said, "is not the kind of place you can push on people."

The frequency with which it was mentioned made it clear that the Wabash men believe a vital part of their experience is involvement, and they are heavily involved. Athletics are important and over 40% are on one of the many varsity athletic squads. And the teams are good. Long ago they earned the nickname "Little Giants" for knocking off opponents from much larger schools. And they have beautiful athletic facilities that are extensive, expensive, and state of the art.

As I was reading the campus paper at lunch, one of the fellows I'd been talking to earlier passed by and said, "We all work for it." Furthermore, faculty members and their spouses are also involved. Three had roles in that evening's production of *The Grapes of Wrath*.

At many of the other colleges in this book faculty members exulted in the wonderful spirit of collegiality they had found at their colleges. At Wabash, they went further. As one put it: "This is an involved faculty. We are getting the best. If someone publishes a paper or a book, we are proud of each other's success. There is an attitude of mutual support, with no sense of competition. There is an esprit de corps."

Even when offers come to go elsewhere, he added, they usually choose to stay. Joy Castro had received several other offers, but chose Wabash, she said, because "I was treated most professionally here."

It's not surprising that what Wabash produces is remarkable:

- Thirteen percent of its alumni have Ph.D.s, a higher figure than most of the Ivies.
- An amazing 12% of alumni hold the title "president" or "chairman." One recent chairman was AT&T's Robert Allen.
- Only two Ivies have a higher percentage of alumni in *Who's Who*.

- ▪ At only four of the 11 Ivies and Little Ivies do the seniors perform as well or better on the Medical College Admission Test.
- ▪ Three-fourths of its graduates go on to graduate or professional school within five years.

In short, Wabash is a continuing repudiation of the idolatry of selectivity. It does an outstanding job of developing productive citizens. What's more, it does so while accepting nearly 70% of its applicants. Fewer than half had SAT verbal scores over 600, and only about a third were in the top tenth of their high school classes, many of them small and rural. This is in dramatic contrast to the colleges that boast of their selectivity.

As President Andrew Ford observed, "With quality now equated in the public mind with selectivity, many colleges work to see how many students' dreams they can break. Colleges encourage students to apply, then reject them."

Wabash is not only inclusive, it is spending its money to help those who need it, whether they have learning disabilities or come from schools where their preparation was not adequate for such a rigorous program. As President Ford noted, "We can't assume students will have similar preparation and skills."

Equally important, Wabash gives more financial aid per capita than any other school, largely thanks to the generosity of Mr. Eli Lilly. About 95% get substantial help; a lot of this is merit scholarships. Each year it gives ten full-tuition Lilly scholarships to outstanding leaders. Every student automatically gets all the need-based aid his family qualifies for; he doesn't have to ask for it. Indeed, Wabash for most is cheaper than a public institution. For many families it is the best financial bargain in the college world.

This financial aid bounty enables Wabash to have a 17% minority population: 5% African Americans, 5% percent Hispanic, and 3% Asian. Each year it gives ten Lilly Scholarships of full tuition to outstanding minority applicants.

The Wabash student gets a truly liberal education. He has to be proficient in his own and in a foreign language. He has to take at least three courses in science or mathematics, and he has to become familiar with other cultures and traditions. He has to examine and discuss his values. As at many other colleges, he is introduced to the academic way in a small freshman seminar examining a topic of the instructor's choice. He has to have a major and a minor and take comprehensive exams. And there is writing in every course, even mathematics.

But the magic of this or any other place is not in what they do; it's in how they do it. Every college in this book achieves its goals by different methods. Here, the how is the pride the whole community takes in its commitment to learning for its own sake. It is the common enterprise.

Long before the end of my overnight visit, I was wishing I'd gone here instead of to its coed rival, DePauw.

Wheaton College
Wheaton, Illinois

J ust an hour's drive west of Chicago is attractive Wheaton College, a place where both students and faculty enjoy themselves, where most of them work hard, and where the friendly atmosphere would impress even a curmudgeonly atheist. But it won't admit you as a student unless you're a Christian. The college's firmly stated beliefs include the parenthood of Adam and Eve and the divinity of Christ. Its firmly stated mission is to "address the needs of the world and to provide leadership for the work of the church."

Within that context it is a community that embraces at least 30 different stripes of Christianity, from liberal Episcopalians to literal fundamentalists. It is also a place that produces many highly respected scientists and scholars. Indeed, over a 70-year period it ranks 12th among all the undergraduate colleges as a source of future Ph.D.s. And just for good measure, it ranks 25th among all four-year institutions in the percentage of alumni listed in *Who's Who in America*. The presidents of 43 colleges went to Wheaton.

How is the teaching of geology, which deals in eons, or biology and the theory of evolution, reconciled with the biblical story of creation?

A biologist put it this way: "In natural sciences, for instance, when 'issues of origin' are taught, the faculty do not try to indoctrinate. They attempt to discover and lead students through discovery processes that discern truth through revelations of God in Scripture and nature. Students are challenged to discern and act upon truth as revealed by God and to do so within a Christian context. Students are given an education designed to help them appreciate the Creator, beauty, and order in God's creation and human creativity in the arts and sciences, and to apply those insights to the pursuit of righteousness in the life of both the individual and society."

A geology professor said, "We have an attitude of humble uncertainty," observing that science is not a place for dogmatism. A professor of Christian thought added that there are different forms of revelation and that "the scientists are not sweating over trying to fit together the principles of organic chemistry and Genesis."

Wheaton is often called the Harvard of the evangelicals, but that moniker does not do it justice because it is head, shoulders, and heart above Harvard in its concern with good moral compasses and strong value systems, as well as in the percentages of future Ph.D.s it has turned out.

Financially, Wheaton is a bargain. Not quite half the students get need-based financial aid averaging about $4,700 a year, and another 16% get merit aid averaging about $800 a year.

Its impressive record of producing contributors to society puts it in this book, even though a "B" student has to have credentials other than grades to get in. Wheaton accepts only 58% of its applicants. The middle 50% of acceptees have SAT scores of 1,100 to 1,300 and their grade point average is 3.6, but one-third of those high averages are from rural high schools. All must have been involved in "quality service to others, not necessarily in church."

They come from all 50 states and 40 foreign countries. There are two groups of applicants; one applies only to Christian colleges, the other applies also to the Ivies, especially Princeton and Yale, and to Virginia, North Carolina, Michigan, Northwestern, and William & Mary. Ten percent are minority. An Ivy-like 93% return as sophomores, and 72% graduate in four years.

Admissions Director Daniel Crabtree says, "I want students willing to think through issues. Wheaton provides an atmosphere that honors the individual. They come here with a set of beliefs but they make their own choices. They spend semesters in youth hostels with atheists and those of many other persuasions. We hope students will leave Wheaton having thought through issues of life and developed a theology of their own. We are not stuck in the 19th century. I rejected one applicant whose well-meaning high school counselor had written that she saw everything in black and white.

"We hope they will learn how their commitment relates to living and learning and are open to discover truth. We are confronting the world with deep moral issues and we have a lab with Chicago right here. Nearly half the student body [of 2,200] is involved in helping roles of several kinds, in jails, shelters, social work, tutoring."

As might be expected, alcohol, drugs, and tobacco are prohibited, along with social dancing. Chapel three times a week is required as are 14 hours of Bible and theology. One administrator said dancing was "a non-issue" but several students disagreed; they said conservative alumni kept the ban in force. One girl seemed to reflect the attitude of resignation when she said, "I do hope that when my daughter comes here they can dance." No one got visibly angry when the subject was brought up.

It is a pleasant place; as I walked across the campus on a sodden gray day, everyone, students and professors, smiled and said "Hi." It is also very Republican and those who said they wanted to work in think tanks or political action groups all had the conservative variety in mind. Everyone was enthusiastic about Wheaton and involved not only in their own education but in any one of an array of social, musical, theatrical, athletic, literary, or other activities. There is a wealth of lectures by people famous in their fields, concerts, and other cultural events.

There is a strong sense of community, partly because one of Wheaton's main attractions is as a Christian school. The thrice-weekly chapel, one senior said, helps create a sense of being one. A girl added, "We have such a wide range of beliefs here but the common denominator is Christ."

Its other principal drawing cards are its reputation for academic excellence and its friendliness. Several had decided Wheaton was as good or better academically than such schools as Northwestern or Princeton, and that its Christian commitment gave it the edge.

A black girl from Chicago was one of those who said that when she visited, everybody seemed so welcoming and so sincere. Or, as another put it, she was disappointed in other Christian schools but when she came here she knew this was it, there was genuine welcoming acceptance. All of the African-American students I spoke with said they felt they were an integral part of the community.

When students were asked what kind of person would be happy at Wheaton the most common answer was that he or she should be motivated and disciplined, interested in learning, and willing to be involved. They were assuming of course, that the person was a Christian. For the most part they offered the same descriptions as did the faculty: The person should not only be serious about education but also have an interest in how Christianity affects life and learning.

But all don't fit that pattern; there are also, one senior said, "non-organized, go-with-the-flow, free-thinkers, objective, open, so there are almost two groups here." Another senior interjected that quiet, reader types are also happy at Wheaton, and that "we have a mix of 'A,' 'B,' and 'C' students, "but mostly 'A.' "

They study hard. An academician there for a weekend conference asked after going to the library, "What kind of students do you have here? The library is full on Saturday morning!"

These students also have to make up their own minds. As a freshman, said another senior, she was frustrated when a professor didn't take a stand on an issue and made the class decide on its own answers. And there is much discussion in the dorms about questions raised in class. She gave a description of the school echoed by others when she said:

"I think a unique part of school is integrating values into academic studies. And I think Wheaton is unique among Christian schools in that we're not only to learn what we believe, but also what other philosophies are so that you have a full understanding of what you believe. If you know only your own fundamentals you can't relate to other people's perspectives, and you see that because of the different backgrounds here. Our beliefs have to prove themselves in the marketplace."

To a visitor several other things are apparent. One is the students' conservatism; three seniors planning to go into public relations all wanted to work for conservative political groups that deal with issues important to the family, such as the Heritage Foundation. One didn't want to work for a Christian organization because "I don't think we should have all the people with morals in one group."

Another is the commitment to service; many go into teaching or ministries. A pre-med senior said he wants to practice in some underprivileged rural area. Great numbers do volunteer work and enroll in a program that prepares them for helping careers in Third World countries.

And the students come across as likable, clean-cut, all-American kids who very much know who they are, and judging from most of those I talked to, why they are here: to improve things, not by evangelizing but by helping.

The faculty of this Christian school could be switched with that of almost any other school in this book and no one would be able to tell the difference, in their affection for their students, their scholarly standards, or their sense of humor. "Nurture" was a word heard as often here as on any other campus, and as elsewhere, professors said in effect that they were in surrogate parent roles. Not only did they frequently have students to their homes for dinner or dessert, go on hikes or picnics with them, or provide help in the evening, but they made it clear that the reason they were here was because "I love these kids."

There is much student-faculty research, and a good many resulting papers are presented at professional meetings. There is—as elsewhere—much collaborative learning because they've found that a person learns more working in a group than in isolation. The school is changing tactics to take advantage of this new wisdom, even though there's always the problem, as Dean Kriegbaum noted, of some pulling harder than others.

To hold his job a faculty member must be a teacher first. Before he or she even gets a job the prospect has to pass muster in an interview with students at lunch. But to get tenure he needs to get recognition beyond the campus in his or her scholarly field.

Professors from a dozen disciplines were at pains to say there was no indoctrination, that they were trying to prepare people for a new world of job mobility and where "they will have to understand where the other guy is coming from."

Although ethics is emphasized across the curriculum, what they called the single most important thing in the curriculum was not religious studies at all, but an innovative new program in Third World issues called Human Needs and Global Resources. After 14 to 18 hours of course work, there's a six-month internship in Third World clinics and schools. The object is to learn about the local culture so as to be able to give help intelligently within that cultural context. This program equips graduates to work in the Third World with missions, development groups, governments, or international organizations, or for a variety of graduate studies. As faculty at other colleges have testified about theirs, Wheaton's students come back "transformed" by the foreign experiences, which fully a third of the students have.

Another imaginative program run by the chair of the music conservatory is a concentration in arts management. A collaborative enterprise of the music, theater, business, and economics departments, it prepares graduates for careers in the burgeoning field of managing orchestras, ballets, theatrical, or other cultural enterprises.

Of long standing is the Christian Sports Ministry, which originated at Wheaton in the 1940s, with track coach and alumnus Gil Dodd, the world's greatest miler of his time, and by Billy Graham, a fellow graduate. The object is not to create a distinction between sports and ministry, but as elsewhere, to affect its values.

Wheaton assumes a set of beliefs in the youths it accepts, but thenceforward it sees its role as nurturing both moral and intellectual growth and development. And each person is to arrive at his or her own judgments and answers. As Dean Kriegbaum said, "We hope they'll be lifelong learners. What they're learning will change, but what they do with their philosophy will be important."

College of Wooster

Wooster, Ohio

The College of Wooster is my original best-kept secret in higher education; for 30 years I've been telling clients that. As I have gotten to know what it accomplishes I can testify there is no better college in the country. Its record is unmatched in turning out scientists, scholars, and other kinds of achievers and contributors to society by multiplying the talents of "B" and "C" as well as "A" students.

Its 320-acre spread, 40 miles south of Cleveland, complete with golf and cross-country skiing courses, looks like it was built by and for millionaires; it is a quintessential college campus. I was struck by its charm on my first visit in the '70s, and even more impressed 20 years later by its expanded grounds, new facilities, and what it has done to protect the area of that attractive town near the campus.

Perhaps a couple hundred or more of my young friends have gone there. Not only do virtually all of them graduate, but I get such comments from their parents as, "Wooster turned Tania's life around, and she still has ties there," or "Wooster is one school I'm giving money to; our other two daughters didn't have such good experiences at Sarah Lawrence or the University of Virginia." A transfer from Davidson wrote me at the end of his first term, "I have noticed quite a difference between Wooster and Davidson. I feel as if there is a much better social life here and I have already made many friends. Academically the work is just as challenging as at Davidson. Also, there doesn't seem to be the rift between the faculty and students that existed at Davidson. The professors here are more personable and seem more motivated. My grades, of course, were affected positively and I earned a 3.4 average. I am impressed by the [baseball] coach just as I am impressed by all of the people at Wooster."

Things like this happen because Wooster is that unusual college with a sense of mission: to produce educated, not trained, people. "Our goal," said Dr. Henry Copeland, a tennis buff and that rare college president with an educational vision, "is a reflective life" and the development in each student of "the sense of self-possession and critical distance which permits an individual to resist involuntary servitude to the intellectual fashions of the day." Besides that, he will have a powerful ability to achieve his goals.

Dr. Copeland rounded out 25 years as president in June 1995 and, unlike so many upwardly mobile college presidents looking for prestige jobs, went back to teaching—history. At commencement, the senior class of 365 gave him a tennis racquet and one by one tossed 364 tennis balls into a large basket on the platform.

Wooster has been producing achievers for a long time; it's a college that has never been particularly selective, often accepting 80% to 90% of its applicants, yet it ranks number 11 among all the 914 colleges in the country in the percentage of graduates who go on to get Ph.D.s. And it has done this for three-quarters of a century, ever since the National Academy of Sciences started keeping tabs in 1920. In percentage of chemistry Ph.D.s it is third in the nation. It also ranks in the top half of 550 colleges whose graduates become executives in leading corporations. Its graduates have been presidents of MIT, Washington University, and the University of Washington, among others, and one was a Nobel Laureate.

Just one of the reasons for Wooster graduates' achievements lies in its senior-year requirement: an original project and a 100-page thesis. It may be scientific research, or a play, or any good idea in between. The entire college experience culminates in this, for the faculty as well as for the students.

This project fosters creativity, resourcefulness, and self-reliance, all attributes students will need in this new world. They have much control over their educational experiences; they can design their own courses or even their major. They have access to a wide variety of internships in government or major companies, as well as foreign study programs, some of which are provided by the college and others by the Great Lakes Colleges Association.

Something important is said about the Wooster experience when more professors and administrators in the Great Lakes Colleges Association send their children to Wooster than to any of the other 12 colleges in that very good consortium.

Wooster is looking for people with potential. They may have had mediocre high school records, as some of my clients have had, but if there is promise of performance Wooster will take a careful look. It will say no if the prognosis isn't promising; some years it has accepted only 60% of its applicants, but often it accepts 80%.

Seventy-five percent of students are on financial aid averaging $10,000 a year for the need-based and about $3,000 a year for the merit aid. Wooster offers so many scholarships ranging up to full tuition that the $3000 average tends to be an underestimate.

Although Wooster has always been innovative and a pacesetter, it did not try to make itself known until the college-going rush was well under way a few decades ago. Its faculty members haven't had to get into the Federal competition for research grants because Wooster has the most generous leave and research-funding program in the world. Not even Harvard's matches it. Not surprisingly, Wooster's faculty does more research than most others, including prestigious Oberlin's.

In Wooster's program, more than 10% of its faculty is on leave every year. Every fifth year a professor can submit a proposal to a faculty committee for a year of study on full pay. Usually there are 16 or 17 proposals, of which 15 will be approved. And if he or she wants to spend a year in Moscow, or study Eastern European countries' transition from Communism, for example, a rich endowment fund will provide the several thousand dollars needed for travel.

The program is also unique in that its purpose is to enable

professors to get all juiced up to work with seniors on their independent study projects. It is not designed to create new knowledge; "we're underwriting no patents in chemistry," said Dr. Copeland. "It's to help them do a better job. After a year in Moscow, you can imagine how excited a professor would be to work with a student whose independent study project is on Russia."

Right from the start, in 1870, Wooster considered the education of women and blacks to be as important as that of white males. Back then, coeducation was a controversial topic and its early doom was widely predicted. A dozen years later Wooster, then a university, not only awarded the first Ph.D. ever given to a woman but was turning out women graduates who made careers for themselves in foreign missions, founding colleges, administering hospitals, and managing printing firms, often doing abroad what they could not do in this country. And female graduates still have path-breaking careers in business, higher education, and diplomacy.

Wooster also has the distinction of being the only institution in the country to have deliberately chosen to change its status from a university to a college, and to have considered that a step forward. By the time of World War I, the college of arts and sciences was a minor part of a medical school and seven other divisions. But its faculty had a vision, and, bucking the wisdom of the day, started a long fight to make it purely an undergraduate liberal arts college.

Today, with more and more colleges becoming vocational training or pre-professional institutions like the universities, Wooster is one of fewer than 60 colleges that gives at least 90% of its degrees in the liberal arts.

Dr. Copeland says about his college: "You need 'A' students; they are essential to the mix. And Wooster, like many others, offers merit scholarships to get them. As a result, Wooster has a range of students, in ability as well as economic, cultural, and geographic backgrounds. The Woosters and the Hirams of the world have students who are just as bright as any in the world and who could have gone to Harvard, Yale, or Princeton. And we have faculty members who can deal with such a mix of students. We want faculty members who can deal successfully with the best students and inspire them, and we also want faculty members who are capable of inspiring and developing the underachievers.

"Wooster can take kids with native intelligence who for some reason have never developed, and turn them on. What Wooster does differently is independent study; each student needs to learn to make up his own mind. Our message is articulated so clearly. We are successful with a certain kind. All of the colleges in this band [of selectivity] are offering something that's a treasure; we can do some things for you here that Yale can't do. What we do for your kids is a liberal education. We give students standing ground, intellectual self-possession; you can make up your own mind, be critical and analytical. We do a better job than Yale," where his own son had "a miserable education."

Stanton Hales, the academic vice president, an Olympic badminton player who had taught at Pomona (the Amherst of California) for 23 years, said Wooster is every bit as impressive in what it does for students. The range of ability is broader at Wooster and "there's an intangible spirit of 'hey, let's try that.' They don't squelch ideas and are open to new ones. Students know they're going to be called upon to be creative. They have to show something and they grow up in the process. This is a place of high expectations."

Wooster's dean of admissions, Dr. Hayden Schilling, is not only a distinguished professor of British history but a tennis coach who produces winning teams.

The smorgasbord of testimonies of a dozen faculty members who had taught at many places, including Stanford, Pomona, Illinois, Emory, Chicago, New York University, Carleton, and the University of North Carolina, gives some insights into why Wooster is a place that doubles talents and changes lives. I wish every high schooler picking a college could read what the people who have taught at the prestige colleges and universities have to say:

- "The Pomona students' approach to the professors was different; they had a sense of entitlement; 'I've paid so much to come here I don't deserve a C in this class.' You don't get that here. You have to work harder here but the rewards are greater when the students finally get it; their sense of appreciation is so much more."

- "There's a lack of pretension here. There are some who come to be credentialed but they all have to take the responsibility for meeting a challenge with a major piece of work that's going to take an entire year, in which they deal with a significant question, marshal the arguments, and present the evidence. If they go on to graduate school it's a leg up. And if they don't, if somebody asks 'What did you get out of college?' he can hold up this. The challenge is there for everyone."

- "We have a phrase in our college culture: 'the Wooster success story.' My favorite is a student who's practically flunking German but who is working so hard and he's coming to me, and if he's willing to give it the time, I am too. It's about students who are not particularly gifted but who make it. The faculty is here to give that kind of encouragement."

- "People in the Midwest come to college for somewhat different reasons than in the coastal culture of the East. In the East going to college assures your success. My friends in high school who went to the Ivies weren't bright; they were wealthy."

- "A former student of mine, now a university department head, said that going to Wooster exposed him to a quite different range of people in ability,

background, and attitudes than had he gone to an
Ivy League school. At Wooster students are naive
enough that they feel comfortable in asking questions; they don't have the same inhibitions. They're
more open."

- "Students here are engaged in the process of their
own education. There's no such thing as a foolish
question. If you've done your homework and it's a
question to you, it bothers somebody else. And
when a prof is teaching out of his field in a freshman seminar it's a case of 'we're all learning together.' That brings a kind of humility to the
shared joys of this new enterprise."

- "The great satisfaction here is in the act of learning and understanding it and being able to apply it,
not just learning it and stuffing it away. One of my
majors last year who got honors is another Wooster
success story. In his first year, he was one of the
worst students, but he got excited about a problem, was allowed to use creativity to approach it,
and he did a fantastic job."

- "These students are having a cracking good time;
there's something very playful about the best of our
students, and that is what helps keep us on our
toes. They challenge our positions and I reserve
the right to be wrong. And there's an atmosphere
here that encourages that. We're constantly being
surprised; I love to encourage half-baked ideas and
I love being argued out of my position. It's sort of
liberating; it's a lot of fun teaching here. It's de-
pressing when people are trying to guess your position."

Even a coach doesn't have to have a winning record. "If the
morale is good and the players are having fun, the coach
doesn't have to have a good won-lost record," was how Dr.

Copeland put it. What happened in a basketball game several years ago is illustrative. The opposing team was playing so dirty the Wooster coach called time out and said to the players, "Gentlemen, I have nothing to say about basketball just now. I want to say if you remember nothing more from your years at Wooster and playing basketball here, I want you to remember this is a class institution and we want to be a class basketball team. Now go out there and show those guys how class people play basketball." They won the game.

In almost 30 years just one client of mine has wanted to transfer from Wooster. During the Thanksgiving holiday she complained that the social life was inadequate. I told her to send me her transcript and we'd discuss options at Christmas-time. I never heard from her again; she got a boyfriend. Now she's a Wooster alumna. Usually my clients visit several colleges and report, "Wooster's a *good* school!" Parents without exception feel they've been warmly received and well-cared-for by admissions people as interested in helping their child as in talking about their college.

The differences between the reactions of students and faculty members were largely governed by youthful enthusiasm. One boy expressed the consensus of many others with, "The professors all know you by name. It's a great place! It's exactly what I was looking for!"

They all spoke of how Wooster had made them examine their values, broaden their views and accept those of others, and realize how important people are to each other. One transfer from the University of California at Berkeley said, when I asked him what Wooster had done for him, "So much I want to stay. I'm leaving now for graduate school but I want to come back. I wasn't a geology major to begin with but I was turned on by a class."

Among those who had been made aware of interests they didn't know they had was a lovely, lively African-American. A top student in her Atlanta prep school class who had been voted most likely to succeed and was wooed by many colleges, she had come to Wooster planning to be a lawyer. But a freshman art history class was so fascinating that became her major instead of political science.

A young man from Virginia found Wooster "everything it said it was; everything I envisioned, as contrasted with conservative Washington and Lee where everybody is exactly the same." A young woman from India was bringing her sister the following fall because the school had done so much for her.

They all valued Wooster for what it had done to give them new powers and new confidence, to help them think critically, to live the reflective, responsible life, to learn how to change and adapt no matter what, and to land on their feet.

Austin College
Sherman, Texas

T he word that best describes the lovely 60-acre enclave of Austin College's world in Sherman, Texas,
is "exemplar," which means ideal, model, pattern. If I were advising a high school senior trying to decide whether to go to
Austin or to Cornell, Penn, Brown, Yale, Harvard or some other
fancy name, I would tell him or her this:

This 150-year-old community of learning, with its 1,200 students, will excite you, stretch you, expand your world, and
make you believe in yourself. This college does marvelous
things to multiply talents and to develop character, something
of no particular concern to the name brands.

Some day, if reality should dispel myth, people will know
that Austin—and colleges like it—have a special magic the
prestige ones don't. You will find the work is harder than at
Cornell or at Penn, and so is the grading. More is expected of
you; you can't hire somebody to take notes for you. Austin will
do more to give you a successful and satisfactory life.

What a high school senior, especially one with an SAT verbal of 500 and a B average, simply cannot imagine is that by
the time a diligent student is an Austin senior his work will be

as good as, or maybe better than, an Ivy senior's who had a 700 or 750 verbal and an A average. Here's some evidence:

The professor in charge of international programs had been curious to find out how Austin students stacked up against those of the highly selective Eastern colleges. She was told by the director of the London program of the Institute of European Studies that Austin students' work was better than that of Haverford or Williams students. It was partly because the Austin students weren't as impressed with themselves, and partly because they had been encouraged to think and to look around a little bit rather than to try to finish the paper that afternoon.

An obviously tough German professor who had taught at Texas and at Williams said the Williams students "were very aggressive, very-well prepared, worked very hard [the Texans were laid back]. When I compare them with the students here, there's a wider range of ability, so it includes people who are very good and some who aren't so good academically. But at the end, in the quality of the research paper that's done I can see very little difference."

"What does this say about our SAT system," the first professor asked, "when you also consider how the graduates of colleges like Austin are more productive or contribute more?" The conclusion is obvious. What it says about SATs as a measure of a person's potential is pretty devastating. It's a phony, one-dimensional measure that serves a competitive, status industry.

At Austin you will have great teachers; they will want to stretch you, and they will want to be your friends. They got their doctorates from, and now could be teaching at, those other places. They just think what they're doing here is more important.

At Austin you will not be cheated, as you will at any of the others, by trying to understand instructors who can barely speak English, by being second-class citizens who get only teaching assistants, by being caught in a competition for grades, or by being unable to have any kind of conversation with a professor.

Nor will you spend four years passively taking notes at lectures. You will be actively involved in your own education, which is the only way, no ifs, ands, or buts. At Austin, in the fall you will take a freshman seminar with 13 others on some contemporary issue to develop writing, speaking, and research skills. The instructor becomes the mentor for that group, the person with whom you plan your program and to whom you must report at least once each semester.

The other requirements are three terms of Western Heritage, and distribution requirements that will expose you to the arts, sciences, social sciences, and philosophy or religion. There is much freedom of choice, and beyond these you may plan your own major, do one-on-one directed or independent study projects you plan yourself, and you may even get into a collaborative research project with one of your professors.

A January term offers all kinds of exciting off-campus as well as on-campus opportunities to go to exotic places or to try something completely different. Austin offers a rich variety of foreign study programs in the fall and spring terms in England, France, Germany, Austria, Spain, Japan, and Singapore.

Also very important is the fact that students cooperate and collaborate. A faculty member said, "We like to encourage the idea that education is not a competitive activity." They've succeeded. As others nodded, a senior girl said, "You hear a lot about cutthroat competition for grades at other schools where you have 400 in a class graded on a bell curve. I've never experienced that here. There's never a bell curve; here we're helping each other get into medical school." In some courses, a junior girl said, you can't make it through unless you have a study group. There is also an honor code, which students said is observed.

If you should ever need help it will be there in full measure, but the chances are the Austin professor will have anticipated your needs. Why? In class he doesn't need to call roll; he knows you're there; he calls you by your first name. He may have guessed your need when he and his wife had you and a couple of others over for dinner or dessert or a cook-out. Students told me that most teachers will come back after hours to help you study, or come in on weekends to help you, "even at ten o'clock at night, and they give you their home phone numbers."

After graduation, when you come back to campus you may have to decide at which professor's home you might have dinner or spend the night. If anything like this were ever to happen at the big name places, or the University of Texas, you could account it a miracle.

Austin accepts more than 80% of its applicants, 90% of whom are from Texas, 16% are minorities. If more people knew about it, it would have 50% out-of-staters because it is such an outstanding academic as well as financial bargain. Sixty-five percent get need-based financial aid, and 80% get some form of aid.

What kind of person would be happy here? Any student planning to go to a mainstream college would find happiness here, whether from the Northeast, Southeast, Midwest, or Far West. This was as friendly, open, and accepting a community as I've seen anywhere, and far more so than most. The kids simply are very nice people.

It ought to be clear that this kind of college isn't for the person who has to have the football weekend extravaganza; he won't be satisfied just watching students play for the fun of it.

This school is for those whose priorities are in order. The only ones who wouldn't be happy here, students agreed, would be those who wouldn't be happy at most of the other good small colleges in this book. Those who don't want to get involved, those who live off campus and want to go home on weekends, or who can't relate to other people—who aren't involved in the life of the community—are not affected by the college experience. They are the ones who feel negative, or drop out, or fail. The satisfied students are always the ones who participate, who make it their life.

Two exceptional juniors, a Latino boy who plans to help other Latinos get a leg up, and an African-American girl, said Austin had changed their lives. The girl said, "Coming here was a big change, it was a white majority but everyone is so accepting I feel like I'm in a majority. When other blacks asked me why I didn't go to a black school I said I wanted the best education, so I came here because I'm going to be competing in a white world. My roommate feels the same way."

This sense of family was one of the big attractions for several others. Two seniors who'd been marked for the University of Texas because their parents had gone there were converted when they visited. As one said, "I could just feel the sense of community; second, it was one of the few schools with an international relations program, and it was easy to get involved here. You can start a group with two people."

The other, a football player, said there wouldn't be so many college transfers or dropouts if teenagers were smarter consumers and looked at themselves and then visited colleges. Then they'd go to places like Austin, he said, "but instead they go where their friends are going and wind up going to three or four schools or dropping out."

Many of the faculty—as at other colleges in this group—had planned to stay a few years and then move on to a university, but got hooked by the place and the people. They talked with obvious pride and pleasure about their students. One said, "We enjoy our students. I like the contact here. There's hardly a week goes by I don't hear, by phone, by mail, by office visit from someone who graduated last year, five years ago, ten years ago, fifteen years ago. And the continuing interest that I have is finding ways to open doors for our students that their life experience up to this point just hasn't opened."

A chemistry professor who 24 years ago had planned to stay a couple of years and then go to the West Coast, his home area, said, "We are particularly effective in polishing up what you might call these diamonds in the rough. They may come from high schools that weren't particularly demanding and suddenly the level of expectation is high. We've been effective partly because of our accessibility and partly because the freshman seminar gets them off to a good start and gives them a real adrenaline rush because they realize there's a level of expectation they've never had to contend with. Then they're off and running. I told my freshman class they were going to give up memorizing and learn to think. At evaluation at the end of the term at least a third thanked me and said they had begun to think."

An English professor said the story of one of her students illustrates how a college like Austin works its magic. "At some competitive place—she was like a tightwire anyway—she would have become more and more aggressive in trying to figure out what the party line was and then trying to beat it. But here it is not competitive, it is collaborative and cooperative, and what has happened is that she has learned to open her mind, relax a little bit, and trust herself."

Students I talked with, most of whom were juniors and seniors, echoed all the good things their teachers had said. Every one said emphatically they would attend if they had it to do over again. They reported they had learned to trust their own minds, to take a chance, and they had been broadened by the general education requirements and by the enthusiasm of their teachers in ways they wouldn't have been at a university. The foreign study terms, the international relations program, and even the service experiences evoked especially good testimonials.

One senior said, "Austin has affected me because I've gotten interested in history and psychology, and I hated history in high school. Working in Habitat for Humanity also affected me; I wouldn't have done that anywhere else. I tried to explain to my parents how contact with other peoples and other conditions was necessary today."

Several said the ease of getting involved had not only given them a lot of pleasure but had also developed their abilities to work with people and improved their leadership skills. Uniformly they felt they had powers they hadn't had a few years ago. And whether prompted or not, they talked about their teachers. One girl said, "I'll be in touch with faculty members over the next few years while I'm working, and when I want recommendations they will remember me and be able to give me good ones." Another boasted, "One of my profs is going to be in my wedding."

For many years I had been aware that Austin was a first-rate school, but until I spent a day there I hadn't been able to know how very special a community it was. It is one of those that is doing the essential work of producing the enlightened, responsible, creative people with moral compasses who make democracy work. We need many more colleges like it.

St. John's College
Annapolis, Maryland, and Santa Fe, New Mexico

S t. John's, one of the two most intellectual (and indispensable) American colleges—along with Reed—has no majors or electives; it has one mission, one curriculum, one catalog; and it has two campuses, two presidents, two faculties, and student bodies that may freely move from one to the other. This unusual duality is the result of the expansionist mood of the '60s when education was a booming industry and the college heads in Annapolis, Maryland, decided to install a clone on a Santa Fe, New Mexico, mountain.

Many years ago as education editor of *The New York Times* I went to Annapolis to do a Sunday article on the coming of age of the St. John's Great Books program in which everyone confronted the greatest minds of Western Civilization by discussing 100 great books. They also took four years each of science, mathematics, and language, and two of music. Grades were neither issued nor discussed, only recorded for graduate school purposes, and they depended on total performance, emphasizing contribution in class discussions, rather than exams. The most important form of evaluation was the Don Rag, in which each student met with all his tutors at the end of each semester for a no-holds-barred discussion of him and his work.

St. John's, founded in 1696 as King's School, became a different kind of college in 1937 with the introduction of this radically classical program. There were no choices and no one could transfer in. All students had to start at the beginning. Even so, nearly a third of the student body were—and are today—transfers who found the ideal college, some after spending three years at another. There are no faculty ranks, and there is no need to publish; their role is to stimulate. All are tutors who may lead discussion in a Greek or literature class this year and in a Ptolemyic geometry class a few years hence. It is a true community of learning, one of only 450 students.

My newspaper story was calmly descriptive but I came away a zealot. This was the kind of education Jefferson had in mind as the sine qua non for American democracy. As democracy's problems grow more complex this kind of education grows more necessary.

As an educational adviser, whenever possible I have persuaded young friends to go to St. John's. One year there were a mathematically improbable eight, two of whom were deep into specialties, one in French literature, and the other in the study of butterflies. They were able to pursue their special interests later and, like their lives, more effectively. At the end of that season, the admissions director said, "Amazing! That's 10% of my freshman class!"

St. John's charming tidewater Colonial campus in Annapolis, with its ancient trees and mix of historic and modern buildings, is on a Severn River tributary. Next door is quite a different place, the Naval Academy. On as dramatically beautiful a campus as any in the country, nestling on the shoulders of Monte Sol in the southeast corner of Santa Fe, New Mexico, a student body of like size is wrestling with the same questions of the human condition.

Intellectually demanding and intense, as it is, St. John's is not selective; it is selected. It accepts 80% to 85% of its applicants, who demonstrate whether they belong there by writing as many as six to ten pages about themselves, sometimes more. Most years a modest 20% to 30% of their applicants will be in the top 10% of their high school classes, compared with Harvard's 95%. More than half the applicants will have verbal SAT scores of more than 600, sometimes nearly three-quarters will.

But scores are not essential. The St. John's criteria are radically basic. What is essential is "desire more than brilliance." A tutor who served as admissions director several years ago insisted that St. John's was as valuable and as necessary for the person with a 500 verbal as for one with a 600 or 700. Dr. Eva Brann, dean at Annapolis, adds, "It is, in fact, a rare tragedy that a person wants to learn here and is unequal to the program on some respectable level. Weaker students may, for example, ask the most useful questions. Moreover, our communal style of learning is antithetical to competition—to competition, not to distinction."

Presidents or deans at most colleges would about as soon admit to taking syphilitics as "B" students, but when Dean Brann was asked what kind of student they wanted, she said, "All we want is people who read and who can do a little mathematics."

St. John's has no need of Establishment pretensions for it produces future scientists and scholars, winners of such things as the major graduate fellowship awards and Rhodes Scholars, at a rate higher than any Ivy school. It turns out writers because good writing is 80% good thinking, and it produces a disproportionately large number of future math Ph.D.s even though there is no math major.

It should be clear that this is a place only for those who read and who are interested in ideas and fundamental questions. The interested person can find out for certain whether St. John's is for him or her by going through the most sensible college-visiting program in the country. In a two-day period the visitor goes through the whole regimen, classes and formal Great Books lecture-discussion. For the latter he gets the reading assignment in advance but may not take part in the discussion. If he gets hooked, he can have an admissions interview and probably be admitted; if not, he should look elsewhere because there is no middle ground; it's excitement or misery.

The students come from every state and nine other countries, and aside from a common interest in ideas, they are as diverse as any group. Although there are no intercollegiate sports, there are as many kinds of intramural and club teams as there are people interested in playing them. Boating and water sports are popular in Annapolis, and one can even build a boat while there. Santa Fe has, naturally, a great outdoors program, with hiking, skiing, climbing, and so on.

Well over half the students get need-based aid averaging more than $12,000 a year.

I recently made my third visit to Annapolis, and my first to Santa Fe, but thought the word would be heard more clearly if it came from someone under 30. She's a former client, Mrs. Virginia Beck, who works and lives in Albuquerque, and she said to me, "I simply couldn't produce an impersonal report of this school, especially not when I spent my whole two days there trying to figure out how I could manage to go there myself . . .

"I first visited St. John's on a clear spring Sunday. The campus was quiet and my visit was brief but two things impressed me. The license plates in the student parking lot came from all over North America, indicating an eclectic mix of students who had traveled far specifically to study at St. John's. The second thing was the atmosphere. St. John's Santa Fe campus is at an altitude of 8,000 feet. The clean, thin air acts as a magnifying glass; pine needles and shadows are distinct from hundreds of feet away. Such clear vision can't help making you feel smarter, more aware, and it was inspiring. Studying at St. John's would be like climbing the mountain to study with Socrates.

"I later went back for a real visit. I spent two days on campus, observing classes and a Friday night seminar and talking to students. I was there just before finals, and while the stress level was high, all the students I met were enthusiastic about their studies and happy to explain what it was like to attend such an unusual school.

"I can testify to many problems with being an undergraduate at a big-name university. My main problem was so big I never recognized it while I was there, and it came from not knowing as much as I thought I did. In graduate school and later, out in the working world, I realized that despite all the classes on all the topics that had interested me so much, I had very little idea of the Big Picture. I had read and learned little pieces of history, literature, science, and philosophy, but I had no way of fitting those pieces into any larger order.

"The Big Picture means 'everything.' It's what the great modern physicist Stephen Hawking says we would understand if, impossibly, we could comprehend every bit of information in the universe for even a second. The Big Picture shows the connection between, say, mathematical logic, Pablo Picasso, and World War I. No one has ever drawn or been able to describe the Big Picture, but for 2,000 years Western civilization has evolved because certain people needed to know more about it. Those great thinkers have investigated the Big Picture from a million angles and have discovered a lot of new territory. You can follow any of those angles at almost any college or university in the country, but only St. John's will give you a guided tour.

"St. John's students are self-selected. It would be hard to convince most high school seniors that four years of college could be fun without frat parties or varsity sports when attendance is required at Friday night seminars and everyone has to do things like study (and even write) classical music. St. John's is a school for the intellectual explorer, the student who likes math because it makes sense or who reads Dickens because he's a good writer.

"For those students, it's important to emphasize the value of a St. John's education. After four years here, you need not find yourself in the fabled position of the Ph.D. washing dishes for a living. The unusual curriculum, with its complete lack of electives and its seemingly outdated reliance on the 100 Great Books, is designed as a tool for each student to use in his own self-development. Simply put, at the end of your four years you should know what you like and what you're good at. Without seeing the whole thing, you should be able to find your place in the Big Picture, should know how to conduct your own explorations.

"The experience of my student guides illustrates the success of St. John's in helping its students figure themselves out. My guides were twin sisters who had started college at the same time, one at St. John's in Santa Fe and one at MIT. The difference in their freshman-year experiences was huge. During my first day's tour, the original St. John's sister told me how she had convinced her MIT twin to transfer, 'just in talking on the phone about the discussions we were having in class and about the kinds of things I was starting to think about.' Those telephone calls often became long-distance debates and discussions themselves, and the MIT sister finally decided she wanted to experience them for herself.

"On my second day, I asked the MIT transfer twin whether she missed MIT. She had gone there to study science but found, she said, that her classes taught her certain facts but didn't help her understand why those facts were true. At St. John's she was learning the same facts, but here the facts were by-products of understanding the concepts. Plus, she said, she was always amazed at how much the classes that at MIT would be labeled the 'liberal arts' helped her understand science. (Pythagoras would not have been surprised; he was as much a philosopher as a mathematician.)

"Even with a year's credit from MIT, the transfer twin had to start at St. John's as a freshman. All St. John's graduates study the same four-year program, thus ensuring everyone not only a quality education but the opportunity to talk to almost anyone on campus about almost anything. St. John's is a true intellectual community. As a sophomore, the original St. John's sister found that she and her freshman twin had plenty to talk about and teach each other. 'It was illuminating for both of us. She was taking classes I had already taken, but it was never like I knew more than she did. She was thinking new things, and since I was a year further along, I could help point out where those concepts and ideas were going to be important. We had a really great year.'

"St. John's is proud to point out, especially I think to parents, that 80% of its graduates go on to graduate school or to study medicine or law. I'm interested in knowing about the other 20%. This is a school that inspires self-confidence, that makes its students believe they can do anything. While that one student in five may look like an underachiever, I'm willing to bet that's the one who has chosen not to follow even the road less taken but is exploring a new angle, a new way to glimpse the Big Picture. Those are the thinkers who will boost us past our fuel, pollution, population, and financial crises into the next millennium; you might be one of them."

Mrs. Beck would have seen and heard the same kinds of things had she visited Annapolis. The testimony of the MIT twins recalls one of my favorite comments from an Annapolis student of about ten years ago. At lunch at a table with eight students, I asked two transfers from Berkeley if it didn't bug them that they couldn't have a course in psychology under someone like the late Eric Erickson at Harvard, then at his peak of fame. "Oh no," they said simultaneously, "we can go to the library and read all that." The others at the table agreed; they made it clear they were engaged in a more important search.

Southwestern University

Georgetown, Texas

S outhwestern University, which encompasses 500 acres of pleasant Georgetown, Texas, a half-hour drive from Austin, is the story of an exciting transformation. Chartered as the state's first university in 1840, until the 1970s it was doing the conventional thing, providing the B.A. union card for its graduates' first jobs. Then, with the catalysts of the new president's vision and the generosity of three Texas foundations, it was born again as a place to prepare for the 21st century.

It takes money, lots of it, to make the kind of top-drawer liberal arts college that President Roy B. Shilling envisioned. Luckily, the Brown Foundation wanted to stimulate giving from alumni of Texas colleges, which had been uniformly low. The Houston Endowment and Cullen Educational Trust were also interested in Southwestern's rebirth. A matching-grant-fund drive doubled and then quadrupled foundation shares as the college did its part. As a result, Southwestern has a still-growing endowment of $205 million, which ranks it among the top 30 colleges and well ahead of most universities.

With all this wealth Dr. Shilling brought in a young, first-rate faculty, created a new curriculum and foreign study programs, and built eye-popping new facilities. The striving for excellence also brought a $6.5 million grant from the Olin Foundation in New York for a state-of-the-art academic building with electronic classrooms. There is a new campus center, an enormous new physical education plant, new residence halls and apartments.

To cap all this, in 1994, Phi Beta Kappa, the scholastic honorary society, gave Southwestern the academic stamp of approval by installing a chapter there. Now it is one of the few jewels of the Southwest whose mission is to prepare a new generation to contribute to a changing society, and to prosper in their jobs, whatever and wherever in the world they may be.

Dean James W. Hunt explained, "We are well underway with an ambitious master planning process looking toward 2010 that will focus on preparing a new generation of leaders whose actions and values encourage contributions toward the welfare of humanity. Southwestern will eventually be recognized as a model for undergraduate liberal arts education."

The conviction on campus is, naturally, that the day has already arrived. Students wax enthusiastic about how close are their relations with their teachers and how strong is the sense of community. They use such phrases as "a new dynamism," and "a changing school." Faculty members talk about what good and interested kids their students are, about "the contagion here," and "the sheltering environment." When I asked the professor who had used that phrase if she would send her own daughter here, she said, "You bet! This is a safe place to be a college student. No sex problems here!"

Ninety percent of the freshmen return, and 70% of students graduate in four years. The retention rate for minority students is even higher than that for the whites. The director of institutional research said proudly, "We are providing the Hispanic leaders of the future."

The college has also seen new alumni interest and involvement. Not only has alumni giving tripled since the '70s, with many substantial gifts, but large numbers are coming back as volunteers. To meet the demand the college started a "days of service" program, but the trouble has been too many volunteers and too few jobs for them.

For now, but probably not for long, Southwestern accepts two-thirds of its applicants, so there's plenty of room for "B" students. Over 60% rank in the top 10% of their high school classes—many of which are small and rural—and over half have SAT verbal scores of more than 600.

Ninety percent of the 1,200 students come from Texas, a

statistic that fails to reflect the student body's actual diversity. Twenty percent are Latino and other minorities. A small percentage of students hail from 36 states and several foreign countries. In a conversation that included a half-dozen students, a Vietnamese senior said his only complaint about "a great school" was a lack of diversity, yet in that group were two Latinos, one African-American, and two whites. At any rate, the college is working to attract students from other parts of the country, and it will.

For out-of-staters, Southwestern is indeed a bargain, and nearly 60% of the students get need-based financial aid averaging a little more than $5,700 a year, with another 10% receiving merit scholarships averaging $2,800 a year.

Why is all this happening? Vice president William B. Jones, who doubles as institutional research director, noted, "We have a sheltering environment, plenty of resources, and a spirit of harmony. We change the perspectives of students. They may not come here with the same vision of doing good as the kids at Millsaps [in Mississippi where he had taught] but here they are awakened. International studies is now one of the top five majors, and 40% of the students have an overseas experience."

It is not only a sheltering but an uplifting environment in which students are given encouragement at every turn, so their self-confidence is reinforced by teachers who want to help. By contrast, said one professor, "at the University of Texas, if a student goes to a professor for help the reaction is likely to be, 'What? You don't know?' "

Just as important is the emphasis on values and on developing the whole person. Dr. Vicente Villa, a charismatic biology professor from a poor Mexican family who won the 1994 National Teacher of the Year award, echoed the views of his colleagues when he said, "We can address values here—unlike a university. There's a hunger and a thirst for it. There's much discussion of issues in class, which is a requisite. Southwestern is a changing school. There's a contagion here!"

Furthermore, he went on, as students develop they may

change majors or shift from pre-med to graduate school and a research or teaching career. Such things happen because their horizons are being widened and their aspirations raised by an energetic young faculty that most other colleges would envy. They are teacher-scholars good enough to be courted by research universities, which was where most of them had been planning to wind up. But something happened when they came to Southwestern, and 14 out of 15 have decided to stay. In a faculty of 112, all but a dozen have been there fewer than ten years. These young profs hadn't expected what changed their minds. After having had to lecture to apathetic classes as graduate assistants, they were confronted by eager, questioning learners. For a real teacher this is a wonderful but rare experience.

From the Southwestern students came emphatic confirmation of the feeling of family. Individual students I encountered crossing the campus and groups in formal discussion agreed that "the strongest feature of this place" and its great virtue is its ability to foster close bonds between students and their teachers. They mentioned being able to work on research projects with faculty members, having dinner at a professor's home, and valuing them as mentors and as friends. Others said their minds had been opened or that a professor's passion for his subject had struck a spark or changed a major.

Several made a point of expressing gratitude to the taskmasters who had inspired and pressured them to make their thinking and writing clear. Others volunteered that Southwestern had caused them to examine and become concerned about their value systems. The new Southwestern, they said, has become "dynamic, open-minded, and there is much sense of community," due in part, no doubt, to the broader view of the world instilled by the new foreign programs.

One of the smart things Dr. Shilling planned was to give students a role in choosing faculty. Every prospect has to teach a class, and the students' reaction is critical, for they not only serve on the search committees but they also vote in the hiring decisions. If the prospect is not the genuine teaching article, he's wasting his time coming to Southwestern.

It's not surprising that every professor I talked to thought highly of his or her young friends. Southwestern, they say, is getting a different type of student now, and his goals are being affected; he tends to choose a graduate rather than a professional school. One prof said, "They are bright and capable; they are also Southern and conservative and it takes longer to bring them out of their shells, but then they're on a par with the best mainstream liberal arts college kids. They are also very nice kids and very good achievers, really good kids."

Another added, "The value-added factor here is turning passive learners into active learners. So many of our graduates are successful. The percentage going to graduate school has about doubled."

Southwestern has done a near heretical thing in Texas by turning its athletic program upside down, ending athletic scholarships, and playing only genuine students on the varsity teams. Now, 92% of the students are on intercollegiate or intramural teams, a vast change that has contributed greatly to the sense of community.

The curriculum has also changed. There are strong general education requirements, beginning with a freshman symposium that develops critical and analytical thinking and requires frequent writing of papers. Along the way students must develop some familiarity with mathematics, the great ideas of Western civilization, and those of at least one other culture. They must take courses in science, the social sciences, and the arts—an area the college is especially proud of—as well as a values analysis course. Every senior must fashion a capstone experience for himself, a major project for the year, but there is great latitude. Depending on the department, it might be a research project or a creative work—an art work, a play, or a novel—but it must be a significant effort that brings together and applies what he has learned in his years there.

What faculty members said is true; the students are indeed

very nice kids and very friendly. That is why a senior girl who'd been accepted by three very selective schools chose Southwestern. She made three visits and every time "everyone was so friendly. I was really impressed that they would remember just a high school senior. The people here were attractive, the campus was attractive; I can't think of anything negative." After working for a year she planned to go to medical school, which had already accepted her. Another said that on her visit a philosophy professor took nearly two hours "to talk to a high school nobody from New Mexico. Now he's my adviser and I talk to him all the time."

Whether African-American, Asian-American, Latino, or white, all said it was a place that had helped them grow, given them self-confidence, and broadened their horizons and their view of the world. It had also made them realize the importance of friendship and of working in their community.

One result has been a surge in community service. In a student-initiated project, half the student body worked with residents of Georgetown to build a city park that has graphic displays on the history and heritage of the region and provides three hours of child care daily. Students also tutor in the public schools and repair homes of low income residents. After Hurricane Andrew, two busloads of students, faculty, administrators, and staff went to help repair the damage, another student-inspired project.

Southwestern is a warm and friendly place that evokes in its teenagers and in its teachers a pride in belonging, and for good reason. It will do the same for those who come from the North, the Midwest, the West Coast, or the Northwest. True, they might as freshmen find their classmates a tad more conservative than themselves, but also probably kinder, more tolerant, and considerate. Four years later as seniors they'll probably have found common ground, and those from afar may have acquired some of the warm virtues of their Southwestern friends as well as an exceptional four years of growth.

The Evergreen State College

Olympia, Washington

Nestled in 1,000 acres of towering forest six miles outside Olympia, Washington, 28-year-old Evergreen State College offers the most unusual undergraduate experience in the Northwest, or in any public institution anywhere. Along with Reed and Whitman, it's one of the three best in the Northwest. It opened in 1971 to prepare its young people to live effectively in a new kind of world. Taxpayers everywhere should demand colleges like this one that change their children's lives.

As one professor said, "I, we, came, come here committed to making a difference."

The campus is unlike any other. Modern concrete buildings and even the open spaces sometimes seem lost in the great evergreens. It also has more than a half-mile of waterfront on Puget Sound, and a demonstration organic farm used to teach students practical applications for the principles of sustainable agriculture.

The majestic setting gives a sense of being one with nature, and everything seems natural and unaffected. Relationships are on a first-name basis. Dress is casual, women wear no makeup or fancy hair-dos, and the few skirts were prairie length, just short enough to reveal the same kind of hiking boots or Reeboks the men were wearing below their jeans and lumberjacks. Backpacks were everywhere. Most of the faculty women wore skirts and the men were all in short-sleeved shirts open at the throat. Mine were the only jacket, tie, and city shoes on the campus.

Evergreen would be unusual anyplace. Instead of grades there are narrative evaluations by the teachers, and by each student of his or her work. Students also evaluate their professors. For a public institution it is more than unusual, it is unique, because values are as important as learning and public-service is strongly encouraged. It is a place where tolerance and civility constitute a social contract, because it is a community that values freedom. As at St. John's, there is a great deal of class discussion where ideas and points of view must be argued on their merits. "There is a good spirit here," said a dean, "our ability to argue and remain friends."

There is a group carrying a torch for every cause. A gay-lesbian alliance is just one of many groups with offices in the student union. The bulletin boards there were like soft sculptures, they were so thick with notices and calls to action, more even than in activist places like Antioch. Some appeared in every building, like the one calling for action to defeat Senator Slade Gorton because of his bad environmental record.

Evergreen appeals to the self-directed student with drive, the person who was unhappy in high school, or who wants to do things he can't do elsewhere. This is not the place for the person who can't help himself, for the person who needs a recipe, or for the passive note-taker. The Evergreen student has to be able to make some decisions. But he has some of the best help I've seen anywhere in the Evergreen catalog. It is a model of intelligent suggestions and guidance. It tells the student that the first order of business is to look at himself, decide what he wants, in college and in life, and make a plan. The plan may change over time, but its basic fundamentals won't, and they are detailed for his guidance, along with such solid tips as: go talk to faculty members, check with academic advising, support services, visit other offices. In short, be an active, do-it-yourself consumer.

After a first-year Core program of general education, the Evergreen student has great breadth of choice. He can choose from the menu of offerings in the catalog, or he can select from a whole curriculum of faculty-initiated and planned "coordinated studies programs." Registration is like a farmer's market with a great array of choices. At each table in the hall is a professor or two to explain the goal and the methods of this science, humanities, environmental, or other program. Some of them build on the Core program, some don't. The student has his pick. There is also an All-Level Program that mixes freshmen and advanced students.

Since there are no majors and no distribution requirements, students do design their own course of study, but it is not loose as ashes, as it is at some no-requirement colleges. The foundation of the curriculum is the planned offerings. Independent study is encouraged only for juniors and seniors. A faculty-planned offering in one area may involve study in several others the student may think are extraneous, but he will discover he was wrong.

Like the young planners at Antioch, Hampshire, and Marlboro, Evergreen students discover the interconnectedness of knowledge. "This," observed a chemistry professor, "is a very subtle requirement for breadth. As you get into a project you find you need to know a lot of things outside this particular area."

In its profile, Evergreen doesn't mention things like class rank or SAT scores of its freshmen, only that 87% of the applicants got in and a quarter of them were from out of state. Indeed, in a full day on campus talking to administrators, faculty, and students, I never once heard SATs, grade point averages, or class rank even mentioned. One girl did say she'd been a National Merit Scholar. The academic dean said, "We have the best luck with misfits." When faculty members were asked what kind of kid would prosper there, several agreed with one who said, "If you want to sit and have someone lecture to you, Evergreen is not the place for you." Others said, "They're risk-takers," or "There's an enormous range of abilities here," or "Our students are idealistic and impatient with the world. They want to do good, and two-thirds of them will do some significant service before they get out, and we have programs that require it."

Although two-thirds of the freshmen had B averages or better, a lot of those were from small rural high schools. The middle 50% had combined SAT scores in a very wide range: 1010 to 1240. What the applicant said about himself or herself, meaning what indication of real desire came through, was often much more important. Indeed, one faculty member said, "A lot of students here have flunked out of other colleges." But they have to bring their G.P.A. up to a 2.00 to be admitted.

About a quarter of the 3,200 students are older than 30, and 17% are minorities. More than three quarters get financial aid averaging more than $7,000 a year. The most unusual statistic is that 22% of the faculty are persons of color, ethnic Americans, of Asian, Pacific Island, African, American Indian, and Hispanic descent.

This is one of the rare places where older students not only feel at home but are also valued. Some professors spoke enthusiastically of their special contribution, especially in the seminars, which are the principal class form. Adults who are having successful careers often can offer authoritative, real-life observations that give the topic being discussed the shock of relevance it otherwise wouldn't have. "I have a mixed class of freshmen, sophomores, juniors, and seniors, and some adults who had degrees who added dashes of reality and real life to the discussions."

Evergreen encourages a freshman to enroll in a Core program, and after that the curriculum is pretty free form. But even the freshman Core is unusually flexible because each year faculty members get together and decide what topics should be focused on the following year, and, depending on his interests, a freshman might choose one involving physics or mathematics, a political or environmental problem, or any one of a number of other things. Each fall at registration time the students can shop around, questioning professors about what their Core has to offer. There may be 48 to 96 students in a given Core who will be team-taught by perhaps four professors from different disciplines. The individual class groups, or seminars, are 23 to 25. In some cases different seminars might meet together to give a broader, more interdisciplinary picture.

As a chemistry professor said, "The programs they choose are all broad interdisciplinary ones that include elements we think are important for their education. For example, in a program on ecology a student has to study biology, soils, chemistry, and have a seminar on the history of agriculture because it's part of the package in my program. They learn things they didn't expect to learn, and they may say, 'I didn't know this was part of ecological agriculture.'"

But the chemist would be only one member of a teaching team. For example, in a history of science and technology program there's an economist, a political scientist, a historian, and a historian of science.

An advanced student may agree on a program-of-study contract, not unlike the plans at Hampshire and Marlboro, with a professor in some broad area as listed in the catalog. At least half of the students have an internship in the field of their projects (compared to a national figure of 2%). Almost a third do independent study.

The contract plan has a powerful effect on the quality of teaching as well as on learning, because with each new contract with a student, the professor is faced with a new problem he has to cope with. It also means trade-offs. "I don't cover as much in chemistry as I did at Harvey Mudd. I have more time to worry if they can do something with their chemistry."

But apparently the professor needn't worry. Several faculty members told stories of employers wanting more Evergreen interns or employees because they can think and act on their own, because they're independent and have initiative. Also, a large percentage of Evergreen alumni have started their own businesses. Their testimony was in full accord with the findings of a 1991 survey of graduates and employers to prove to the legislature, and taxpayers, that Evergreen was giving them good value.

At the end of a semester, every student writes an evaluation of his work and of the teacher, and the teacher writes a page or two on the student. The students are often harder on themselves than are the faculty—which also happens at Hampshire and Marlboro. Faculty members say this is much more effective than letter grades, and I didn't run into any student who would have preferred letter grades; they were all firm believers in Evergreen's evaluation system.

There are precious few public institutions where the faculty feels as close to the students or values them as highly. Students and faculty host potluck dinners and take three-day field trips together. Also, the Core seminars and group projects provide opportunities for bonding. More than once I heard a professor say that people come to Evergreen because they want to make the world a better place to live, while at other places they were just preparing for jobs. They said they "loved" working with these kids, that they speak up, that they influence the courses and their content, and that they "are truly involved in their own education." A physics professor observed that this is the ideal place for those who want to do things they can't do anywhere else, adding, "We've done brain research here that students couldn't do elsewhere." Another said proudly, "My own kid is planning to come here."

The closest thing to a disaffected student I found was a junior changing her major to psychology who wished there'd been more general education requirements because now she has gaps to fill. All the others were enthusiastic about what the

Evergreen experience was doing for them, including a couple of recent graduates who'd come back just to have lunch. They said all kinds of things:

- "It has helped me figure out who I am and has taught me to analyze."
- "It has made me more well-rounded."
- "I like the diversity, and you can do what you want here—you can start a group or you can design your own program" (a girl from Mexico).
- "It teaches you how to go about learning. You learn in seminars how to present your own ideas, and the more you do the more you find you can do."
- "This is a good community; there's a good spirit here. Your opinion counts."
- "What it does for you is not described in the catalog, but it's to be able to think for yourself, and to think your opinion is valid."
- "It teaches communication skills. The classes are small group discussions and you're asked your opinion often. There are no cookbook courses; you help design your own, often in your first year."

The National Merit Scholar, a senior from Minneapolis who had chosen Evergreen over several prestige institutions, was editor of the school paper. Was she happy with her choice now? "Absolutely! I would do it all over again. But, it's really hard here if you don't know what you want or if you have to be pushed. But what you want may change. You have to think for yourself. The person who comes here should be a self-starter or have a willingness to ask for help—and there's a lot of help available."

Here, as at some of the other colleges in this book, the students feel they're a part of the institution and take great pride in it. They may in the past have been misfits or malcontents, but now they're movers, shakers, and people who are going to cause trouble because they'll see that the emperor has no clothes.

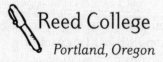

Reed College
Portland, Oregon

f you're a genuine intellectual, live the life of the mind, and want to learn for the sake of learning, the place most likely to empower you is not Harvard, Yale, Princeton, Chicago, or Stanford. It is the most intellectual college in the country—Reed, in Portland, Oregon.

Furthermore, Reed's president, Steven S. Koblik, was one of the few with the courage to refuse to participate in the *U.S. News and World Report*'s inherently phony idea of rating of colleges by statistical data, like trying to quantify a human being. The simplistic results do a great disservice to society. The magazine took its revenge in its ratings.

On the lovely 100-acre campus with great trees and expanses of lawn are slightly fewer than 1,300 students, but Reed has an unmatched record of turning out high achievers; winners of the major graduate fellowships, future scientists and scholars, and notables in many fields.

Then what is it doing in this book of colleges that take "B" students? Before long it won't be, for each year it gets more selective, but right now it is an admissions bargain. It is only 80 years old, and just in recent years, has become more widely known. A few years ago it got 800 applicants for a class of about 280. In 1994 it got 2,000 and accepted about 70%, but only 27% came. As its reputation catches up with reality, the numbers eager for the Reed experience will climb and the competition to get in will be a lot stiffer. Right now, 60% of the freshmen have SAT verbal scores over 600, 69% have math scores at least that high, and well more than half come from the top tenth of their high school classes.

It also has a number of students whose high school records were mediocre but who clearly had potential and gave some evidence they were ready to develop it. An administrator said, "We're looking for that crazily brilliant kid." One such was a junior who'd been a turned-off "D" student in high school, discovered Reed, spent a year proving himself in a junior college, and now rhapsodized, "This is paradise!" (Furthermore, Reed is paying three-fourths of his way.) As another student put it, "If you took all the kids in high school who are bright but bored, that's Reed."

A phenomenal 25% of its alumni have Ph.D.s, a figure that only very selective Haverford and Harvey Mudd can match. One consequence is that Reed alumni are scattered through the faculties of the most prestigious colleges and universities and across the hilltops of the professional landscape, from designer Emilio Pucci to Apple Computer's co-founder, Steve Jobs.

Only one institution, California Institute of Technology, has produced a higher percentage of future scientists and scholars. But in the science category alone, Reed is number one, although it is a liberal arts college. No college has topped its 30 Rhodes Scholars, and only one—Williams—has equaled it. What's more, Reedies have won 42 Fulbright and 51 Watson fellowships and, in the two dozen years they have been awarded, 59 National Science Foundation Fellowships. In addition to two dozen undergraduate winners of Mellon, Carnegie, and Goldwater Fellowships, one alumnus has won a MacArthur genius award, two have won Pulitzer Prizes, and an amazing total of nine have been chosen as members of that intellectual holy of holies, the National Academy of Sciences.

Reed's title of most intellectual might be contested by Caltech, which recently had a freshman class whose every member had scored 800 on the Level II math achievement test, or by Harvey Mudd, where the median one year was 790, or by MIT, where the median is consistently in the middle 700s. But at those schools they are specialists learning to be biologists, chemists, engineers, or physicists. Reed students are in love with learning. This is also true of tiny Marlboro in Vermont, and of the two St. John's colleges with their Great Books program. Such schools are Reed's closest relatives, but not its clones.

Where else but Reed would you hear a senior say, "I had the most rewarding week of my life last week working on my thesis." Or hear another say, "Everything here revolves around intellectuality; there is a deep appreciation of learning." Or still another say, "People are proud of how hard they work. It's almost a masochism; you drive yourself to the edge. Because of the drive to learn it's hard to achieve a sense of balance between social and academic needs. There are more students in the library on Friday nights than you would ever expect. And they're not cramming for an exam. They take breaks and there are chats and there are talks on issues of the day: what is power, the nature of government. There are all kinds of interesting conversations going on on campus."

Why does all this happen here? Years ago, a professor at a neighboring college gave me a sour-grapes explanation: "Their faculty isn't all that good; they just get kids with a commitment to learning." The truth is they get kids with a commitment to learning for the very good reason that that is what pervades the institution. And the faculty *is* all that good. Some kind of osmosis or magnetic vibrations work for the very few distinctive colleges such as Antioch, Earlham, Evergreen, Marlboro, Reed, and St. John's that draw the appropriate pilgrims to each.

The word was out from the beginning that Reed wasn't the place to come for a degree or a job, but to become an intellectual novitiate. Reed has never wavered in its faith in its ideas of what constitutes a liberal education, even in the '60s when Amherst, Brown, Oberlin, and others abandoned required courses so kids could satisfy their own desires for "relevance."

As Jacques Barzun, former provost at Columbia, said, "If students were competent to decide matters of curriculum they'd be in the faculty, not in the student body."

Reed also attracts people with a commitment to learning because it takes great care to select faculty members who will feed that commitment. In 1994, for example, a few vacancies attracted hundreds of applicants, but the deans and departments didn't make the final decisions. Every lucky winner, whatever the discipline, had to convince students during long lunchtime interviews that he or she was not only on the cutting edge of his or her field, but also loved teaching and would be a friend as well as a teacher.

At Reed such rapport is vital because so much of the learning process is in one-on-one conferences with faculty members or in small discussion groups. And I've never listened to a discussion group that was sharper or more probing, even at St. John's, where it is standard fare, than those at Reed.

Every student must fulfill distribution requirements that provide the framework of a liberal education. He must take a junior qualifying exam given by his division or department before he can begin the major task of his senior year—the thesis. Just preparing for this often means an extra independent study project.

The thesis is not just a long paper. It takes all year under the guidance of a faculty member. It must develop new knowledge and it permits the student to integrate all aspects of the academic experience, or, as the catalog says, it is "the sustained investigation of a carefully defined problem—experimental, critical, or creative—chosen from the major field. At the end of the year he submits to community scrutiny a thesis describing the problem and its attempted resolution."

In the basement of the library are a few long rows of carrels, with bookshelves rising above them, one for each senior; it is The Thesis Ghetto where they spend many, many hours. The labor and the pressure that are part of these creations are intense. More than one senior has told his or her adviser, "I just can't do it." The teacher reassures, "Everything will be all right," and it is. On Thesis Day in May the lid blows, and there's a week-long party. As befits all the sweat and tears and pressure, every thesis is bound and filed for public inspection in a room on the top floor of the library.

The senior must also pass a two-hour oral exam that may cover every course he's had, and on which he may be examined by professionals from outside the college. Oh yes, in addition to the thesis, one senior told me she'd written 54 other papers that year.

What about grades?

Grades are not revealed to students so long as their work is C or better, but they are recorded for such purposes as graduate school applications. Believe it or not, few bother to find out what their grades are. The director of institutional research who served as registrar for several years said he was always amazed at how few requests he got to see a grade.

The college says it doesn't want to divide students by levels of achievement. Instead, it encourages them to measure academic achievement by self-assessment of their grasp of the course material and of their intellectual growth. Their work is frequently evaluated by faculty members with oral or written comments, as might be expected at a place where so much of the learning is one-on-one, in small groups, or in independent study, and where people are on a first-name basis.

Evaluation is reciprocal and collegial, "because we're learning together," as one student said. "We talk to the prof about how the class is doing as well as how we're doing. If I feel uncomfortable, for instance, because certain people are talking too much, or if something isn't being emphasized, the prof may restructure the class. This is not arrogance but a search with colleagues."

This sense of being a community of learning gives Reed its gravity. A senior from a self-described "stuffy, conventional background" had planned to transfer after her freshman year because her mother had been leery about Reed. She herself had been shocked to see pot smoking, but then, "We'd have a reading and people would come prepared. I'd say maybe the point is this and people would turn around and say, 'That's an interesting idea.' And I thought, 'Wow!' and I was converted. Like children with blocks, we're building together—you learn so much that way. It's really fantastic."

Reed's reputation for pot smoking, long hair, and hippie attributes came under vehement attack from many students. "There are a lot of myths about all this," a senior girl said. "It's just that here people are not afraid of being themselves or of being unique, or of being intellectual. There's pot smoking here just as there is everywhere else, but people are just more open about it. At Reed it's a matter of being yourself, of individuality. Things are much more focused on thinking and learning and on experiencing that intellectually than on drinking." In two day-long visits to Reed a dozen years apart I didn't see any more green hair or earrings in male ears, or grungier outfits, than on most other campuses.

This is the testimony of another girl who was student body president and who had been commissioned by IBM to design software for use in schools that would encourage girls to enter careers in science:

"With all its wonderful qualities, Reed is not perfect, and I nearly left my freshman year. Here were a lot of bright kids not knowing who they were and trying to find their identity. But whatever I did people didn't care, only did I have integrity, was I intelligent, did I cheat, and it was really hard. I never had anyone say, 'Will you have a drink?' and I told a freshman girl worried someone might ask her to, 'Don't worry. Nobody's going to ask you to or pressure you. You can be yourself.'

"Here you make your own choices. They expect you to be an adult and that's hard, and that's why attrition is high. [About 55% graduate.] The adjustment is difficult. You're in charge of your own life. What kept me here was the faculty. One counseled me to find a dorm situation where I'd be comfortable. I went on a 12-mile hike in the summer with a couple of others and I realized I'd have a hard time finding that kind of concern anywhere else."

There are no easy classes at Reed. An administrator who'd gone to Duke said it was easy to skate through there, but "you couldn't do it here." Any student I talked to would have called that a rank understatement, they were so full of how hard they had to work. But they wouldn't have it any other way. Nor does anyone avoid science and math courses for fear of getting low grades. Since 1950 only Caltech and Harvey Mudd have produced higher percentages of future Ph.D.s, and no place starts up as many women scientists per capita.

If things get too rough and a change of venue is needed, there is a variety of study programs in Europe, England, Asia, South America, and this country. A very large percentage of the students take advantage of them, and like the foreign study participants at other colleges, they say those experiences helped "change my perspective of the world."

For recreation and sports the word is "informal." There are no official intercollegiate teams, but there are club teams that compete with those of other colleges in rugby, basketball, fencing, rowing, squash, soccer, sailing, and volleyball. A hundred different sports are available in the required physical education program, with the emphasis on lifetime sports. In addition to most of the conventional ones except baseball and football, they include Aikido, backpacking, canoeing, all forms of dance, horseback riding, rock climbing, rugby, sailing, skiing, Tai Chi, white-water rafting, and water polo, among others.

To faculty members, teaching at Reed is like going to heaven. They got their doctorates from and taught at all the top schools, but never before had the pleasure of teaching students interested in learning. A psychology professor said, "At Duke they wanted the knowledge delivered to them. 'Is it going to be on the exam?' It's such a thrill to work here. They learn to trust their own ideas and intuition."

A history professor who had taught at Berkeley for eight years said, "Reed students are much more active and take more risks, and share ideas and welcome the ideas of others from other backgrounds. Furthermore, it was possible to go through that prestige institution without ever writing a paper. Here they write at least one paper in every course."

Just like the students, they talked like members of a family involved in a common endeavor, one that teaches people to think critically, to present and defend their views in discussion groups and conferences, and to learn about themselves. Learning at Reed is a communal affair and that affects value systems, one reason Reed students don't cheat.

"Also," said an economics professor, "they discover how what they learn in economics may apply in other areas; they learn to recognize bullshit when they see it, and that's a very valuable skill nowadays."

Demanding as they are, these teachers aren't trying to produce ivory-tower types. A history professor said, "I don't so much want my students to get Ph.D.s and become historians as I want them to be able to rule the country."

The research experience and having so much responsibility for one's own education have a lot to do with the large percentages going on to graduate school. They have designed a project for their senior thesis and have carried it out, which gives them an edge in the job market, especially in the sciences. The high-tech companies, one professor noted, "are well aware" of the Reed student's experience.

Reed is a precious asset of American democracy. It develops people with intellectual openness and honesty, clear thinkers who are not afraid of new or unpopular ideas, men and women who have the character and the ability to make the increasingly tough decisions in an increasingly complex and troubled society. Only those willing to pay the price are either likely to come or to prosper here. But in an ideal society, everyone's education would do as much as Reed does to empower a young mind and spirit.

Whitman College
Walla Walla, Washington

W hitman, in Walla Walla, Washington, at the end of the Oregon Trail, provides not only a 55-acre, parklike setting in a cultural center of 27,000, but also one of the three best undergraduate experiences in the Pacific Northwest. The others are Reed and Evergreen State College; each of the three appeals to a very different kind of teenager.

Whitman is for the gregarious youth, a good student who is willing to get involved in his own education and participate in a strong and active community. The kids at Whitman dress well, not outlandishly, and they are as outdoorsy as any.

Indeed, when asked what kind of person should come here, the first thing a Whitman student is likely to say is, "If you're not willing to get involved, don't bother to come." By "involved" that student would mean in one's studies, with one another, with the teachers, and in campus life. Another student would emphatically add that academics come first here, you have to work hard, and "there's a lot of heavy lifting, but we have a lot of fun too."

A faculty member enlarged on those comments with, "We're attractive to a broad spectrum, to the traditional, to the granola liberal, and to people who enjoy life; there are no monastics." Professor David Deal added that the Whitman prospect should be self-motivated, have some kind of achievement, enjoy learning, and know how to learn. Whitman's students, he said, are socially adept, gregarious, very civil, omni-competent, and as befits Pacific Northwesterners, outdoorsy with healthful living styles.

A history professor who had taught at Princeton said, "Our students are sophisticated, they're concerned about cultural diversity, the environment, and feminist issues. They compare very well in ability with Princeton's; they're the same at the top but there's a larger lower end." In the matter of sophistication, another professor said it was a mix, but that they "are willing students who intend to work hard and who are enjoyable to work with," and develop a hunger for knowledge as they progress.

A junior from Seattle said, "Big-city kids are happy here; it's not just the nurturing environment, the town provides a safe community for breaking away from home, and there's so much going on here." This is a point worth enlarging on, because so many high school seniors think the size of a city determines the quality of social life at a college. This is decidedly not so. At Whitman there's more going on in the way of lectures, musical or theatrical events, or dances on a weekend than any one person could take advantage of.

The Seattle junior was talking not only about the many campus activities but also the region's vast recreational resources. For this college, with its Blue Mountains and three rivers, including the Columbia, either at hand or close by, a city is overkill. Any outdoor activity you can think of is right here. To help take advantage of each and every one, the student union runs a formal Outing Program, both to organize such activities as hiking, biking, kayaking, whitewater rafting, skiing, rock climbing, fishing, and so on, and also to teach basic outdoor skills. It's a complete resort program that also rents equipment.

Students talk enthusiastically about their relations with teachers, relations that include going on whitewater rafting or hiking trips with them or being intramural teammates. This is as it should be, because the various degree requirements dictate a lot of student-faculty collaboration. Every student has to take a large measure of responsibility for his own education, such as planning his major and doing a senior thesis, both of which mean much consultation with a teacher along the way. He must pass both oral and written comprehensives in his major.

Students are made to feel they're part of the organization

and have a voice in its governance, for they serve on the important college committees. It is indeed a nurturing environment. With the thesis he had yet to master weighing heavily on his mind, a senior said, "Every student has had a teacher say, 'You can do it.' " A freshman testified he had already experienced that kind of morale-and-confidence booster. A senior girl said that a math professor's going out of his way to compliment her on her piano performance was the kind of thing that characterized the warm familial atmosphere. Another added, "The best profs admit they are learning, too."

The experience obviously affects them because after they graduate they are loath to cut the umbilical cord. They are eager to offer their services in admissions, in providing internships, and in finding jobs for new graduates. Whitman has such a broad network of alumni in professional and executive roles that it makes the job hunt a lot easier than it is for most graduates. But the real proof is that over 50% of alumni contribute financially; only a dozen other institutions in the country can boast greater allegiance, and none west of the Mississippi comes close.

Two-thirds of Whitman's students come from the Pacific Northwest and 15% from California, with smaller delegations from other Western and from Midwestern states.

The admissions statistics look more fearsome than they really are. The median, or middle, grade point average is 3.83, and 64% are in the top 10% of their high school classes. The middle 50% of the class had SAT verbals in the 610 to 710 range (before SAT scores were recentered to make 500 the average verbal). The middle math score range was 600 to 700.

However, a prospect shouldn't be scared off by that 3.83. Many applicants come from small high schools in rural Washington and Oregon where few go on to college and where good grades are relatively easy to come by. A "B" student with a solid program in a big competitive suburban high school where nearly everyone is going to college has usually accomplished a heck of a lot more. In 1999 Whitman accepted nearly 60% of its applicants. It's a great place and they'll certainly be glad to get a "B" student who means business; besides, they want more from outside the West.

Of Whitman's 1,300 students, slightly more than half get need-based financial aid and another 15% get merit aid. Professor Bob Withycombe, who's also the debate coach and therefore should know, called Whitman's students "bright and articulate, capable of reasoning through a problem as well as anybody." It is a writing-intensive college where all faculty expect papers. Also, because seniors have to pass written as well as oral comprehensives and do a thesis based on original research (and there is much cooperative research as well), he says "the whole experience here is of an intensity one usually gets only in graduate school."

Whitman has no business courses, he added, but "our economics majors have an in at the University of Chicago." They are also welcome at the best graduate and professional schools, the route that two-thirds of the seniors take, with the majority going to professional schools.

As freshmen many of them have no such grand plans, but Whitman is a place that raises their sights. "Whitman," Dr. Withycombe said, "changes people, adds to their values, and affects the quality of their future lives. A student may come in planning to be a lawyer and go out planning to be an architect or something else entirely different because of the exposure to new things and ideas. Furthermore, he gets to design his own major to follow up on his interests."

The close working friendships with faculty that students talked about is conducive both to opening students' eyes and to encouraging them to take a beckoning new road. A wise college policy stimulates all this by giving faculty members modest allowances for having students over to dinner or dessert or to go rafting, camping, or canoeing with them. The sums are small but catalytic. So there is, as one professor said, "a lot of neonannyism, but there's also a lot of pushing them out to test themselves."

Instead of competing with one another, students do a lot of collaborative learning in which members of a class may work as a team or in small groups, either on reading assignments or for an exam.

A religion professor's classes are examples of how this works and how the faculty gets the students involved in their own education:

"In the freshman Core I've turned over the text discussion to students. Everyone signs up, and three work as a team, leading discussions, planning questions, and so on. There is visible growth in the discussions and in the disagreements. I only participate as another student. This is learning by doing, making the class work."

Undergraduate research, conducted by the students and by students and faculty together, achieves a like kind of involvement and collaboration. And it has produced students who perform at the top of their class in the 3–2 transfer program at California Institute of Technology, the country's top science school.

Whitman's program ensures that students get a broad as well as an intensive experience. The General Studies Program begins with a year-long freshman core, Antiquity and Modernity, goes on with distribution requirements in the arts, humanities, sciences, and social sciences, and winds up with the senior thesis and comprehensives.

As at other colleges in this group, the students testified that the result of these enforced exposures and of working with teachers who are constantly pushing them to stretch themselves is a steadily growing confidence in their powers.

Also, because there is so much cooperative research with faculty members, students' names are often on faculty publications as co-authors, or on papers presented at professional meetings. Such things not only foster a strong sense of community but also have a considerable market value. Not many college graduates are able to list a co-authorship on a job ré-sumé or graduate school application.

It is not surprising that Whitman produces what Dean Deal called "rabidly enthusiastic alumni" who have great success getting into graduate or professional schools and who continue to testify that Whitman has made a difference in their lives.

Admissions Directors and Addresses

NORTHEAST

Allegheny College
Megan Murphy, Director of Admissions
Park Avenue
Meadville, PA 16335
800-521-5293

Clark University
Harold M. Wingood, Dean of Admissions
950 Main Street
Worcester, MA 01610
508-793-7431

Goucher College
Carlton Surbeck III, Director of Admissions
1021 Dulaney Valley Road
Baltimore, MD 21204
800-638-4278

Hampshire College
Audrey Smith, Director of Admissions
West Street
Amherst, MA 01002
413-582-5471

Juniata College
Michelle Bartol, Director of Admissions
1700 Monroe Street
Huntingdon, PA 16652
800-526-1970

Marlboro College
Katherine Hallas, Director of Admissions
South Road
Marlboro, VT 05344
800-343-0049

St. John's College
John Christensen, Director of Admissions
P.O. Box 2800
Annapolis, MD 21404
800-727-9238

Ursinus College
Richard DiFeliciantonio, Vice President for Enrollment
Collegeville, PA 19426
610-409-3200

Western Maryland College
Martha O'Connell, Dean of Admissions
2 College Hill
Westminster, MD 21157
800-638-5005

Agnes Scott College
Stephanie Balmer, Director of Admissions
141 East College Avenue
Decatur, GA 30030
800-868-8602

SOUTH

Birmingham–Southern College
DeeDee Bruns, Dean of Admissions and Financial Aid
900 Arkadelphia Road
Birmingham, AL 35254
800-523-5793

Centre College
*Carey Thompson, Dean of Admissions and Student
     Financial Planning*
600 West Walnut Street
Danville, KY 40422
800-423-6236
www.centre.edu

Eckerd College
Dr. Richard Hallin, Dean of Admissions
4200 54th Avenue South
St. Petersburg, FL 33733
800-456-9009

Emory and Henry College
Deborah Thompson, Dean of Admissions
Emory, VA 24327
703-944-4121

Guilford College
Randy Moss, Dean of Enrollment
5800 West Friendly Avenue
Greensboro, NC 27410
800-992-7759

Hendrix College
Rick Jones, Vice President for Enrollment
1601 Harkrider Street
Conway, AR 72032
501-450-1362

Lynchburg College
Director of Admissions
1501 Lakeside Drive
Lynchburg, VA 24501
800-426-8101

Millsaps College
John Gaines, Director of Admissions
1701 North State Street
Jackson, MS 39210
800-352-1050

Rhodes College
David Wottle, Director of Admissions and Financial Aid
2000 North Parkway
Memphis, TN 38112
800-844-5969

St. Andrews Presbyterian College
Dale Montague, Dean of Admissions and Financial Aid
Laurinburg, NC 28352
800-763-0198

MIDWEST

Antioch College
Michael Murphy, Dean of Admissions
Yellow Springs, OH 45387
800-543-9436

Beloit College
James Zielinski, Director of Admissions
700 College Street
Beloit, WI 53511
800-356-0751

Cornell College
Florence Hines, Director of Admissions
Mount Vernon, IA 52314
800-747-1112

Denison University
Perry Robinson, Director of Admissions
Granville, OH 43023
800-336-4766

Earlham College
Jeff Rickey, Director of Admissions
National Road West
Richmond, IN 47374
800-382-6906 (in state); 800-428-6958 (out of state)

Hiram College
*Monty Curtis, Vice President for Admissions and College
    Relations*
Rodefar House
Hiram, OH 44234
800-362-5280

Hope College
Jim Bekkering, Director of Admissions
69 East 10th Street
Holland, MI 49422
800-968-7850

Kalamazoo College
John Carroll, Director of Admissions
Mandelle Hall
Kalamazoo, MI 49006
800-253-3602

Knox College
Paul Steenis, Director of Admissions
Office of Admissions
Galesburg, IL 61401
800-678-KNOX

Lawrence University
Steven Syverson, Dean of Admissions and Financial Aid
706 East College Avenue
Appleton, WI 54912
800-227-0982

Ohio Wesleyan University
Margaret Drugovich, Director of Admissions
Slocum Hall
Delaware, OH 43015
800-862-0612 (in state); 800-922-8953 (out of state)

St. Olaf College
Barbara Lundberg, Director of Admissions
1520 St. Olaf Avenue
Northfield, MN 55057
507-646-3025

Wabash College
Steve Klein, Director of Admissions
P.O. Box 362
Crawfordsville, IN 47933
800-345-5385

Wheaton College
Dan Crabtree, Director of Admissions
501 East College Avenue
Wheaton, IL 60187
708-752-5011 (in state); 800-222-2419 (out of state)

College of Wooster
Carol Wheatley, Dean of Admissions
1101 North Bever Street
Wooster, OH 44691
800-877-9905

SOUTHWEST

Austin College
David Dillman, Director of Admissions
900 North Grand Avenue
Sherman, TX 75090
800-442-5363

St. John's College
Lawrence H. Clendenin, Director of Admissions
1160 Camino Cruz Blanca
Santa Fe, NM 87501
505-982-3691 (in state);
800-331-5232 (out of state)

Southwestern University
John W. Lind, Vice President for Enrollment Management
University at Maple
Georgetown, TX 78626
800-252-3166

NORTHWEST

The Evergreen State College
Jesse Welch, Dean for Enrollment
Olympia, WA 98505
360-866-6000, ext. 6170

Reed College
Nancy Donehower, Director of Admissions
3203 Southeast Woodstock Avenue
Portland, OR 97202
503-777-7511 (in state);
800-547-4750 (out of state)

Whitman College
John Bogley, Director of Admission
Walla Walla, WA 99362
509-527-5176

Index of Colleges